Motor Boat Manual

First published in 2009

A catalogue record for this book is available from the British Library

ISBN 978 1 84425 513 9

Library of Congress control no. 2009923759

Published by Haynes Publishing,
Sparkford, Yeovil, Somerset BA22 7JJ, UK
Tel: 01963 442030 Fax: 01963 440001
Int. tel: +44 1963 442030 Int. fax: +44 1963 440001
E-mail: sales@haynes.co.uk
Website: www.haynes.co.uk

Haynes North America Inc.
861 Lawrence Drive, Newbury Park,
California 91320, USA

While every effort is taken to ensure the accuracy of the information given in this book, no liability can be accepted by the author or publishers for any loss, damage or injury caused by errors in, or omissions from the information given.

Printed and bound in the UK

Risks

Boating and working on boat maintenance can safely be enjoyed but involves risks and some dangers. It is vital that you follow instructions provided by the manufacturers when using boats, equipment, tools and materials for maintenance and repair.

HM Coastguard (HMC) and The Royal National Lifeboat Institute (RNLI) provide comprehensive safety advice for boating. Readers are advised to consult and follow their advice at all times; in particular you should wear a lifejacket, and be aware of navigational and weather hazards.

As can be seen in some of the photographs in this book, some people decide to take the risk of not wearing a lifejacket, and that is their choice. But as the RNLI states, a lifejacket can only save you if you are wearing it. People have been known to fall from boats in the calmest of conditions.

The Boat Safety Scheme

The Boat Safety Scheme (BSS) provides an inspection system, compulsory for cruising boats on inland waterways. The Scheme's manual is also an excellent source of safety information for boats used in coastal locations.

Electrical, gas, fuel and safety installations

Readers are strongly advised that all work on electrical, gas, fuel and other installations affecting safety should be inspected by properly qualified engineers before use. Gas installations must be carried out by an appropriately qualified Corgi-registered engineer experienced in work on boat installations.

Further information on safety

Details of how to obtain HMC, RNLI and BSS information are included in the Appendix.

Suggestions in this book concerning particular boats and products do not guarantee or endorse the reliability of particular companies or their products.

Motor Boat Manual

Haynes®

Dennis Watts

BUYING, USING, MAINTAINING AND REPAIRING MOTOR BOATS

1

Introduction

Cruising through tranquil countryside warmed by summer sun.

Get afloat without spending a fortune

New and experienced boat owners will find plenty here to help them enjoy using and maintaining a boat without spending a fortune. It's true that motor boating isn't the cheapest of leisure activities, but our aim is to help you find affordable ways to get afloat by minimising the costs of buying, equipping and maintaining a boat.

This book is about a range of different types and sizes of motor boat, including small to medium-sized motor cruisers with outboard motors or inboard engines, open day boats, sea angling boats, motor launches and inflatable boats with outboard motors – boats that are mainly suited to coastal waters, estuaries and inland waterways. A great many such waters are waiting to be explored and enjoyed by those who want to get afloat without undue expense.

Boating in a scenic sheltered estuary.

Finding boat bargains is now much easier. In the past boat sellers had to pay to advertise in a few specialist magazines, but today the Internet's boat-selling websites make it possible to advertise to a much wider audience very cheaply or even free of charge. Some of these websites are also linked to the increased number of boating magazines and newspapers that are now available.

Motor boats of a variety of types and sizes are great for coastal creeks, inshore cruising, inland waterways and fishing trips.

Being captain of your own boat is a great thrill, whatever its size.

A classic speedboat of the type the author enjoyed as a boy in Cornwall.

Skills used in do-it-yourself tasks at home can be adapted to tackle the improvement of an inexpensive, neglected motor boat. You can even build one from plans or a kit of parts. New materials and methods have helped to make domestic DIY much easier, and the same applies with boats. You don't have to be a shipwright to tackle many straightforward maintenance and improvement tasks.

Personal experience

My earliest experiences of motor boating were as a child. Whilst on a family holiday in Cornwall we admired a beautifully varnished classic speedboat moored in Padstow harbour. The owner noticed our interest and invited us aboard. We set off on the most memorable and exciting high-speed tour of the magnificent Cornish coast.

Other early enjoyable trips were in a boating club launch with my Uncle Maurice, from whom I gained much of my knowledge of boating matters. I frequently helped my uncle with his enthusiastic renovation and refitting of many of the boats he improved and used throughout his life. It was hard work, but worth it when we launched a brightly painted and varnished old boat into the estuary following its rescue from decay in the corner of a boatyard.

Buying a neglected boat in the autumn, renovating it on suitable days in the winter, using it in the summer and selling it (for a good price) to buy another – and bigger – one is how my uncle progressed over the years from open boats to substantial cruisers used on the coast and on the local canal.

Holidays on hired motor cruisers on the Norfolk Broads at various times of the year increased my desire to own one for myself. On one occasion we returned from a hire boat holiday to find my uncle negotiating the purchase of a motor cruiser from the same boatyard we had returned to. This was the start of his involvement with inland waterways, which led eventually to his ownership of a boat with substantial accommodation. He also worked part-time for a canal company, helping to maintain and skipper the boat *Victoria*, used to take passengers on Chelmer canal cruises. His own boat gave members of the family many opportunities to drift through glorious countryside, operate locks and take the helm.

Buying a boat, improving it and enjoying the benefits is very rewarding.

Enjoy the countryside from a different perspective as you cruise along inland waterways.

Some interesting experiences await you on waterways – as on this canal which crosses a valley near Llangollen via the Pontcysyllte Aqueduct.

My first motor boat was one of the first to be made of fibreglass – a small, old, dilapidated cruiser needing substantial improvement, but very cheap to buy. With its cosy little cabin, it became as much a retreat beside the sea and salt marshes as a means to enjoy actual boating. I used the skills and methods I had learned earlier and after several years of improving and using this boat on the coast and a canal it was sold for a substantial profit that was put into a succession of further boats. I subsequently improved, used and sold these until I could afford a much larger and more substantial motor cruiser suitable for both inland and coastal cruising.

You may want to try the same process, buying, improving and selling a succession of progressively larger boats until you have a substantial motor cruiser, narrowboat, sea angling boat or high-speed boat such as a rigid inflatable or a powerful sports boat for waterskiing. It can be compared with ascending the bricks-and-mortar property ladder. It's even possible to make a small profit each time you sell, to reinvest in the next boat.

You may, of course, be perfectly happy with the first motor boat you buy if it suits your particular needs. But whatever boat you decide on, this book will help you enjoy the experience.

Casual cruising or challenging voyages

Some seek challenges by cruising far and wide. They voyage to foreign parts and have stories to tell of their adventures and experiences. By all means enjoy doing that, as safely as possible, when you've gained the necessary skills, knowledge and suitable boat in which to do so. But before doing that – or instead of taking on that challenge – much enjoyment is to be gained through relaxing in an entirely different environment from that so familiar at home or work. Escape from the stresses of normal everyday life in a watery world where sunlight flickers over the ripples like a million diamonds and the natural surroundings soothe the soul.

Once under way, the concentration that's needed to navigate creeks, waterways and waves blocks out any aggravating thoughts. You can leave them behind on dry land, enjoy the scenic coastal or river landscape, broad seascape, breathtaking sunsets and the company of friendly boating folk.

Arthur Ransome's famous *Swallows and Amazons* book series, about children enjoying adventures afloat, is responsible for many people – young and old – wanting to get afloat on scenic lakes, rivers and coastal waters. Ransome's children used sails on small boats, but if the physical effort involved in sailing doesn't appeal the alternative is a boat with its own source of power.

Sheltered estuaries can be explored in a small motor boat capable of venturing into shallow waters.

Relax and unwind on water

The United Kingdom has nearly 8,000 miles of coast including plenty of sheltered inlets, estuaries and sea lochs that provide sheltered boating when used sensibly and carefully. Nowhere in the UK is more than 72 miles from the sea, and few places are far from a safely navigable waterway where you can relax with a leisurely cruise.

Many people combine motor boating with relaxing and absorbing angling using rod and line. At sea this can be quite exciting as you hunt for elusive shoals of fish, never being quite sure what will appear on the surface when you bring up a creature from the depths. Inland waterways provide a variety of fishing experiences from the comfort of your floating fishing platform, rather than a perch on a muddy bank. Fishing from under the canopy of a motor cruiser with heat, hot drinks and food from the cabin means you can comfortably fish all year round if you so wish.

The phrase 'messing about in boats' will be familiar to most. Some think boating is much too serious to be thought about in such terms, but in reality it's the 'messing about' that many enjoy most. Obviously, venturing out onto the more challenging rivers and coastal waters demands a more serious approach in order to be safe and secure, but the phrase still conveys the pleasure many experience in just being aboard a boat on the water.

Learning the necessary boating skills is not difficult and if you take precautions, detailed later, the risks involved in boating can be minimised. You then have the opportunity to explore creeks, visit remote beaches and, in the cabin of a cruiser, enjoy overnight stays in idyllic surroundings.

Family fun

Most children's fascination with water will lead to an interest in boats at some stage in their childhood. This can provide a way to get them into an enjoyable outdoor environment away from the overused technology at

Idyllic spots can be found for overnight stays.

An interesting night-time mooring on the River Thames, with a Whisper motorsailer providing the overnight accommodation.

Cruising along waterways you can encounter quaint and interesting city scenes, as here in Lincoln.

home. You may have to include some extra electrical entertainment equipment on board, but try to point out the natural attractions and the fun involved with fishing. On a warm sunny day the whole family can learn the skills of boat handling and set off for new experiences together.

Families used to camping or caravanning will find it easy to adapt to the accommodation on a motor cruiser. This enables them to enjoy the adventure of mooring or anchoring overnight in remote, scenic locations or within easy reach of a restaurant or interesting town centre.

Excitement and speed if you want it

For older children, teenagers and many adults there's also the thrill of high-speed boating experiences on suitable waters with boat owners or instructors who know what they're doing. With careful supervision, the delights of being towed behind a motor boat on various devices, such as inflated deck tubes and donuts, may lead to learning how to waterski and wakeboard with suitably qualified instructors.

Left: Motor boating can bring the family together for new experiences.

Below: Mooring near a pub or restaurant is an attraction for many and makes a change from catering aboard the boat.

High-speed thrills appeal to many – here combined with scenic surroundings.

Scope of the book

Any book has limits on its content, and the huge variety of boats and equipment available mean that motor boating and boat maintenance is a vast subject. Many books concentrate on particular aspects of boat ownership and use, and go into great depth and detail on their chosen subject. This book by contrast covers a wide range of topics, but concentrates on those that are within the capabilities of the majority of motor boat owners.

The emphasis is on simple and basic maintenance tasks on the boat itself. The very large and extensive topics of boat modifications and the installation and maintenance of additional equipment, including luxurious domestic appliances in the cabin of a motor cruiser, are not covered, as this would need a whole series of books to cover them adequately.

Having coped with the basic topics covered, more advanced boat handling skills and more complex boat improvements can be learned. You can go on to take courses in offshore motor cruising or high-speed powerboating, navigation, advanced engine maintenance or boat building. You can also buy more specialised publications such as books on modifying motor boats for particular purposes, and the monthly magazines (see the lists in the Appendix) that thrive on such topics as the addition of the latest equipment. But you should always remember that, in the interests of safety, a number of practical aspects are best left to the professionals. These are indicated in the appropriate chapters.

Nautical terms are often confusing for new and experienced boat owners alike, and are therefore explained in the text, in the diagrams in Chapter 2 and in the detailed glossary.

2 Parts of the motor boat

The following diagrams identify the principal parts of motor boats. The Glossary has more detailed definitions, and explanations of most of the parts will be found in the appropriate chapters.

Motor boats vary considerably in size, features, shape and layout. These diagrams represent an amalgamation of features in order to illustrate the parts most commonly found on motor boats.

Parts of an open motor boat, speedboat or sport boat

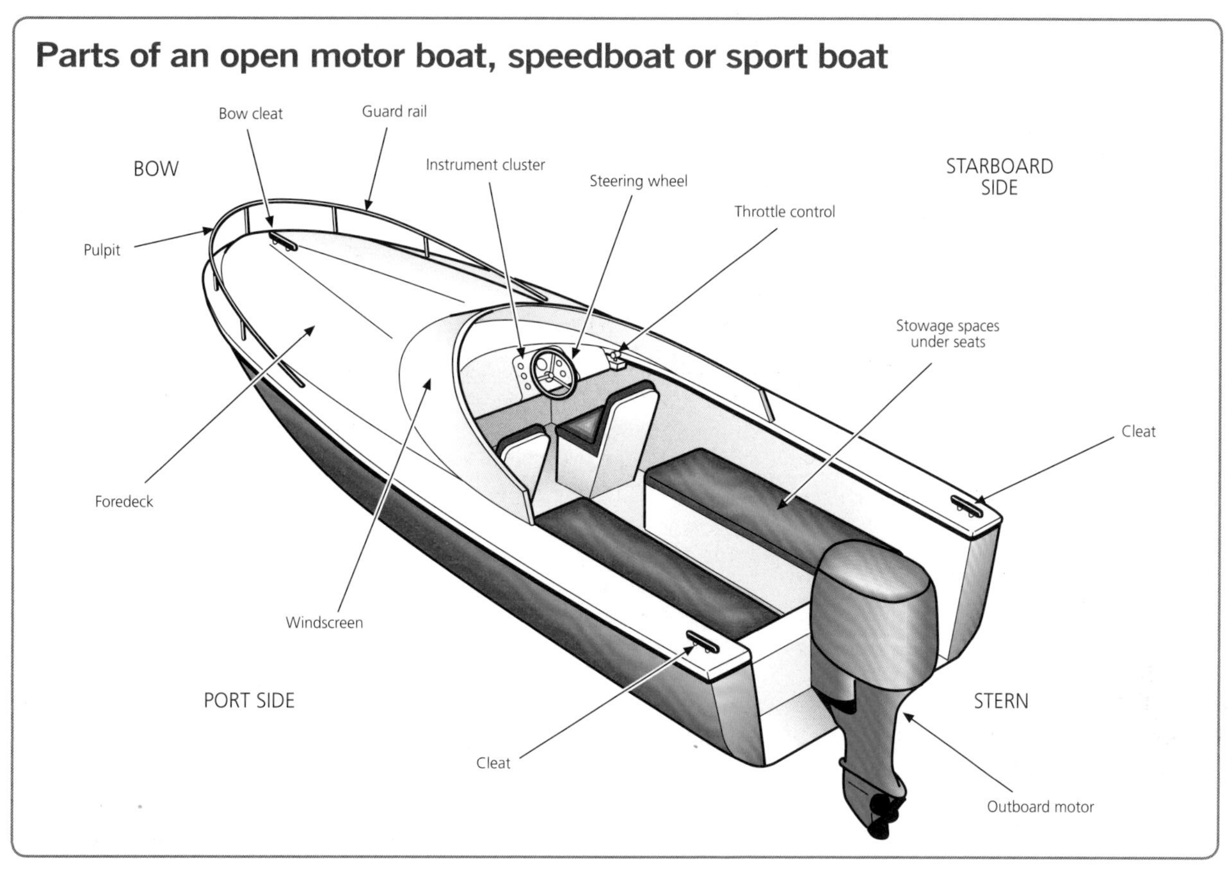

Parts of a seagoing motor cruiser

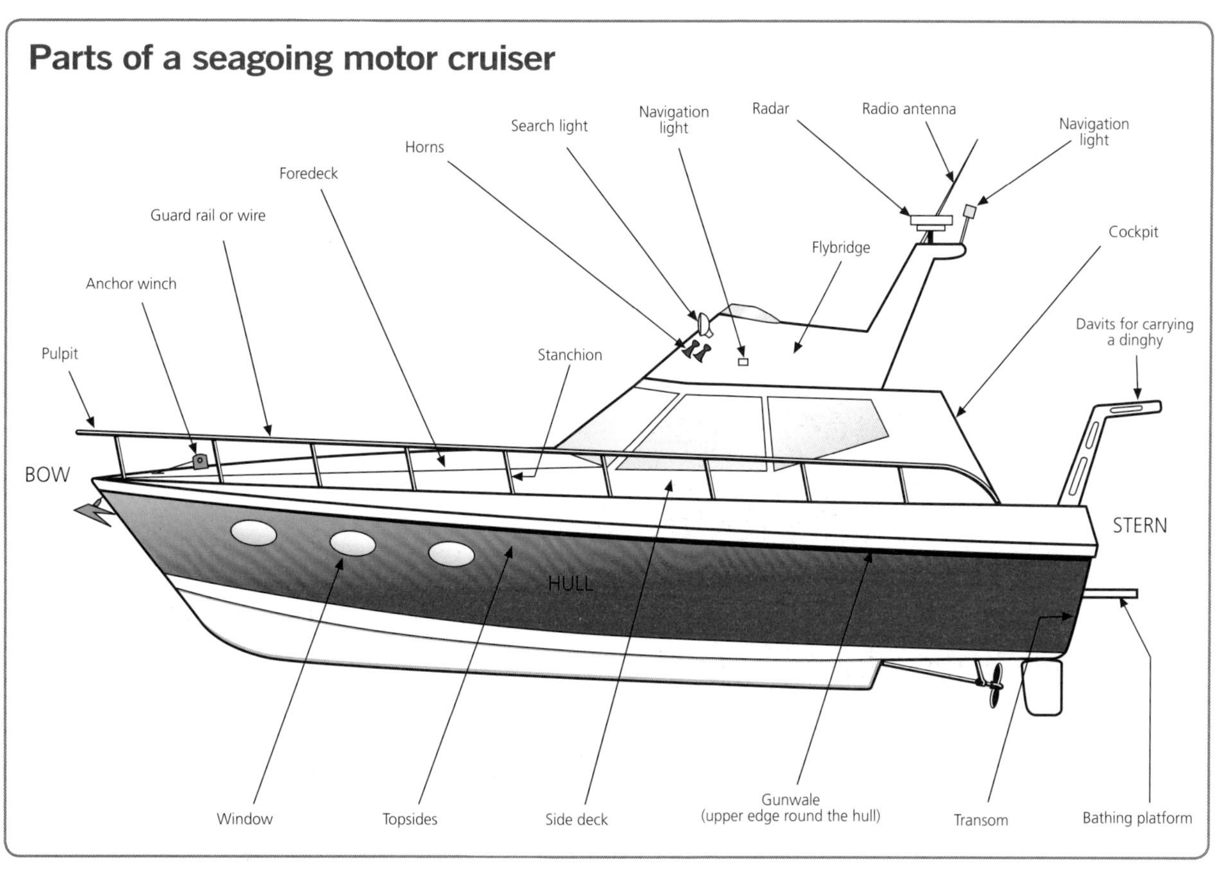

Parts of a typical motor cruiser normally used on inland waterways

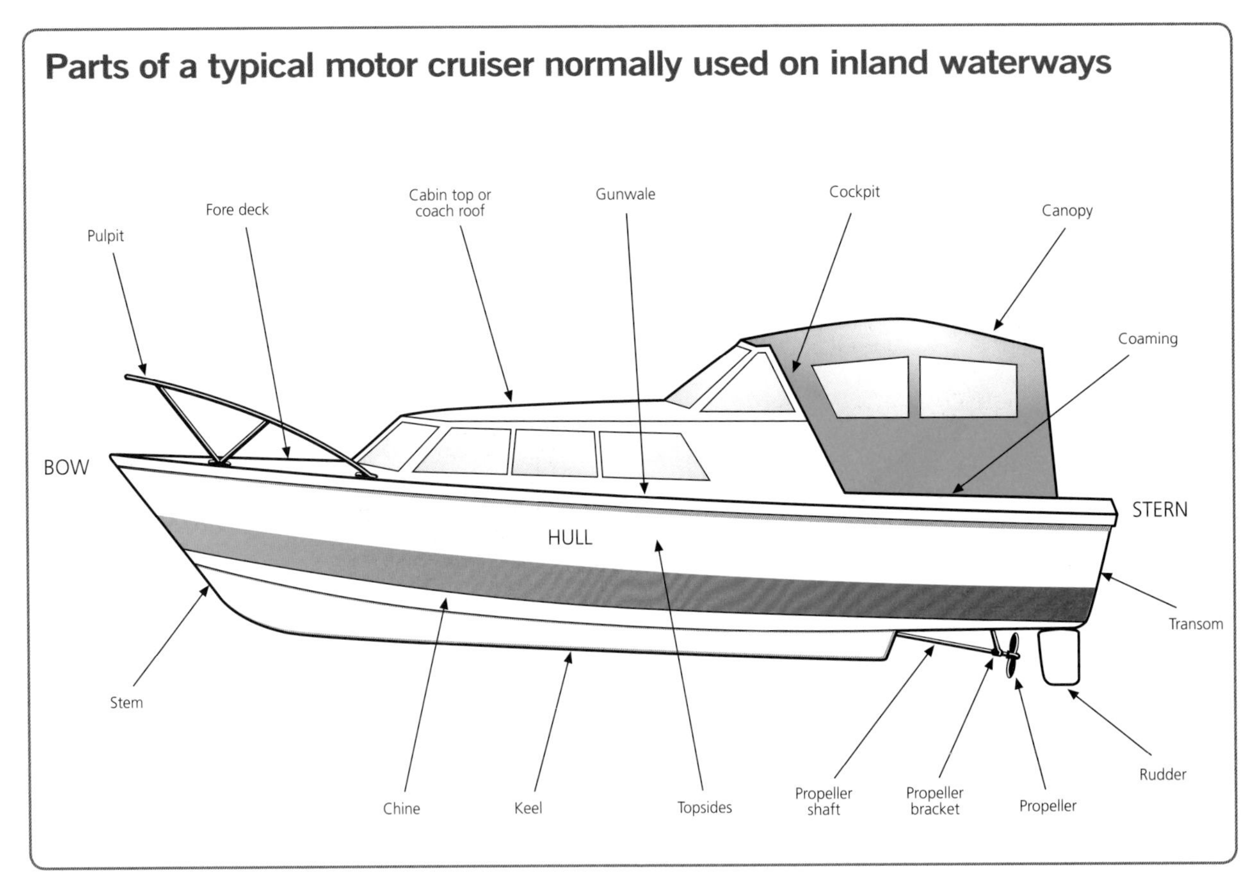

The main parts of a rigid inflatable boat (RIB)

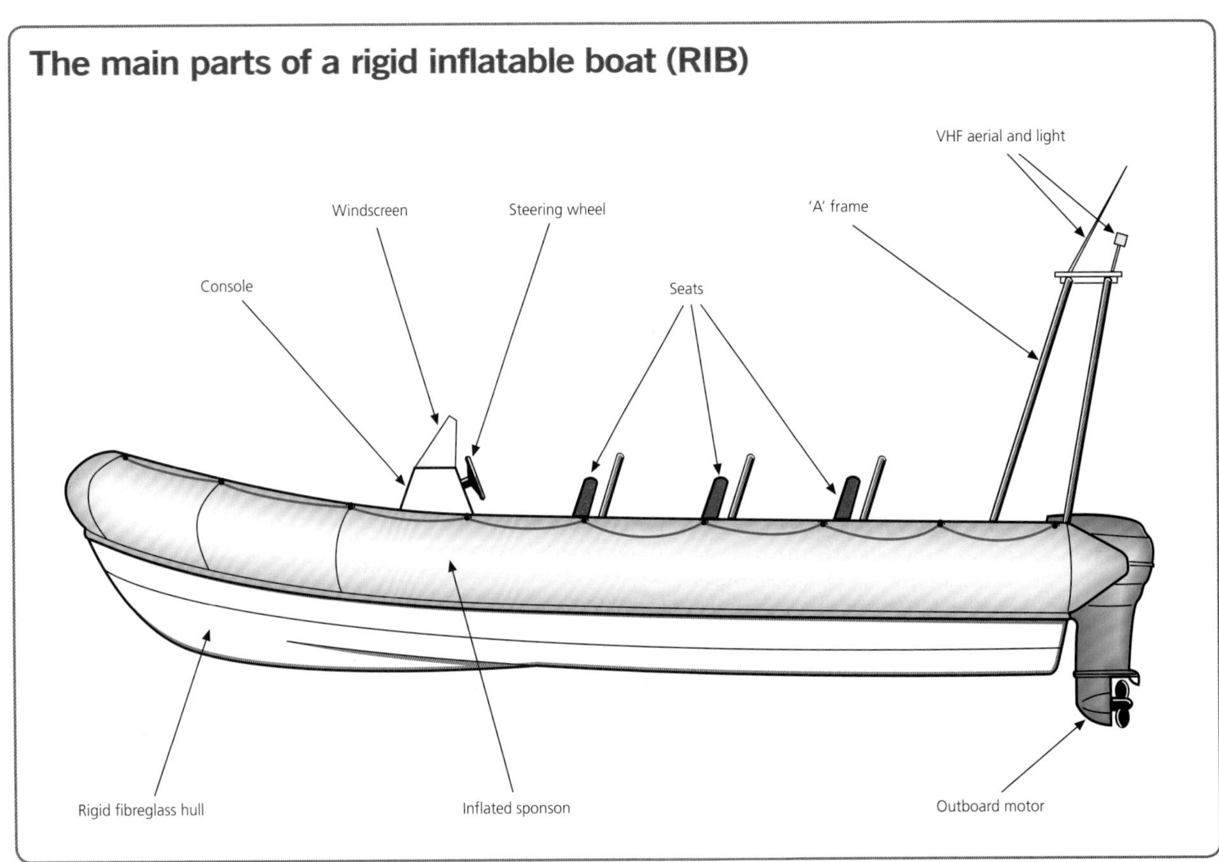

Simplified diagrams of the main engine installation types on motor boats

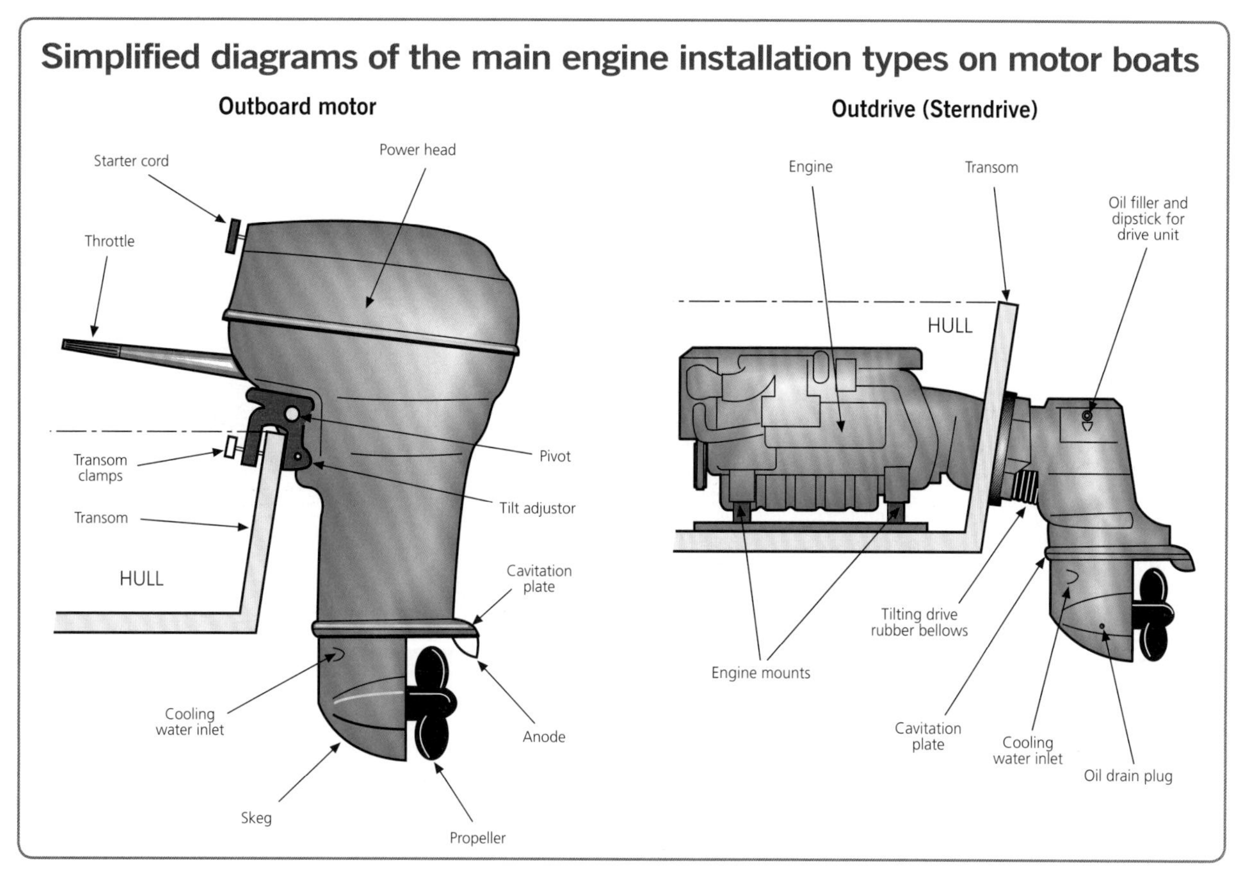

Inboard engine with drive shaft

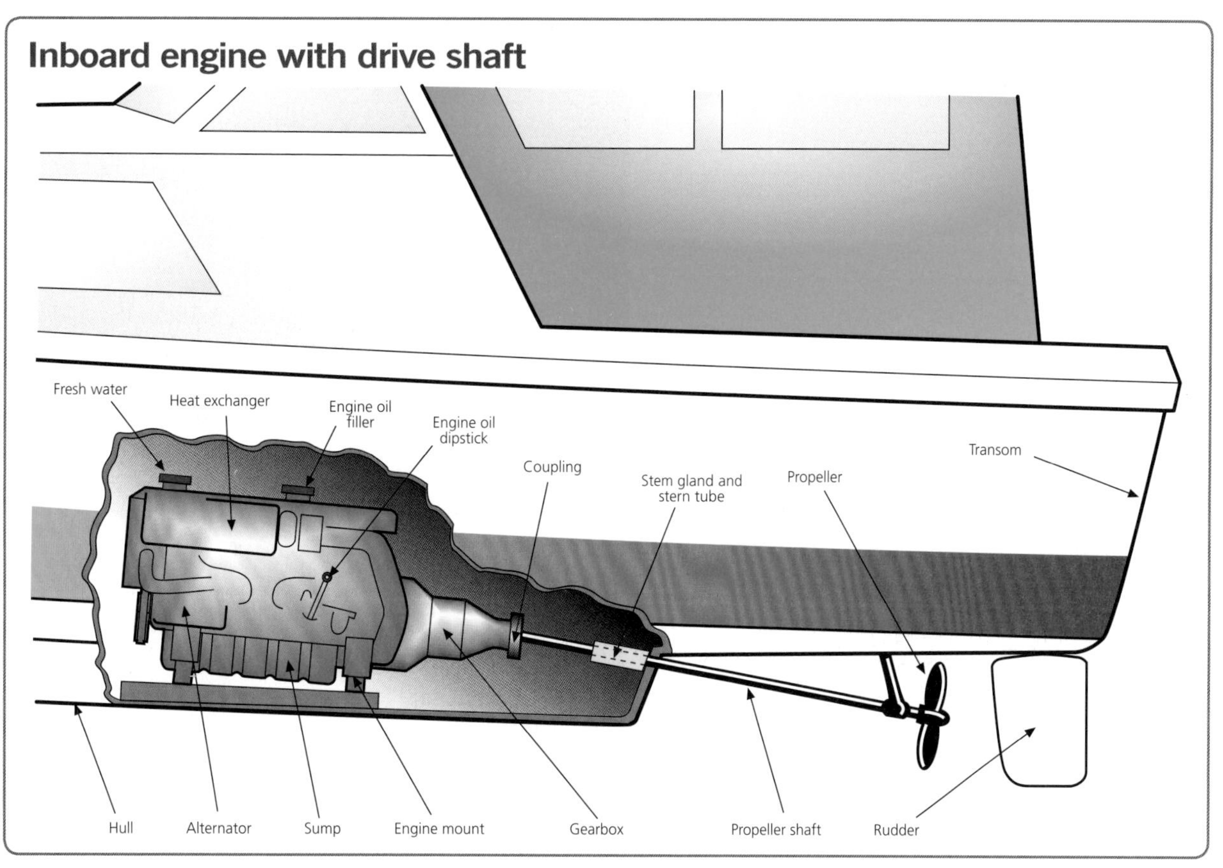

Motor Boat Manual

3 Choice of boat

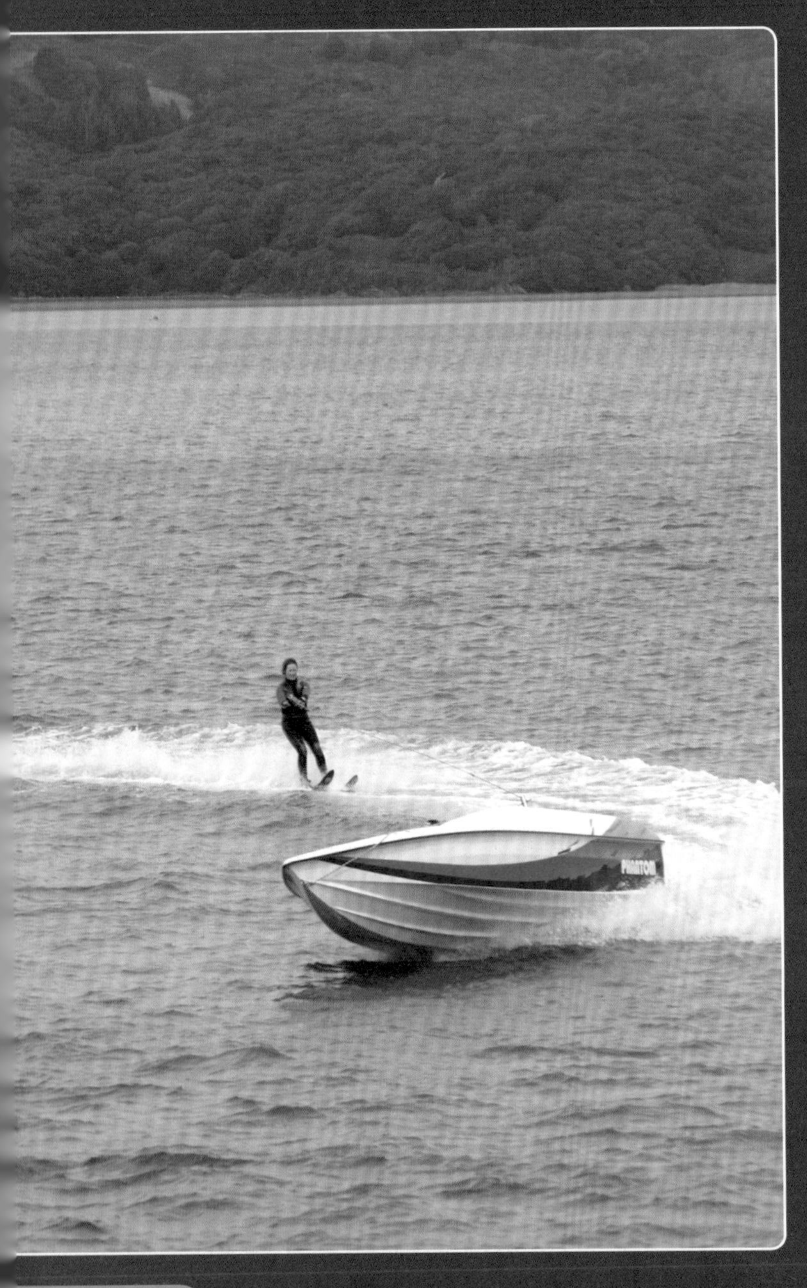

A powerful boat suitable for towing waterskiers may be the choice for some family members.

Reading most of this book before making a choice will reveal a variety of motor boat types and the enjoyment potential for each. This should help you with making a decision on which type to seek and buy. The chapter on buying second-hand and the sections on repair and maintenance have much information on minimising the costs involved.

At this stage it's worth considering some more research and possibly trying several different types. Visit the various boating clubs, marinas, boat shows and boat dealers or brokers. These often offer the chance of getting afloat. Hiring a suitable boat will be possible in many locations – particularly on inland waterways such as the Norfolk Broads and the River Thames. A holiday in a hired boat can establish the suitability of motor boating for the family. If enjoyed by all, it develops enthusiasm and some of the necessary skills. If not, it avoids future family disagreements and may guide you towards a boat more suitable for day trips with those who will find this more agreeable.

Motor boating clubs usually welcome visitors and applications for membership, and provide help for beginners.

Some boating clubs have had the reputation in the past for being rather exclusive and not particularly welcoming unless the newcomer is already well known to existing members. This situation has, fortunately, changed with many clubs. The days when most had waiting lists for membership have passed, and many now need to attract new members. This more enlightened and less exclusive attitude means beginners are much more likely to be welcomed, helped and encouraged.

It could be worth becoming a member for the chance of gaining experience by going for trips in other members' boats before actually buying your own.

Boating forums may arrange cruising in company, *eg* events organised by the Norfolk Broads discussion forum website http://www.the-norfolk-broads.co.uk.

A town or club regatta provides opportunities to learn about different types of boat, as here at Maldon Regatta.

Club activities and boating events provide great opportunities to see a variety of craft afloat and being put through their paces. Enthusiasts for particular boat types abound. They can be very helpful but also tend to get carried away with praise for their particular boat, so keep an open mind and try to talk to owners of a variety of boats that interest you.

Many motor boat dealers will arrange for customers to try boats on the water.

Considerations

Deciding how to start making a choice requires careful thought about your reasons for wanting a boat. A desire to get on the water is a good starting point and excellent in itself.

Making two lists might help – one list is for the things you want from boating and the other is for things you might dislike about it. You might want to go fishing in freshwater or seawater locations. Leisurely cruising on tranquil inland waterways may appeal. Or will you want to attend courses and learn to navigate a suitably equipped boat in the more sheltered coastal cruising areas? Do you want to have the engine power and hull shape suitable to enjoy higher speeds? Does waterskiing appeal? Some might just want a boat to relax and sit on in the sun, enjoying good food and a glass of wine out on the water.

Dislikes might include getting wet and ill from the spray and violent motion caused by high-speed motor boating, or the lack of excitement to be found in gently progressing along an inland waterway. Some may dislike the noise, fumes and maintenance of diesel engines or outboard motors and prefer clean and quiet electric boating.

Others who may join you on the boat should contribute to the lists. Family members could add a score out of ten for each of the points listed to reveal what they really prefer. It's far better to find this out before buying the wrong type of boat, which will inevitably lead to domestic discord later.

Some families have been observed having arguments on boats with little or no shelter after the inexperienced skipper has shouted orders at his wife. Already wet, cold and miserable from rain and spray, she would much rather have been on a boat with a warm, dry cabin. If only they had established this before buying the boat!

Your choice of boat size will be influenced by the size and number of the people likely to use it. A particularly heavy person moving about a small boat will cause problems with its stability, and too many people could cause it to turn over. This has actually happened on a few occasions when boats have been hired and overloaded. Age and agility will also influence your choice. The young and the agile of any age may enjoy the excitement of speed and activities such as waterskiing, whilst plenty of people of all ages prefer more comfortable, leisurely cruising and fishing.

Where will you use your boat?

Inland waterways and the more sheltered inshore coastal waters are the venues for most of the boats covered in this book. These minimise the hazards and maximise the pleasure for those new to motor boating and provide

An open sports boat may appeal to those looking for thrills.

Many people will favour a boat with a comfortable cabin for gentle cruising, such as this smart and well-maintained Freeman cruiser.

Sheltered coastal locations, as here at Salcombe, provide pleasant boating, but accessibility from home needs to be considered.

A scenic river or canal may be within easy reach for relaxed cruising.

experience on which to build when considering voyages further afield in a more substantial craft.

The availability of nearby water for boating and the distance to be travelled are considerations. Work out the time it will take to travel to the water and the time it takes to launch and prepare a motor boat if trailed. Discuss this with existing boat owners if possible to get an idea of the time and effort involved. This can influence the type of boat you'll choose and where you'll keep it. Investigate the tides and depths of water where the boat is to be launched or moored. Will there be times when the tide levels or river conditions prevent use of the boat at your chosen location?

The more exposed and colder the boating location, the more you may be inclined to choose a boat with sufficient shelter in the form of a cuddy, pilot house or cabin. Suitable windproof and waterproof clothing can help here, but bear in mind that the temperature is almost always lower out on the water than on nearby land. Wind chill can be significant and the weather can change quickly.

A caravan afloat?

A consideration with a cruiser with a cabin is its caravan appeal. This could be a controversial point amongst dedicated motor boating enthusiasts, who may feel it's sacrilege to think of a boat on its mooring as a facility for fun in its own right. But if it's your boat, you can use it how you like.

Many people enjoy a cruiser, with reasonably comfortable cabin accommodation, as a weekend retreat on the water – a floating holiday home. They may prefer a tranquil stay beside a riverbank and only occasionally leave their mooring when weather and water conditions are ideal for a relaxing cruise. A 'cottage afloat' is a term sometimes used.

In many marinas and inland waterway mooring locations, fewer than half the cruisers actually go very far and some may never leave their moorings at all. The owners nevertheless enjoy owning their boats to use as weekend retreats in locations at the seaside, or near plenty of attractions close to the waterway. Such entertainments and activities can be enjoyed whenever circumstances or the weather discourage a cruise away from the mooring's attractive location.

Some cruisers are luxuriously equipped with all the comforts of home, making them more like a houseboat than a cruiser. Many thousands of people live full-time in large cruisers, narrowboats or houseboats. It's become so popular that secure, permanent, residential moorings are difficult to find for this purpose. However, using a boat as a second home for weekends and holidays is possible on most motor boat moorings.

Surprising amounts are paid for beach huts on the coast and astronomical amounts for second homes in attractive coastal and waterside locations. Plenty of boat conversions have been made to increase the cabin accommodation in order to have a similar holiday home on a mooring: this is usually much cheaper than a beach hut or holiday property. Some of these conversions may make the boat top-heavy and unsuitable – even unsafe – for cruising, but the purpose of the alteration is to make the boat more like a houseboat. Anyone

One appealing aspect of boat ownership is keeping it in an attractive rural environment.

Some boats are used as houseboats and become comfortable weekend retreats.

Larger day boats can have a cuddy or small cabin to provide some shelter.

who decides to use a boat in this way should not be criticised if that's how they choose to enjoy their boat. It means more people are around at night, which increases supervision and security for the benefit of all the local boat owners.

Affordability

The amount of cash available to buy a boat will have a big influence on choice. The websites mentioned in this and the following chapters and in the Appendix provide current prices of new boats or contact details to pursue your own enquiries.

Open day boats with outboard motors, used for fishing with rod and line or for exploring inland waterways and sheltered coastal waters, cost a few thousand pounds new. A small second-hand open day boat, fishing boat or small speedboat can often be bought for less than a thousand pounds – perhaps only a few hundred – depending on condition.

The larger day boats with some shelter such as a cuddy or small cabin cost rather more new and second-hand. New small to medium-sized motor cruisers or power boats with cabins, plus larger outboard or inboard motors, are mostly

Small open motor boats range from a dinghy with an outboard motor to a rigid inflatable.

A range of small to medium-sized motor cruisers with cabins is available new and second-hand.

between £9,000 and £70,000 – or much more, depending on size and equipment included. A huge range of such boats can be found second-hand and bargains can often be picked up for a few thousand pounds as explained in the chapter on buying second-hand.

The huge range of boats with motors

The above paragraphs having mentioned just some of the many types of motor boat to be considered, more are briefly introduced here before we take a more detailed look at the most popular types.

Most boats can be fitted with an outboard motor or engine and, apart from some pure sailing dinghies designed for racing, many sailing boats have an auxiliary motor for use when the wind drops. Some are actually called 'motorsailers' and are designed to combine both means of propulsion.

Most inflatable dinghies can be fitted with an outboard motor. In fact the 'RIB', or rigid inflatable boat with a solid bottom, is meant to be driven fast with a powerful outboard motor. Even the smallest rowing dinghy or canoe can be propelled by a motor. The petrol outboard is common for these but can be replaced with the rapidly improving range of electric outboard motors popular with anglers on inland waterways. As explained in Chapter 17, electric motors are now a viable – and very quiet – alternative or auxiliary power unit for small to medium-sized boats.

Some traditional open day boats are referred to as 'motor launches', a term that tends to conjure up images of very smart varnished wooden motor boats cruising the River Thames. Launches are likewise often referred as 'day boats' and include the very popular open boats up to about 20ft (6m) long. These can carry several people for a day out on the water in fine weather and may be used for fishing with rod and line.

Other open boats are often called speedboats or sports boats when they have a suitable hull design and a powerful

Sail cruisers have motors and some with inboard motors are called motorsailers

Above: An RIB with an outboard motor.
Below: Even large canoes can be propelled by outboard motors.

A fast fishing boat with a wheelhouse (called a 'pilot house') providing substantial shelter.

Plenty of boats with cuddies and small cabins can be transported easily on a trailer and many types are exhibited at boat shows.

enough motor for high speeds and for towing waterskiers or equipment for high-speed fun on the water. More popular, however, are the fast boats between 17 and 26ft (5 to 8m) with a cuddy, pilot house or small cabin. These may have basic accommodation for a weekend afloat and most are quite easily transported on a trailer. They are frequently the choice for those keen on sea fishing.

Motor cruisers with small cabins and a canopy over the cockpit are available from 16ft (5.8m) to 22ft (6.3m) or more with outboard motors for trips on inland waterways. With increased size and power, suitable equipment and knowledgeable skipper, the cruiser becomes suitable for sheltered estuary and coastal cruising.

The terms 'power cruiser' and 'powerboat' are used in the USA for motor boats, and 'powerboat' is now being used more frequently in the UK too, but is best applied to the

A wide range of motor cruiser sizes exists, providing plenty of choice.

Mayland boats are a popular second-hand purchase.

The Guernsey is an example of a more substantial seagoing cruiser.

Viking cruisers are available new and second-hand in a range of sizes.

The Wilderness trailboat is similar to a narrowboat but is made of GRP and is light enough to be trailed behind a suitable vehicle.

Narrowboats are motor boats designed for the narrow canals of the UK.

Motor yachts are beyond the scope of this book, and beyond the budget of those who aren't lottery winners or earners of very large bonuses!

high-speed versions with particularly powerful motors. Here we're more concerned with the majority of motor boats that you're likely to be able to afford rather than the most powerful – and most expensive – vessels.

Narrowboats are motor boats designed to navigate the canals of the UK. These have engines designed to push their heavy steel hulls slowly along the extensive inland waterway network, and most have substantial accommodation. This specialised type of long and narrow boat is consequently more costly to buy, run and maintain than a smaller fibreglass cruiser, but the slow pace of life cruising gently through the countryside makes it the choice of many.

Sometimes the term 'motor yacht' is heard, but this should really be reserved for very substantial, expensive, luxuriously equipped motor cruisers, with which we are not concerned here. Like the larger powerboats which are cruised and raced out at sea, these are beyond the means of the vast majority of potential boat buyers and are often only rented ('chartered') for a few weeks at a time or are owned or sponsored by commercial concerns.

Cruisers for inland waterways

Rivers such as the Thames, Severn and the rivers of the Norfolk Broads provide plenty of scope for using motor cruisers. On these waterways, progress is leisurely – often restricted by speed limits – so displacement hulls are common. The cruisers used in such environments may not need the power required by seagoing boats, but bear in mind that river currents can vary according to rainfall and time of year, and nearer to the coast the tides will affect the speed and direction of flow. Strong winds can blow you off course too, so some reserve power is useful.

Most small cruisers have a forward cabin with beds (called 'berths'), an area for cooking and preparing food (often called the 'galley'), and a lavatory compartment for the toilet. This is, rather strangely, often referred to as the 'head'.

On rivers, cruiser maximum dimensions may be governed to some extent by the height and width of bridges and the depth of water at various levels. For example, some of the low bridges on the Norfolk Broads prevent access to some areas for boats with too much height ('air draught'). On the other hand, many cruisers have canopies that can be lowered to get under low bridges.

The canal system of the UK is a different matter and much more restricting. Many canals have locks built to take boats with a width (beam) of less than 7ft (2.1m), so clearly, if you want to navigate the canal system this important restriction must be borne in mind, along with the low height of many bridges and tunnels. Investigate these limitations for the waterways you want to navigate before

A canopy like this can be lowered to get under low bridges.

Navigating narrow canals causes inevitable scrapes and knocks, which steel narrowboats are built to withstand.

Tidal currents can be strong, as here under the Conwy bridge, and need enough power to cope with them.

deciding on the type and dimensions of boat to be purchased. Details of such restrictions are available from the organisations that issue navigation licences and guidebooks for particular waterways (see Appendix).

Canal cruisers are narrow beamed to cope with the narrow canals. The long cruisers, mostly made of steel, are called narrowboats. Some are replicas of the original 19th- and 20th-century working boats. The heavy steel construction of most narrowboats helps them cope with the scrapes, knocks and bounces that tend to happen when steering such long vessels through restricted openings into locks and in negotiating other features of the narrow canals.

Suitably narrow glass-reinforced plastic (GRP) cruisers can, of course, be used on the canal system too. Again, check the dimensions of the waterways you intend to cruise, as they are not all narrow and a wider beam cruiser may fit the locks of your chosen canals and rivers. However, a point to bear in mind here is that lighter GRP cruisers are not as resistant to damage as the heavy steel narrowboats, and clearly it's wise to avoid any chance of a collision with one, or of being crushed by one, particularly in or near a lock. This thought may affect your choice of boat if heavy steel narrowboats abound on the waterways where you intend to cruise. You may prefer to be similarly protected by buying a steel-hulled vessel.

Estuary and coastal cruisers

Estuaries may seem sheltered and suitable for some larger cruisers used on inland waterways, but you should investigate them carefully and bear in mind the likely current flowing from the river, combined with tidal streams at different states of the tide. The local harbour master, coastguard, RNLI station and boating clubs are good sources of this information. Tidal conditions usually mean much more engine power is necessary than on inland waterways to overcome currents and the short, steep waves that can occur, especially when the wind is against the tide in shallow water.

Your boat will need to be able to cope with the above without too much water and spray coming inboard if conditions worsen. Generally a boat needs to be over 20ft (6m) in length to cope well with tidal conditions, although smaller open boats with reliable outboard motors are often used by experienced boat owners in calm conditions when the weather forecast is good. Cruisers between 25ft (7.6m) and 35ft (10.7m) are the most popular for estuary and coastal cruising in reasonably safe and sheltered areas.

Whether the boat will be trailed has a big influence on size and weight. Lengths up to about 25ft (10.7m) can be trailed, launched and recovered by suitable vehicles. Check your vehicle's handbook for towing limits, instructions and details, and check that your driving licence and insurance cover include towing the size and weight involved.

Cruisers to be kept on a mooring or in a marina can be more substantial and the range of possible equipment and facilities increases with the size of the boat – but so do the costs involved.

Motor boats suitable for use in the estuary and at sea moored at Essex Marina.

Most boats can be used for a spot of casual fishing as here on the Norfolk Broads, but for more serious angling – particularly on the coast – requirements are more specific.

A cuddy provides some shelter when fishing.

Boats for fishing

The desire to go fishing with rod and line is a very common motive behind buying a motor boat. Most boats can be used for fishing inland waters such as the Norfolk Broads and some may be suitable for sheltered coastal waters.

Even a dinghy with oars and an outboard motor will give you access to many shallow inland waters plus the very sheltered creeks to be found in estuaries where you can drift in with the tide to catch flatfish and bass. There are, though, aspects that make boats more suitable and safe for seawater fishing with rod and line (often referred to as 'sea angling' to distinguish it from commercial fishing). Many of the considerations in this section apply to the choice of boat for this sport.

Much of your time will be spent out in the open wielding a rod and using fishing tackle that needs to be easily accessible. Space for this is important. A large cockpit will be needed, along with storage for bait and tackle. Two or three people using rods take up a considerable amount of space. A boat with ample beam (width) helps to provide this space, and its width will make it more stable when anchored and riding any waves. An open boat may be satisfactory in suitable weather and calm conditions, but a cuddy or small cabin will be greatly appreciated to make tea, to eat sandwiches, to use a toilet, and to escape from the sudden blast of a squall of rain and wind.

Although a boat over 20ft (6m) is recommended above, smaller boats designed for sea angling, with powerful outboard motors, have recently become popular. These provide the angler with the speed both to reach fishing 'marks' rapidly and to return quickly if the weather and sea conditions deteriorate. However, this ability should not be relied on as a substitute for adequate safety and navigation equipment and appropriate experience, plus, preferably, qualifications in handling the boat.

Small speedboats with shallow hulls can tend to get blown about by the wind and waves at slow speeds and can be uncomfortable when anchored for fishing.

Small motor boats with powerful outboards help sea anglers reach fishing marks quickly.

Larger motor boats with large cockpits can accommodate groups of anglers comfortably. Many are operated as hire boats with skippers. A trip on one of these will help you decide whether sea fishing is suitable for you. This one operates from Aberdovey in Wales.

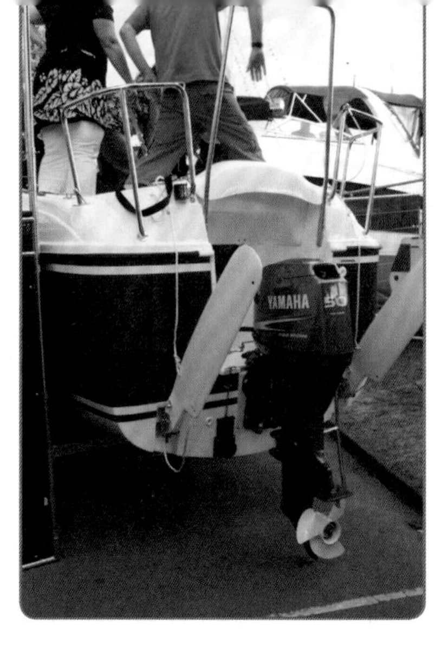

The MacGregor 26M is an unusual combination of sail cruiser and motorboat. With its powerful outboard motor it can get up on the plane at high speed.

A website providing reviews of boats suitable for fishing and the equipment needed is can be found at http://www.fishing-boats.info. The articles are written by boat owners, who give personal opinions about their boats and equipment for sea fishing. More on fishing websites, magazines and books is provided at the end of Chapter 18 and in the Appendix.

Motorsailers

Most sailing boats can have a motor fitted but some have been designed to combine the advantages of a motor cruiser with a sail cruiser. This arrangement was initially criticised as providing a boat which neither motored nor sailed particularly well. This is a matter of opinion, but more recent designs have achieved a good compromise. It's certainly useful to have sails if the engine lets you down! Using the wind also saves on the increasing cost of fuel, and the steadying effect of the wind pressing on the sails reduces the rolling motion experienced when motoring into or across the waves.

Some points to bear in mind are that the keel needs to be substantial to prevent the boat from moving sideways when sailing. This increases the draft (depth) and requires deeper water. Obviously a mast is needed too, and this will have to be lowered if cruising into waterways where there are low bridges and other obstacles, such as trees.

Sailing involves acquiring substantial additional skills which can greatly increase enjoyment of boating but require practice with an experienced skipper and/or instructor on an appropriate sailing course. Sailing and sailing equipment maintenance is not covered in this book but many aspects are covered in the Haynes *Sailing Boat Manual* by Dennis Watts.

Cruiser accommodation

It's often been said that most women tend to prefer boats with comfortable cabins rather than open boats. This point may be debatable but, as the majority of people buying boats are male, it's a consideration to be borne in mind if the company of the opposite sex is desired. In fact comfortable accommodation away from it all can have a romantic appeal to many…

A major selling point of motor cruisers is the number of berths. It may be theoretically possible to have a certain number of people lie down on bunks in the cabin or cabins, but what happens when they all get up and move about? In the case of a caravan someone can go outside and sit in a chair, allowing more space inside for the others. With a boat, though, that chair would have to be floating beside the boat! Storage space for water, supplies, clothing and personal possessions will influence exactly how many can realistically live on the boat for any length of time.

Of course, you need to decide whether the boat will be used for weekends or for longer periods. This can make a substantial difference to the amount of storage space needed.

Some family members may prefer a boat with comfortable, well-equipped cabin accommodation as in this Viking cruiser.

With a centre cockpit a cruiser can have two separate cabins, which may be an advantage for owners with a family.

Some cruisers have a central cockpit with two separate cabins. This can give more privacy but does tend to split the accommodation up into rather small units. The aft cabin can then seem particularly cramped and airless.

The position of the cooker, sink and work surface should be considered, bearing in mind that the person working there may block the route through to the rest of the cabin. On many small cruisers this cannot be avoided, but for obvious safety reasons the cook should not be pushed past and disturbed whilst busy with hot pans.

Consider the size, arrangement and facilities of the toilet compartment. On small inland waterway cruisers the compartment may have a portable chemical toilet with rather limited capacity. This has to be emptied into suitable discharge points at boatyards. Somewhat larger boats have a fixed toilet linked to a much larger holding tank which, when necessary, is pumped out into the sewage system at a boatyard. All of which needs to be taken into consideration in relation to the number of people who'll be using the boat and for what length of time.

A compact, well-designed toilet compartment.

The smallest toilet compartments won't have room for a washbasin and washing will need to be done at the sink in the cabin. However, cruisers built more recently have a washbasin in the toilet compartment, and very compact designs of washbasin, vanity unit and shower have been developed to fit small spaces. Bear in mind aspects such as ventilation, storage, and handholds for when the boat is moving.

Headroom in the cabin may be an important factor. The young and the agile may be quite happy to bend and crouch inside a very small cruiser, but tall people, those liking more comfort and those with less than perfect backs may well prefer full standing headroom. Decide how important this is at an early stage and include the investigation of headroom in your research of various boat types before even viewing them.

Hull types and shapes

Displacement

The displacement hull is the traditional type, designed to move through the water by displacing it rather than by planing or skimming over the surface at high speed – in other words it goes *in* the water rather than *on* it. The engine pushes the boat through the water efficiently but quite slowly.

The displacement hull has good directional stability. Its maximum speed is limited and dictated by the length of the hull. If you're not in a hurry and want a reasonably smooth ride using fuel economically, the displacement hull is suitable. In fact on most inland waterways and in many parts of estuaries there are speed limits, so if this is where you'll use the boat there's little point in spending more on one with the shape and power to exceed them.

A displacement hull with typical rounded shape.

The virtually flat-bottomed hull shape of the Wilderness Trailboat is fine for inland waterways and provides maximum interior space.

A keel extending down from the hull helps with directional stability.

Shallow vee or flat bottom

Many boats designed for inland waterways have vertical sides and a very shallow V-shaped or completely flat bottom. This design provides the maximum space inside – important in boats that have to be narrow to fit many inland waterways. Because they tend to be top-heavy, this shape is not recommended for waters where waves can cause dangerous instability.

Some of the earliest designs for speedboats had virtually flat bottoms but, again, the problem here is with stability, particularly at slow speeds. They also pound heavily onto waves, making for an uncomfortable ride.

Semi-displacement

This type has a deep V-shaped hull forward, which changes to a flat or rounded shape towards the stern. This design combines the benefit, at slow speeds, of the displacement hull's stability, with the capacity to rise up and plane when provided with a powerful enough engine. The speed may not be as high as a true planing hull but provides a useful compromise if you desire the opportunity to go faster at times.

A V-shaped hull enables a boat to get up onto the plane. Semi-displacement (or 'semi-planing') hulls have a V forward, which flattens towards the stern, providing the option of planing when needed.

Keels

With all three of the above types of hull there may be a small keel extending down from the centre line of the hull bottom. This improves directional performance and helps to stop the boat drifting sideways in a crosswind at slow speeds. On a motorsailer keels are more important, ensuring the boat moves forwards rather than sideways when sailing; twin bilge keels are a common arrangement for this type of boat.

A skeg may be an extension of the keel or a fin in front of the propeller. This also provides some directional benefit and helps to protect the propeller and rudder.

Deep vee

This style of hull is used for high speed and is designed to slide up and over the water instead of through it. This means there is much less resistance than with a displacement hull. The engine has to be powerful enough to push the boat up onto the plane; once up, speed then increases. This is an exciting sensation and many people find it a main attraction of motor boating. Waterskiers can be towed and more distant fishing marks can be reached quickly.

A deep V-shaped hull can plane over the water at high speed.

A cathedral hull.

On a smooth sea the exhilaration of high speed is a big appeal. Unfortunately, if waves are encountered, bouncing over and crashing into them quickly becomes much less appealing, and at slow speeds the boat may very well be less stable than a displacement vessel. Wind, waves and currents can cause the boat to wallow uncomfortably, move slowly and make it difficult to steer, particularly with smaller speedboats or sports boats. Larger boats with planing hulls may cope better, but bear in mind that the powerful engines necessary for high-speed use large amounts of fuel.

Cathedral hull

Designs using multiple hulls include the cathedral and dory. The two planing hulls combine extra stability with increased internal space and the option of reasonable speed in suitable calm conditions. However, they give a rather rough ride in choppy conditions.

Rigid inflatable boats

RIBs have a rigid V-shaped planing hull which is surrounded with a tough inflatable tube. Divers use this type of boat and don't mind getting wet, but the fact that the boat is low-sided and easy to get into when diving also means that spray can enter when speeding across the water. Nevertheless, many people find the speed and spray appealing aspects of RIBs. The larger ones have one or two very powerful outboard motors pushing them at high and exhilarating speeds.

Smaller RIBs can be used like an ordinary dinghy or small day boat and the fact that they can be reduced in size by deflating the tubes can make storage easier.

A rigid inflatable boat or RIB.

Inflatables

Small flat-bottomed inflatable boats are very popular. They can be taken, deflated, to the water in the boot of a medium-sized car and inflated rapidly with a 12V inflator or foot pump. Various types of folding or inflatable floors provide a firm base, and an outboard motor is attached to the transom. Although quite stable they can be blown off course by wind because they are sitting *on* the water rather than *in* it and are quite light. Indeed, one of the main problems with inflatables, particularly the very cheap lightweight ones, is their dangerous tendency to be blown out to sea by an offshore wind. Many inflatables are quite difficult to row if the motor fails, as the effort of pulling on the oar can get absorbed into the flexibility of the inflated tubes.

Small inflatable boats are popular for use with an outboard motor in sheltered waters, and as a tender to reach the shore from an anchored or moored boat.

Often when a larger motor boat or cruiser is owned a smaller boat is bought as a tender and kept on deck or hung on davits at the stern. If this is not possible, an inflatable boat could be packed away and inflated when needed. The inflatable itself can then provide extra enjoyment when fitted with an outboard motor.

Engines and outboards

Here we are concerned only with such engine considerations as will affect your choice of boat type. Much more on engines will be found in Chapter 17.

Outboard motors

Some have been put off boating by seeing the difficulties sometimes experienced by people repeatedly pulling at the starter cord as they try to start an outboard motor. However, a well maintained outboard motor should be quite easy to start and if pulling the cord puts you off, electric-start outboard motors are quite common.

A boat with an outboard is usually cheaper than one with an inboard engine, and it's much easier to remove and replace an outboard than an inboard engine. Smaller outboards can easily be removed and carried home for storage and maintenance. It's also quite easy to get at the propeller if anything gets wrapped round it or it gets damaged.

Steering with an outboard motor is positive when under way and when reversing, although the lack of a rudder can cause problems at very slow speeds. Two-stroke motors tend to be noisy but modern four-stroke units are comparatively quiet and more economical on fuel. Older two-strokes also tend to produce substantial smoky and smelly exhaust. Because of regulations restricting exhaust emissions, most new outboards are four-stroke. These do not need oil to be added to the petrol as two-stroke motors do.

Storage of sufficient fuel for an extended cruise can be a problem for outboards compared with inboard engines, where a large fuel tank is usually permanently installed. The Boat Safety Scheme (BSS) regulations for inland waterways require petrol to be stored in safe well-ventilated positions where petrol vapour cannot enter the boat. The availability of petrol along the waterways where you'll be cruising needs to be checked, since it's not necessarily as readily available as diesel.

Petrol inboard engines

Boats with petrol inboard engines are normally cheaper than those with diesel engines. They also run smoothly when well maintained and are quiet compared with many diesel engines. As stated above, though, check the availability of petrol at boatyards and marinas in your area. Strict regulations concerning storage of petrol have made it too costly for many boatyards to supply it.

A most important consideration is that petrol vapour is highly inflammable and heavy. In a car's engine compartment there's scope for vapour to escape, but any leakage in a boat will accumulate and can be ignited by a spark from the electrical system. For this reason it's essential that the petrol engine be very carefully maintained to avoid such risks. Inland cruisers must have a BSS certificate, requiring a compulsory inspection every four years that includes checking the petrol engine and its fuel supply. However, much more frequent maintenance and checking must be carried out and it's important to run the venting fan (often called a 'bilge blower') in the engine compartment to remove any vapour before starting the engine.

Another problem is with the ignition system, which can suffer from the damp environment of a boat. Although engines in boats get much less use than in road vehicles and should last much longer, condensation is a major cause of deterioration in petrol engines.

As with road vehicle engines, the consumption of petrol may be higher than diesel but the prevailing cost per litre also needs to be considered in connection with this. For serious cruising, the vast majority of boat owners in the UK prefer diesel engines.

Diesel engines

In the UK, diesels are the most common type of inboard engine. A major advantage in the past was the availability of diesel for use in boats at a price much lower than the price of road diesel and petrol. However, this 'red' diesel is no longer available at a low price as engine fuel in the UK because the European Union required the privilege to be

An outboard motor can easily be unclamped and removed for servicing and repair.

The damp environment may affect the ignition system of a boat's petrol engine.

More recent diesel engines are quieter than older models.

withdrawn from leisure boat owners. The full price for diesel is now charged, including the relevant taxes except for diesel used for heating purposes. The cost of fuel has, therefore, become a more significant consideration and may affect your choice of a boat with a large thirsty engine. Fuel consumption is related to the size of engine and speed. In particular, high-speed boats with large engines can consume alarming quantities very quickly.

Diesel engines can be more reliable in a damp environment compared with petrol engines. The fuel is also less volatile than petrol, although once ignited it can burn fiercely so safety is still an issue. Many older diesel engines produce noise and smells that are quite penetrating and persistent. Recently developed engines, though, are significantly quieter.

Bear in mind that some aspects of diesel engine maintenance and repair require specialist knowledge, equipment and tools, making it necessary for such work to be carried out by suitable engineers.

Inboard engine installation types

There are two main types of inboard installation: shaft drive and outdrive (see the diagrams in the previous chapter).

Shaft drive

The engine is connected by a shaft through the hull of the boat to the propeller, and steering is by a rudder. This is a comparatively simple arrangement, with the engine and gears sited in a compartment which can be accessed from the cockpit or cabin, and is likely to be easier for a DIY mechanic to understand than the outdrive system. Directional stability is good forwards although not necessarily in reverse. A disadvantage is that the propeller is not easily accessible.

Outdrive

The engine is hard up against the stern of the boat and connected through it to a 'leg' which has gears and a propeller and which pivots to provide steering, making for good manoeuvrability. The outdrive has some similarities with the lower parts of an outboard motor, and like an outboard motor it can be tilted up to access the propeller. Maintenance is more complicated than with a shaft drive and can become comparatively expensive, particularly if it's not regularly serviced. The outdrive is also rather vulnerable to damage, as it's on the outside of the boat.

Twin engines

Larger boats may have twin engines to produce plenty of power. Obviously they require more expenditure and effort to maintain and need more fuel than a single engine. A major advantage is safety in the event of one engine failing. However, this safety feature can be provided on a boat with a single inboard engine by having a suitable auxiliary outboard motor mounted ready for use in the event of engine failure.

Electric motors

Although very few boats currently have electric inboard motors, their popularity is rapidly growing. In the not too distant future electric propulsion will take over as the world runs out of adequate oil supplies, and the Electric Boat Association is experiencing a very large increase in interest. The Association's website at http://www.electric-boat-association.org.uk has much information on electric motor boats, and more about the potential for quiet and clean electric propulsion can be found in Chapter 17.

An outdrive can be tilted up like an outboard motor.

4 Buying a second-hand motor boat

Looking for and discovering a suitable motor boat can be a most enjoyable part of the boating experience. Walking along the sea wall or riverbank, watching all the different boats, arouses a strong desire to join them. Buying what seems the ideal boat is an exciting and emotional experience as you anticipate the pleasures and enjoyment of ownership. But try to keep in touch with reality. Ideally, you should read not only this chapter but also the rest of this book before buying. The extra knowledge will help towards a wise decision.

Where to keep it

Before buying a boat a most important consideration is where you'll keep it. Some of the boats covered in this book will fit onto a trailer and could be kept in a suitable space at home. If this isn't possible, storage at an appropriate club may be available. The availability of storage and moorings varies greatly according to location and should be arranged before purchase. Sometimes it's possible to take over a mooring or storage space when buying a boat, but don't rely on it. More on storage and moorings will be found in a Chapters 6 and 7.

Second-hand for choice and value

A large budget is needed to buy new, but for a fraction of the price of a new boat you'll find a much wider range of choice among the thousands of second-hand boats advertised for sale. In fact there are many excellent boat types that are no longer built and the only way to obtain one is second-hand.

Many small open boats sell for hundreds of pounds second-hand compared with several thousand for new versions. Motor cruisers costing tens of thousands new can often be found second-hand for a few thousand pounds. Whether a good outboard motor is included will, of course, make a difference to the price of the smaller boats, as will the condition of an inboard motor in more substantial cruisers. More on motors can be found later in this chapter and elsewhere in this book.

A second-hand boat will often include many of the accessories and extras that have to be purchased separately when buying new. Equipment such as anchors, auxiliary outboard motors and their spare parts, mooring ropes, oars, fenders and lifejackets usually have to be bought as extras to the cost of a new boat, so when they come with a second-hand boat they're a major asset and cost saving.

A good condition outboard motor may be included with a second-hand boat.

Buying second-hand is also an excellent example of recycling, which we are all encouraged to do. Buying and restoring an old boat recycles one that might otherwise be left to deteriorate to the point where it would have to be scrapped.

Mooring included?

Some boats are advertised as having a mooring or storage space available to be taken over by the purchaser. This can be really worthwhile in an area where moorings are difficult to find. In fact, some people have been known to buy a cheap boat sold with a mooring simply to take over the mooring. The boat is then sold on separately, thereby releasing the mooring for use with a better boat.

All this depends, of course, on the co-operation of the person or organisation that owns and rents out the mooring, so it's important to confirm that it can be

A mooring may be included with a second-hand boat, but don't rely on it.

WEBSITES SELLING BOATS

The Internet is now accessible to almost everyone, whether or not a computer is available at home or work. Local libraries have expanded the number of computers available to the public, with assistance available if it's needed.

Some websites not only provide free or cheap advertising but also publish adverts in printed form. Conversely, several boating magazines have website listings of their classified adverts. The most popular boat buying and selling website is probably http://www.boatsandoutboards.co.uk, several reports indicating it has more visitors than any other such site. However, other websites are also well worth searching, and a selection of these are listed below. A list of the motor boating magazines' own websites is included in the Appendix.

- **http://www.boatsandoutboards.co.uk**
- **http://www.apolloduck.co.uk**
- **http://boatshop24.co.uk**
- **http://www.boats4sale.co.uk**
- **http://www.allatsea.co.uk**
- **http://www.ybw.com/ybw/boatsale.htm**
- **http://boatsforsalenow.com**
- **http://search.ebay.co.uk**
- **http://www.boatshed.com**
- **http://www.boatbrowse.co.uk**
- **http://www.boatsforsale.co.uk**
- **http://www.noblemarine.co.uk/boatsforsale.php3**
- **http://www.look4boats.com**
- **http://www.boatandyachtbuyer.co.uk**

A great many websites specialising in general classified advertising also do an excellent job in encouraging the recycling of all manner of items, including boats. Many of them are online versions of the classified ads in local newspapers that wouldn't easily have been available to people outside their local area in the past. Other sites exist mainly to provide free or cheap advertising. Some classified advertisement websites which include motor boats are:

- **http://www.adtrader.co.uk**
- **http://www.friday-ad.co.uk**
- **http://www.loot.com**
- **http://uk.freeads.net**
- **http://www.findit.co.uk**
- **http://www.preloved.co.uk**
- **http://www.classifieds.co.uk**
- **http://www.ukclassifieds.co.uk**

A road trailer included as part of the deal is a big asset.

transferred and what costs are involved. Sometimes there's a transfer fee and the annual rental charge may be increased above that paid by the existing owner. If the boat is stored at a boating club, will membership and the storage space be available to you as the new owner of the boat?

Trailer included?

The inclusion of a road trailer with a second-hand boat is a big attraction, particularly if you're keeping the boat at home. A road trailer in good condition may add something to the second-hand price when included with a boat, but a suitable new trailer will cost far more, possibly more than the second-hand boat itself!

Where to look

Recent years have seen a huge increase in opportunities to advertise boats cheaply, often free of charge and to a very big range of potential buyers, mainly via the Internet. Websites now provide many opportunities to find a bargain. Lower-priced boats needing some work which in the past were often only advertised in shop windows are now much more widely promoted. Buyers no longer have to rely on adverts in a few magazines.

Photos of boats for sale

Another advantage of using the Internet is the easy availability of photographs. Plenty of website adverts include photos, and sellers are often able to supply more by email. It's worth asking for extra views of boats that genuinely interest you. For example, it's a good idea to see the interior of a motor cruiser as well as several views of the hull and decks. Photos of a reasonable resolution can be copied into appropriate software to be enlarged on your computer's monitor. This way, so I've found, it's possible to get a good idea of a boat's condition before travelling some distance to view it. When viewing the pictures just bear in mind that there's a tendency for photographs to be flattering if taken in bright sunshine or when the boat is wet after a shower of rain.

A website that's taken the approach of providing plenty of photos to a particularly helpful level is www.boatshed.com. Advertisers have to pay a broker's fee, but the help provided can make it worthwhile both for seller and buyer. Someone is sent by Boatshed to take up to 65 photos of the boat for sale. However, this is mainly for sail and motor cruisers – you won't necessarily find the cheapest small motor boats here.

Before making a journey of any distance to view a particular boat always telephone to check it's still available. Even websites aren't always completely up to date.

If a particular type of boat is not currently being advertised a 'wanted' advert can be placed on most websites, often free of charge. State where you are and how far you're prepared to travel to view the boat. Another way to find the type of boat you want to buy is to find a good example of one which isn't necessarily for sale. Most owners will be flattered to think you like their boat enough to want to buy it, so find out how to contact them via the boatyard, club or marina. Alternatively leave a polite note on the boat. The author has successfully bought boats this way.

It's also worth keying 'project boat' into the search facility on boat-selling websites in order to find neglected boats available cheaply and worth improving.

Internet auction

The eBay auction website has a section for 'Boats and Watercraft' – rather strangely included under 'Car Parts and Vehicles' – which is certainly worth searching on a regular basis. More boats are included under 'Sporting Goods'. Sometimes a boat has to be sold in a hurry because of a change in family circumstances: unexpectedly inheriting a boat, for instance, can mean that it needs to be sold quickly, and eBay provides an opportunity to dispose of it fast – which means a possible bargain for the buyer.

A disadvantage of eBay is the short time available to visit and view a boat being auctioned. It's essential to inspect the boat before bidding, whatever assurances are given by the seller. Remember: bids are legally binding once you click on the bid button. Advice on inspection, surveys and trying out a boat on the water are included later in this chapter.

Boating magazine adverts

Don't forget to look at boating magazine classified sections. In fact you'll probably be tempted to buy magazines such as *Motor Boats Monthly*, *Motor Boat and Yachting* and *Practical Boat Owner* anyway, because they contain many interesting articles and trade adverts as well as boats for sale. For boats on inland waterways try *Canal and Riverboat*, *Canal Boat and Inland Waterways* and *Waterways World*. Boating magazine websites with contact details for subscriptions are given in the Appendix. Their websites also include boats advertised for sale.

Boating clubs and owners' associations

Motor boat and yachting club websites often have a page of boats for sale. The Royal Yachting Association provides a list of clubs nationwide. Just go to http://www.rya.org.uk and select 'club' from the 'find' box. Select 'Motor boating' to find contact details and websites for clubs in your area. Most will have lists of members' boats of many types for sale.

Associations for owners of particular boat types also advertise examples for sale on their websites and in their newsletters. Examples of boat owners' associations that often have boats for sale are listed below, with the name of the actual make or model of boat being included in the website name. Such websites include galleries of pictures of their boats, and the discussion forums are a good source of advice.

To find boats up for sale, in most cases you need to click on 'boats for sale' or 'members' adverts'. If this option isn't available, select the contacts option and email to enquire about any boats for sale.

The selection below is intended to show the range of boats for sale that can be found by visiting association websites. A full list is regularly updated on the Royal Yachting Association website at http://www.rya.org.uk.

Additionally, try a Google search for any particular boat type or class to find other boating organisations and discussion forums currently advertising boats for sale.

Owners' associations

http://www.vikingowners.org.uk/
http://www.wilderness.org.uk/
http://www.nauticus.co.uk
http://www.normanboats.co.uk/
http://www.shetland.owners.org.uk
http://www.dawncraftowners.com/
http://www.seamasterclub.co.uk/
http://www.microplus.dk/
http://www.hardy-owner.org.uk/
http://www.fairlineownersclub.com
http://www.faireyownersclub.co.uk
http://www.freemancruiser.co.uk
http://www.freemancruisers.com
http://broom.woodleyheadland.net/
http://www.hampton.owners.org.uk
http://birchwoodboats.aceboard.com/
http://www.elysianboats.co.uk/

The Association of Waterways Cruising Clubs provides a map showing clubs to be found in each region of the UK on their website at http://www.awcc.org.uk. An inland club list can also be found at http://www.ukcanals.net/clubs.html.

Notice boards

Don't neglect the old-style advertising methods. Although Internet access is widely available, not everyone advertises on websites. Club notice boards and the windows of newsagents, chandlers, boatyard offices and supermarkets

A shop window may be the first place a boat is advertised.

may therefore still be the first place a bargain boat is advertised. Some boat types are popular in particular locations and could be sold quickly this way.

Knock on the door of a boating club and introduce yourself. As a non-member of a club you can ask a club steward or a committee member permission to look at their notice board showing boats for sale. It's also worth asking members if they know of any boats likely to be for sale in the near future.

Plenty of small second-hand motor boats can be found for sale in boatyards such as this one in Woodbridge, Suffolk.

Boat brokers

Dealers in boats are called brokers or yacht brokers. Most of them have a catalogue of boats for sale on their websites. Their fee is normally a percentage of the boat's selling price, and is charged to the seller, not the buyer. The fee that the seller has to pay to the broker may consequently increase the price above that for similar privately advertised boats.

If a suitable boat is available, there should be advantages in buying from a broker, who can provide plenty of advice about particular types of boat. Bear in mind, though, that brokers are similar to estate agents, and are keen to sell you a boat; so if you go on a mailing list they tend to assume that you can afford more than you may have mentioned. On

A brokerage, as here at Essex Boatyards, can provide a wide range of larger second-hand and new boats for sale.

Investigate moorings and the corners of boatyards for neglected boats. Some may have 'For Sale' signs.

the other hand, you could receive details of the boat of your dreams before someone else buys it.

Brokers may be members of appropriate associations, such as the Yacht Brokers, Designers and Surveyors Association, which has its own website at http://www.ybdsa.co.uk. Such membership can increase the confidence in the services provided. These can include checking the paperwork that comes with most motor boats to ensure legality of ownership, and ensuring that deposits and payments are handled correctly. At additional cost, they should be able to arrange any necessary surveys and boat safety inspections, and provide transport facilities for the boat.

Boatyards

These can vary enormously. Large boatyards may have a substantial brokerage business with plenty of boats to view on hardstanding and on their moorings. Smaller yards may just have a notice board in their office window or on their gate with a few cards giving brief details of boats for sale. Some vessels in the boatyard may simply bear a handwritten 'For Sale' sign.

Small motor boats are sometimes abandoned by owners who have lost interest. They might clutter corners of a

A boatyard will have equipment to lift, launch and transport boats.

boatyard and the boatyard owner may be keen to arrange for them to be sold and cleared away ASAP. It's worth investigating and asking to see the boats. The response could vary according to the job on hand: a boatyard owner busy deep inside the hull of an old boat may give a short sharp reply, but catch him at a better time and he could be the most helpful boat expert you'll ever meet.

Boat owners often ask the boatyard that provides them with maintenance services to sell their boat. The main advantage of dealing with a boatyard is the availability of skilled craftsmen to deal with work you don't want to do yourself. Part of the deal might include the cost of hauling out and relaunching or servicing the engine. A further advantage is the possibility of being given priority for renting a temporary or long-term mooring or storage space at the boatyard.

Auctions

It might be possible to find a bargain by attending an auction, depending on the level of risk involved. Items are sold 'as seen' and much depends on whether you have sufficient opportunity to inspect a boat, have it surveyed and check its equipment before the auction. Few boats are now put up for sale at real live auctions – mostly they go on website auctions or are advertised in the ways described above.

Boat jumbles

Events called boat jumbles – the low-cost alternative to boat shows – can be fascinating. Major boat shows are an

Boat jumbles are worth searching for bargain boats.

experience not to be missed, but they tend to include a high proportion of boats and equipment priced beyond the reach of many new to boating. The main attraction of boat jumbles is the range of low-cost new and second-hand equipment for sale, but there are usually a number of actual boats displayed for sale as well – to pay for in cash and take away on a trailer. The bargains go quickly, so get there early and join the queue before the opening time, which is usually 10am on a Sunday. The friendly atmosphere and fascinating boating conversations alone make boat jumbles worth visiting, whether or not you purchase anything.

Some concern has been expressed about the quality and legality of a few items for sale at boat jumbles, but the police now often attend such events, acting as a deterrent to fraudsters and reducing the possibility of stolen goods being offered for sale. However, you'll still need to take care when buying equipment or boats to check that they're suitable and safe for their intended use.

A list of most of the main boat jumbles can be found at http://www.boatjumbleassociation.co.uk.

Finding a bargain

Privately advertised boats and neglected ones in boatyards and boating clubs' storage areas provide the greatest chances for finding a bargain. Occasionally a boat with a 'For Sale' sign can be seen in an unexpected location such as the front garden of the boat's owner.

Damaged or neglected boats can be difficult to sell and are often called 'project boats'. The price may be very tempting and there could be much scope to reduce it further. Don't get carried away, though. Check the later chapters on boat maintenance and repair to be sure you want to take on, and can cope with, the tasks that may be involved. Having done that, an informed and level-headed decision can be made to spend winter weekends renovating and refitting a project boat so that you end up with an outstanding bargain ready for summer boating.

Sometimes a really shabby, dirty boat with green algae all over it is actually in sound condition – particularly a fibreglass boat where rot is not a problem. Where the owner does not have the time, inclination or ability to clean the boat, its appearance reduces the asking price substantially – or provides you with a good reason for negotiating a reduction.

Boats can be found for sale in unexpected places. This one was in a field beside a country road.

Sometimes a boat is advertised for sale in the owner's front garden.

Careful use of a pressure washer, cleaning compounds and some paint or polish may produce a bargain boat.

Prices

There is no frequently updated guide to boat prices as there is for cars. Try to find several advertisements for the same type of boat and compare their prices, bearing in mind age, condition and the items included in the sale. The Internet has made it easier to establish the value of a boat. Putting the type or class of the boat into an Internet search engine such as Google will not only provide you with details of the prices currently being asked but will often indicate where boats of that type are up for sale.

The auction website eBay provides a list of boats recently auctioned, showing the final bid. Click on 'completed listings' in the column on the left. This shows the bids that won particular boats and those that did not meet the reserve price. This helps to establish how much you might have to pay for a particular boat, and a print-out could be used to help negotiate a price reduction on a boat advertised elsewhere – if you're lucky!

When to buy

Understandably, the greatest interest in boat buying tends to be aroused when the weather improves in late spring and early summer – the start of the main boating season. However, prices tend to be higher and more 'firm' at that time, with plenty of buyers about.

By contrast, a boat advertised in late autumn or in winter, by someone who needs to sell it quickly, is likely to attract fewer buyers and there is the potential for a bargain to be found. One exception tends to be in January, when publicity for the annual London Boat Show encourages thoughts of getting afloat in summer sunshine, and interest in boat buying increases for a while – until it subsides again when confronted by the reality of February weather.

Minimising risks

As with buying anything second-hand, there will always be some risk involved in buying a used motor boat, but the risks can be minimised by adopting a commonsense approach and taking some precautions. The risk of being sold a stolen boat is small compared with road vehicles. However, though there are registration schemes, boats – unlike motor vehicles – do not currently have to be registered. The latest details of the current voluntary registration scheme for pleasure craft and small ships can be found at https://mcanet.mcga.gov.uk/ssr/ssr/. If a boat *has* been registered, this helps to confirm ownership and whether there are any outstanding financial charges, such as a marine mortgage, to be cleared by the owner.

Ask to see the bill of sale or receipt from the previous sale. Check the name and details on this with those on any other paperwork. An insurance policy may be available for this purpose. If you feel uneasy about the seller it helps to check their name, telephone number and address in a telephone directory or with directory enquiries. Two websites listing stolen boats are http://www.stolenboats.org.uk and http://www.newtoncrum.co.uk/stolen.html.

When buying from a private individual it's advisable to visit their home address to make the payment – ideally collecting the boat from there if it's on a trailer. A boat bought from a broker should come with some assurance that it is legitimate and free of any financial charges.

The Recreational Craft Directive was established by the European Union in June 1998. This introduced minimum standards for all new pleasure boats between hull lengths of 2.5m and 24m and required such boats to have a hull identification number. Part of the rules includes a requirement that the seller of a second-hand boat built since June 1998 must pass on the paperwork – including proof of compliance, the hull number and proof of ownership – to a purchaser, so check this is available before you buy. The number is known as the HIN (Hull Identification Number). Check that the number on the hull agrees with the number on the paperwork.

As with many such EU sets of regulations, the Recreational Craft Directive is changed frequently, and if you want to read the latest version full details should be available at http://www.berr.gov.uk. Put 'Recreational Craft Directive' in the search box.

Most boats built before the introduction of the Directive in 1998 will have a number somewhere on the hull and/or engine. Ask the owner to show you where this is on the boat and check the number against that on any paperwork the owner has. Outboard motors have serial numbers, which can also be checked.

VAT should have been paid on any boat built in or imported into the European Union since 1985. Receipts should be available with the boat showing that VAT has been paid. Availability of this proof is important and makes life much easier in the future when selling the boat or trailing it for a holiday abroad. Boats large enough and suitably equipped to cruise to other countries will also need to be registered.

Whilst dealing with paperwork, ask to see any bills for

Boat shows increase interest in boat buying.

servicing and maintenance of the boat and engine. Even if the boat seller has done this himself there could be receipts for parts, which will show that regular maintenance has been carried out.

Thorough inspection and testing

Buyers of second-hand boats are often advised to carry out a considerable number of tasks, stage by stage, to check a boat thoroughly – particularly the more expensive motor cruisers. These include viewing it several times, in and out of the water, trying it afloat and getting a professional survey done. However, this is the ideal situation in a perfect world and requires considerable co-operation from the seller.

Being more realistic, boats widely advertised at a reasonable or bargain price will attract many enquiries and the seller will be inclined to accept the first buyer to put cash in his hand. A buyer who goes away thinking he can take his time to make a decision frequently misses the opportunity to buy. It's a careful balancing act between rushing in and buying on impulse – which may lead to later regrets – and thoroughly considering the purchase before buying.

It makes sense to inspect the boat as thoroughly as possible on the first viewing, bearing in mind all the points raised later in this chapter and elsewhere in this book. Ask if a recent survey report is available. A cruiser to be used on inland waterways in the UK must have a currently valid Boat Safety Scheme Certificate. Ask to see this. If you're satisfied with the boat's condition, a cash deposit can then be paid to secure it before someone else comes along. Final payment should be agreed in writing subject to a satisfactory survey and engine test – and subject to negotiation on price if the surveyor finds any faults not already declared or immediately obvious.

Whether buying second-hand or new it's always best to take the boat out for a trial before committing yourself.

Taking a friend with you when you go to view a boat is a good idea – preferably a friend who knows something about boats, though even someone with no relevant knowledge can help you check for the various aspects mentioned below. Two pairs of eyes are better than one.

Surveys

A boat surveyor will charge several hundred pounds. For small motor boats costing less than a couple of thousand pounds it can be difficult to decide whether the expense is worthwhile. However, a serious fault may be hidden to anyone but a qualified surveyor, and you could be saved from wasting a large amount of cash. More likely, the surveyor will find some minor problems which might enable a reduction in the price to be negotiated. This reduction may well be much more than the surveyor's fee. Ensure the surveyor will provide a written report, including a valuation.

If you have any doubts about the safety aspects of a boat, either don't buy it or get a survey done to establish exactly how safe and seaworthy the boat and its equipment are.

Check that your surveyor has professional indemnity insurance against any possibility of errors on his part. Ask if he can check the mechanics, including the engine. If not, get an engineer to go out on a sea trial with the boat. Three websites listing registered and qualified surveyors are:

- **http://www.ybdsa.co.uk**
  (the Yacht Brokers, Designers and Surveyors Association)
- **http://www.iims.org.uk**
  (the International Institute of Marine Surveying)
- **http://www.boatsurvey.com**

Be aware of insurance matters

Another point to bear in mind is that most insurance companies will want to see a survey report before insuring a motor boat, particularly if it's over 15 years old. It's wise to check the type of boat you have in mind with several insurance companies before viewing boats, to establish their requirements and get some idea of insurance costs. There is more on insurance is in Chapter 6.

Inspection: what to look for

Fortunately, with smaller motor boats, spending some time carefully looking over the boat and under the hull, and checking associated equipment, will reveal most problems. Plenty of the faults likely to be found can be repaired with sufficient enthusiasm, time, effort, DIY skills, some expenditure on materials and the help of this book.

In order to inspect the boat fully it must be out of the water and supported safely off the ground. Be absolutely sure that the boat won't fall on you before going under it.

Magazine reports

Boating magazines have published a great many reviews and reports on new and second-hand boats. These can be purchased from the magazines via their websites (see

Old antifouling paint can look shabby, as it's designed to dissolve in order to deter the growth of marine organisms on the hull.

Appendix) or by telephone. Boat report reprints from several magazines can also be ordered via http://marinedirectory.ybw.com/reprints/search2.jsp.

Reports should include indications of weaknesses that have emerged over time for particular makes of boat. These provide a pointer to aspects that warrant investigation when you view a boat. More reassuring are the positive comments on a boat's resistance to wear and tear. A brief description of each of '100 Favourite Power Boats' is available by clicking on the list at http://www.ybw.com/mby/boats/100/.

Some motor boats have active owners' associations, such as those already listed earlier. Their list of committee members usually includes a technical expert willing to give advice on what to look for when inspecting one of their type of boat prior to purchase. Remember that this person is providing help on a voluntary basis, so don't be too demanding. Remember too that they'll be enthusiasts for the particular type of boat, so may be a little biased and unwilling to be too critical.

At the end of a boating season most boats will look rather shabby so bear this in mind if viewing them in the autumn. It's surprising how many people put a boat up for sale without smartening it up. This can be an advantage, as any defects may be easier to see than if polish, paint and varnish have just been applied.

The antifouling paint used to stop the growth of water plants and pests on the hull of a motor cruiser normally kept on a mooring will look very patchy and thin when hauled out. Again, this can make it easier to spot any problems with the hull. Antifouling paint is usually applied in spring within a few weeks or days of launching. If it's been applied at some other time of year, could this be to cover any faults?

Hull materials

The vast majority of motor boats are made of fibreglass or steel. Aluminium has also been used. Many wooden boats have been neglected and have rotted away, but some may be found in good condition for purchase second-hand.

Many fibreglass boats have parts of their superstructures and interiors made of wood, and much of the ensuing section on wooden hulls applies regarding these.

Wood

An old wooden or plywood boat may be cheaper than a fibreglass one but there are more potential problems, depending on how well the wood has been cared for. Superb examples of beautifully varnished wooden boats can be found, lovingly restored and maintained by enthusiasts, and these can be a delight to own. A website with much information on such 'classic' motor boats is http://www.tradboat2.co.uk/editorial/motor.htm.

The important point to remember if considering buying a wooden or partly wooden boat, in good condition, is whether you want to spend the amount of time necessary to keep it in the same condition. It's often said that at least an hour's work repairing, scraping, painting and varnishing is needed for every hour of boating.

Wooden boats more recently constructed and thoroughly

These classic motor boats made of wood, exhibited at Basildon Motor Boat Museum, include one used in a James Bond film.

A well-maintained wooden boat looks superb but takes a lot of work to maintain.

treated with epoxy resin are much more durable than older boats without this protection.

On older wooden boats not maintained by enthusiasts, rot, cracking of dried-out timber and fillers, possible attack by wood-boring organisms, delamination of plywood and poorly carried out repairs to damage are the main problems. These tend to be quite obvious on close inspection but are sometimes concealed under layers of fibreglass and resin or filler, applied in an attempt to strengthen, repair or replace rotten wood. Rotten areas may feel spongy. With the permission of the seller, you could try pressing the blade of a screwdriver on to suspect areas. If permission is not given, be suspicious.

It's very important to inspect wooden structures inside hulls built of GRP and steel, as well as inside wooden hulls. Rainwater is a serious enemy of wood. Where it has accumulated in places such as the bilges – perhaps concealed under the floorboards – wet rot can do much damage. Condensation shouldn't be as great in the cabin of a wooden motor cruiser as in the cabin of a fibreglass boat, but if it does accumulate in corners without enough ventilation to dry it out, rot can set in.

Bulkheads, which are walls that divide up the interior space, are frequently made of wood whatever the building material of the hull. Check for rot where bilge water or leaks from windows may have caused it. The bulkheads contribute to the structural strength of the entire boat, and could be compromised by rot.

Black stains under varnished wood indicate water damage, which can be dealt with if it's only superficial, but the risk of deeper penetration and rot is substantial. Bubbles under paintwork can also show water damage.

The plywood in a boat should be marine grade or at least 'water and boil proof' (WBP). Many boats constructed with plywood, or with parts replaced with new plywood, have been constructed or repaired by amateur boat builders. They should have used epoxy resin and marine plywood, but if marine-quality plywood has not been used water is likely to have penetrated at an early stage and started to cause the layers of the ply to come apart, a process called delamination. This is unsightly and seriously weakens the structure. Ask the seller if he or she knows what was used in the woodwork being examined.

Wood not adequately protected with paint or varnish or reinforced with epoxy resin can quickly rot and crack.

Bubbles under paintwork can lead to this situation, where rot may be well established under the paint.

Plywood delaminating.

Rot along the corners and edges of woodwork can mean that substantial replacement is needed.

Delamination can be seen as swelling and raised edges along joints. Pressing down on suspect areas may show the surface flexing. Tapping suspect areas with the handle of a screwdriver should produce a solid resonating sound. If a dull thud is heard there could be a problem. Unfortunately even top-quality marine plywood can eventually delaminate if damaged or neglected. A boat with delaminating plywood is best avoided. Repair can be difficult and the cost uneconomic.

Fibreglass (GRP)

Most motor boats for sale will be made of glass-reinforced plastic (GRP), often referred to as 'fibreglass' because the glass is actually a woven matting of glass fibres. The word 'plastic' tends to be avoided, as the materials that bind the fibres are actually sophisticated and strong synthetic resins. You'll find more on GRP below and in Chapters 10 and 11.

Parts of many fibreglass boats are made of wood or plywood – bulkheads, interior fittings and even the whole deck and cabin or wheelhouse of some older motor cruisers. Consequently the points raised in the preceding section on wood should be checked carefully.

A particularly difficult type of build to check is 'sandwich construction', where plywood or some other type of wood is sealed between two layers of fibreglass. If this seems spongy it shows that water has penetrated into the plywood core, which can rot and greatly weaken the structure. If this is suspected, either avoid the problem by not buying the boat or employ a surveyor – if doing so is really worthwhile.

To check the sides of the hull when the boat is ashore, put your eye close to the hull at the stern and look along its length. It should be smooth and regular apart from points where a bulkhead or part of the internal structure is attached. Any other bumps, ridges or flat spots that interrupt the curve may indicate damage, poorly executed repairs or distortion. This type of inspection can be helped by shining a torch along the surface of the hull to reveal irregularities. In some circumstances wetting the hull can also reveal such problems.

Also look along the top of the hull from bow to stern. Look for any distortion or twist in the shape of the hull. Such defects could indicate serious structural weakness, damage or poor-quality construction.

Expect boats that have been used for several years to have some scratches and minor blemishes. See how well they have been repaired or whether this needs to be done.

Impact damage is often shown by stress cracks, either as a bullseye pattern of cracks or some other regular pattern. Gently tap round the cracked area with the handle of a screwdriver. A dull thud, rather than a sharp report or more resonating ringing sound, may indicate delamination, where the layers of fibreglass and outer gel coat are parting company and allowing water to penetrate. Check the inside of the boat at the location of the cracks to see how serious any damage is: has it broken the glass fibres? If there *has* been impact damage, the shocks from the collision can also get transmitted through the boat and further damage may result, such as delamination or distortion where bulkheads are fixed to the hull.

When a fibreglass boat is hauled out of the water on a dry day, it should dry out in a few hours. If there's still a damp patch it's likely that water has penetrated through a crack, which may be concealed under paint. Checking for this 'weeping' of water is particularly important around the rudder and any keels protruding from the hull.

A motorsailer will have keels to stop sideways movement when sailing. Many motor boats also have keels or skegs. These are made of steel or reinforced GRP. Keels consisting of steel plates attached to the hull have bolts through the hull and into reinforcing plates on the inside. Check the condition of these both inside and outside. Corrosion of the bolts weakens the structure, loosens the fixing, and can allow water to leak into the hull. Check for rust, which could indicate weakness and cause leaks. If the keel contains

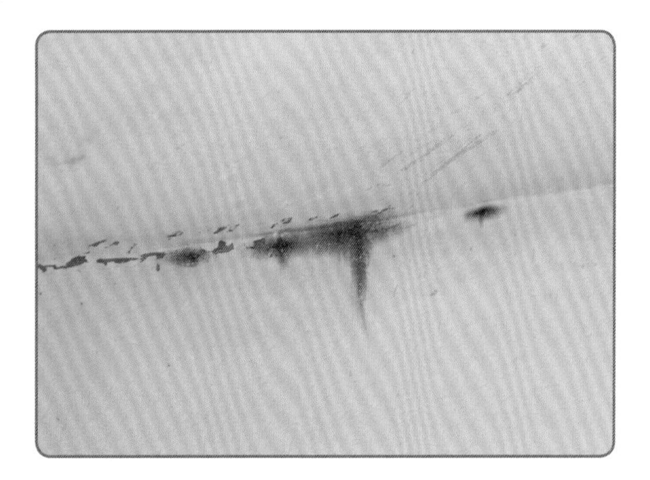

Rust where a keel is fixed to the hull indicates problems.

Bolts securing a keel can usually be seen inside the hull. Extra reinforcing plates have been bolted through in this instance.

encapsulated iron ballast this could be rusting, expanding and causing serious damage.

Repairs to the hull that have been done well will be as strong as the boat, but look carefully round the inside as well as the outside to find evidence of any problems. Question the owner about any repairs. How were they carried out and were they done by the owner or by a boatyard?

Osmosis and blisters in GRP

The word 'osmosis' has caused considerable anxiety to owners of GRP boats. Much contradictory advice has been written on the subject, and this has led to some confusion. The intention here is to identify any problems a second-hand boat might have with osmosis, without going too deeply into the technicalities.

The gelcoat which forms the plastic surface coating of GRP boats isn't 100 per cent waterproof. On some boats, where there may have been either faults in their construction or damage that wasn't adequately repaired, tiny drops of water are drawn through the gelcoat surface by a process usually called osmosis. This water then combines with chemicals and is unable to escape back through the gelcoat. The build-up of this liquid then exerts pressure which causes blisters in and below the gelcoat.

A bad case of osmosis, shown as blistering.

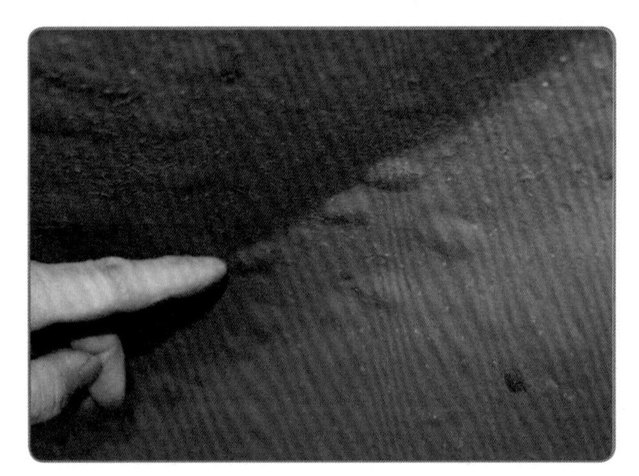

The more a boat is in the water, the greater the risk of osmosis. Small motor boats kept ashore on a trailer most of the time are unlikely to suffer from it, unless water has been left in them or rainwater has been allowed to accumulate. Cruisers kept on moorings are more at risk, but if they're laid up ashore and dry out every winter the risk is minimised. The increased tendency for motor boats to be left on moorings in marinas all year round has accelerated osmosis in the hulls of some boats.

Osmosis blisters can be as small as a ladybird or bigger than your hand. Generally, the longer a boat has existed without blisters, the less osmosis is likely to become a serious problem in the future. For instance, a boat over 15 years old with a few well-scattered blisters, each no bigger than a ten pence piece, is unlikely to develop a serious osmosis problem during the next ten years of its life, although this cannot be guaranteed.

On the other hand, if large blisters are found this could indicate delamination and weakening of the hull. If a rash of hundreds of blisters cover the hull of a motor boat this is often referred to as 'boat pox'. This is expensive to have repaired and involves grinding away the gelcoat over the whole of the hull, which then has to be replaced with new gelcoat. This sort of repair isn't a task for the amateur.

It helps to inspect a boat for osmosis blisters as soon as it has been lifted out of the water, since some blisters can shrink and disappear as the hull dries out.

Sometimes blisters may be in a layer of paint rather than in the actual surface of the hull. Repainting could solve this problem.

It's important to wear goggles and gloves if closely inspecting blisters. Sometimes boat owners are advised to burst a blister to see how deep the problem goes. This can cause the acid liquid to spray out under pressure, potentially into your eyes and onto your hands.

Light-coloured discolouration on this hull responded to the treatment described in Chapter 11, and the original gelcoat colour was restored.

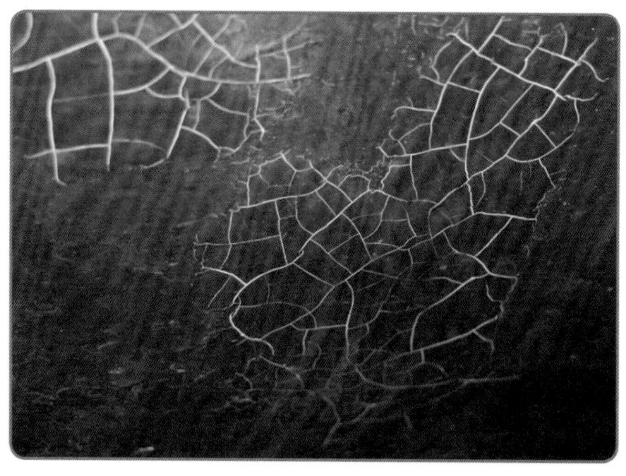

Cracked paint on this hull betrays poor-quality repairs.

If there are just a few small blisters a boat may still be worth buying if it's good value in other respects. They can, in fact, give grounds for reducing the price. The decision will then be whether to leave the blisters to see whether or not they get worse over a number of years, or whether to remove and fill them with marine grade filler. Boat pox and large blisters indicating possible delamination are good reasons to look for another boat without such worrying problems.

Bear in mind that evidence of osmosis will usually reduce the resale price of a boat when you come to sell it on.

Painted GRP

The surface of a GRP boat can stay in good condition for many years and you may be lucky enough to find a second-hand boat with shiny, well-polished, original gelcoat. Sellers often make a point of advertising such a boat as 'unpainted'.

GRP that's had heavy use and not been polished with protective products will show discolouration through oxidation. This can show as yellowing on a white hull and a cloudy, chalky surface discolouration to the gelcoat. It may be possible to bring this surface back to a much more attractive finish as described in Chapter 11, but if not, painting is an option. This option has been chosen by many boat owners, and older second-hand motor boats frequently have painted gelcoat.

Painted GPR isn't a problem if the paint has been carefully applied to an undamaged or properly repaired surface. But herein lies the problem: paint is sometimes used to cover and disguise damaged or poorly repaired areas of the hull and decks. A coat of paint is, therefore, the cue to be particularly careful when carrying out the inspections described in this chapter.

Of course, once painted the hull will need repainting every few years, and too great a build-up will eventually necessitate removing all the paint and starting again. This task needs to be balanced against the work involved in polishing unpainted gelcoat annually to keep it in good condition.

Antifouling paint will be found on the underside of boats normally kept on a mooring. This, too, can disguise damage and repairs, so once again you need to look carefully at both the exterior and interior surfaces. Many types of antifouling can be quite easily rubbed or scraped from areas needing closer inspection – with the owner's permission. Bear in mind that antifouling paint is poisonous. Only scrape it when wet, and wear suitable protective gloves, clothing and mask.

Steel

Steel hulls withstand abrasion and knocks better than GRP but suffer from corrosion. A steel narrowboat is protected from corrosion by having its underwater areas painted in bitumastic every few years. This is black and tarry. The areas above the waterline are painted instead with layers of appropriate protective paint. Unfortunately some boat owners continue the thick tarry paint above the waterline in order to disguise dents and scratches. This then comes off onto anything with which it comes into contact, causing the owner to become unpopular with boaters whose white GRP

The hull thickness of steel boats will reduce over time, particularly if inadequately protected from rust.

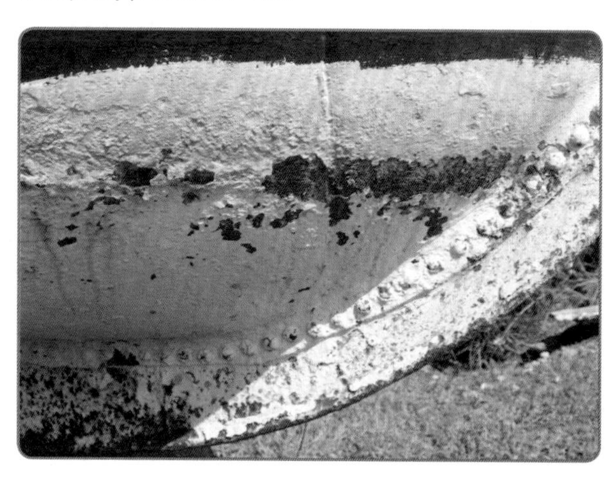

hulls are disfigured when they come into contact with the black paint in a lock.

With the steel boat out of the water, look for rust and the pitting caused by corrosion. Older boats will have started with an adequate thickness of steel plate but this will reduce over time. A surveyor needs to be involved to be sure that an adequate thickness remains.

Water accumulating inside can cause rust and weakening of the hull. Check for puddles of water causing rust where the framework that supports the plates of steel is attached in the bilges.

Sacrificial anodes, which are lumps of zinc or silver-coloured magnesium, should be seen attached to the hull below the waterline. These corrode instead of the hull and protect other metal fittings from corrosion by electrolytic processes.

Aluminium

Though steel is much more common, some motor boats have aluminium hulls. Oxidation of aluminium shows as a white powder. Where denting of the aluminium has occurred it needs to be checked for possible weakening of the hull. Like steel, aluminium also needs to be protected from electrolysis by having appropriate anodes attached to the hull.

Decks and deck fittings

The decks of boats take a lot of wear. The crew clamber about on the deck and often grab fittings that they expect to take their weight as the boat goes along. Everything therefore needs to be strongly constructed and secure.

The joint between the hull sides and the decks needs to be checked inside and out. See if the fastenings, such as bolts, rivets and screws, show signs of corrosion or looseness or are actually missing. Any gaps may mean bolts just need tightening and the join needs resealing. Any distortion is more serious.

This wooden rubbing strip can be replaced with a new one screwed into place.

All deck fittings need to be securely fixed.

Inside the cabin, leaks of rainwater from the deck join or other deck problems may show as marks on the hull interior. Inspect the outer surface for cracking that will need repair to make waterproof.

Rubbing strips round the edge of the boat are designed to absorb impact and take some wear. Expect some scuffing and damage on a second-hand boat. A new rubbing strip can usually be screwed on or slotted into place.

Non-slip surfaces moulded into the deck of a motor cruiser or painted into surfaces should still be rough enough to stop you slipping when wet – they can get worn smooth and lose some grip.

Hatch covers made of wood tend to come apart at the corners while the more flimsy fibreglass hatch covers may have split round the edges. Open and shut the hatch to check the hinges or slides and look for any distortion. Similarly, check the fittings and operation of locker doors, locker lids and the doors into the cabin on a motor cruiser.

These windows have been given new rubber seals to make them watertight.

Stanchions and fittings have to be strong enough to take the weight of your body falling against them.

All deck fittings should be gripped firmly and pressure applied to check for looseness. Cracks in the gelcoat radiating from bolts show stresses have moved a fitting such as a stanchion. Bolts for deck fittings should go through the deck and into substantial backing plates reinforcing and strengthening the GRP to prevent damage. All fittings, including windows, should be bedded in a thin layer of sealant or suitable gasket. These have a limited life and, once hardened or perished, can allow water penetration. Check inside the hull for any evidence of leaks: a powerful torch will help show up water stains, corrosion, streaks of dirt or rust, and a concentration of mildew stains where sealant has failed. The corresponding fitting then needs to be removed and re-bedded in fresh sealant.

A motor cruiser with lifelines or 'guard rails' stretched between the supporting posts, called stanchions, provides some safety for crew moving around on deck, but only if the stanchions can take your weight and the lines or rails aren't frayed and about to break.

The canopy

A canopy covers the cockpit of many motor boats. After about five years of use the fabric tends to become stiff, faded and cracked. Check the stitching and the zips, as these tend to fail before the actual fabric. The fastenings may be missing or weak and the window panels could be losing their transparency and strength. The high cost of replacing a canopy can come as a shock after a boat is purchased!

The interior

The interior finish of the cabin is much less important than all the other aspects already covered. Attractive and well furnished bunks, cabinets and lockers with a shiny varnished finish are good to see and may be a major attraction for some members of the family, but they can distract you from thoroughly inspecting the boat's structure and fittings. In fact, some furnishings and woodwork may actually make it difficult to inspect the interior of the hull.

Having stated that, a shabby interior is a good bargaining point, whilst bearing in mind that cushions can be replaced and wood can be re-varnished.

Have a good look at how furnishings are attached and whether any fixings are coming adrift. This also applies to the partition walls (called bulkheads in a boat). Sometimes they crack away from the hull or get distorted if the boat has been involved in a collision.

When inspecting the cabin, use your nose as well as your eyes. Boats left locked up for some time without sufficient ventilation will develop musty smells, but after airing out for a while are there still persistent and worrying odours?

Sources of odours include the head, or toilet, and leakage from tanks storing liquids such as sewage and fuel. Tanks, including the holding tanks for sewage, should be vented to the outside to remove methane and other gases. Wiping over any pipes with a damp cloth and then sniffing it may show up leaks not obvious to the eye. Check that the toilet operates as intended and that waste is efficiently dealt with.

Lift the floorboards and look into the bilges. Are they free

Don't let a smart interior divert your attention from the rest of the boat.

Check the operation of all equipment such as gas cookers and the water supply to the sink.

of water, or are they dirty, oily and a source of the odours you discovered earlier?

Check whether the cabin windows are scratched or cracked. Windows made of Perspex eventually craze and crack with age. Window replacement is covered in Chapter 15.

Ask the owner to demonstrate that all equipment and fixtures are working effectively and safely, including the cooker, refrigerator, water system and navigation equipment. Gas appliances should be checked regularly by a qualified engineer – ask for recent evidence of this, and if not available arrange for an inspection by a suitably qualified Corgi-registered specialist.

The boat you're inspecting should be viewed afloat as well as on land. This not only helps you check that the hull is sound but enables the motor to be tried out. All other relevant equipment can be tested under way and, providing the owner's insurance cover allows it, you should be given a chance to take the helm to experience how the boat performs.

Electrics

12V batteries included should be checked for age and condition. This is likely to include a deep-cycle 'leisure' battery and a heavy-duty marine battery for starting the engine. Check electrical connections for condition and switch on any electrical equipment, such as navigation lights. If the boat is not afloat, take care not to switch on and start the engine or any other equipment that might get damaged – like the bilge pump – if it is run dry.

The pointed skeg below the propeller should be checked for any damage indicating a collision, which could have caused other damage and distortion.

Outboard motors and inboard engines

Most small motor boats will have an outboard motor. To inspect the engine, remove the cover or 'cowl' and look at the general condition. Any salt corrosion around the cylinder head indicates leaks and gasket problems.

With the motor clamped on the transom, check for wear and looseness in the engine mounts and swivel bracket by trying to shake it.

At the bottom end of the leg there is a pointed tail called the 'skeg'. See if the bottom of this has been damaged. If so, it probably means the motor has hit something. This may have caused further damage and distortion. Check the condition of the propeller. With the engine out of gear and the ignition switched off, rotate the propeller slowly. This will show whether the propeller shaft is bent.

If it's not possible to try the outboard with the boat afloat an alternative is to try operating it securely mounted in a tank of water. Running it whilst out of the water is dangerous and causes immediate damage, as the cooling system relies on a water supply to lubricate it as well as to cool the engine.

Many outboards have a 'kill cord' which stops the engine. Check that this works as it should. If the outboard motor starts easily and runs well with cooling water coming out, it's probably as good as any second-hand one you may come across.

Ask the owner for details of when it was last serviced, and whether a manual is provided. If you have doubts about

Above: A stern gland, where the propeller shaft goes through the hull, prevents leakage whilst allowing the shaft to rotate.

Right: Bearings and fastenings for the rudder should be examined for wear.

the motor or engine, make the purchase subject to a satisfactory check by an engineer.

Much of the above applies also to checking an outdrive leg. If there are oil leaks coming from an outdrive, replacing the seals and any parts worn because of a lack of oil can be very costly.

Boat engines generally get far less use than car engines and are unlikely to actually wear out. However, neglect and lack of servicing in a damp environment cause corrosion and deterioration. This may be clearly evident as soon as you look into the engine compartment. It should be clean and not showing salt deposits, rust or oil leaks. The bilges below should not show evidence of oil leaks. If the engine has a new coat of paint ask why.

Water for cooling comes through the hull via a seacock, which is a tap or handle that can be opened and closed. Check that this moves freely so that it can be shut in an emergency.

Withdraw the engine oil dipstick. The oil on it should be brown or black unless it has recently been changed. It should also be runny: if it is very thick it could indicate that it hasn't been changed for a long time and neglect is a problem. If it is a milky colour it shows water has mixed with the oil, indicating expensive repairs are needed. Gearbox oil should be clean and clear.

Some fuel filters have a transparent bowl enabling you to see if there is any contamination, such as black slime or a jelly-like deposit which shows that biological growth has contaminated the diesel fuel.

Inboard engines should start easily. Running the engine at a mooring is not good enough to test it properly. An engine can run perfectly well at a mooring and then display faults when required to actually propel the boat out on the water. If the engine is already warm when you arrive for a sea trial it could be that the owner is disguising something such as difficult starting.

Where a shaft runs through the hull to the propeller a stern gland stops water entering the boat. This can be expected to drip slightly when the engine is running, as it must not be too tightly fitted round the shaft. However, continuous dripping when the engine isn't running means the bilges will eventually fill unless steps are taken to tighten or repack/replace the gland. At least one electric bilge pump should be fitted in the hull to deal with leaks, and obviously needs to be in good working order.

For more on outboards and inboard engines, see Chapter 17.

Steering

On a boat with shaft-drive from an inboard engine, the rudder bearings should be checked for play and the rudder itself for damage. In the case of an outboard motor, check the fastenings for steering and controls.

Check the free movement of all steering and control cables, which, on a boat not used for some time, can seize up. Rudder steering controls should be positive, without excess play or looseness. In the case of hydraulic steering check the oil level and look for any oil leaks.

Inspecting inflatable boats and RIBs

Much of the above guidance also applies in the case of rigid inflatable boats (RIBs), particularly for the GRP hull and the outboard motor or engine. Some additional points follow for RIBs and the inflatables often used as tenders to reach a boat on a mooring, or as a motor boat when fitted with an outboard motor.

Ideally they should be inflated and left for a few days before checking that the tubes have remained fully inflated, although this can be difficult to arrange.

Thoroughly check the inflated buoyancy tubes for leaks, which can occur at valves as well as on the tubes. Look for repairs. If a patch has raised edges or is only half stuck on this is likely to be the work of an amateur and will need to be replaced. Where a tube is attached to the hull of an RIB check that it's secure all round, paying particular attention to the seam at the transom, the bow and the underside of the hull. On many boats a cone shape has been fixed at the stern end of each tube. Examine the joint here for any sign of repair or deterioration. Repairs are often accompanied by stains from excess glue nearby. Any such repairs at seams need to be checked for strength by pulling at the fabric.

Many seams have tape covering them. On some boats the tape may simply cover the main seam, protecting it, and in such cases glue can be applied to refix it. If, on the other hand, the tape itself is the main attachment the problem is more serious and expensive to repair.

Inflatable boats should have several independent air chambers so that, if one is punctured, the others will still provide buoyancy. The divisions between each chamber should not leak. To check this, deflate one section at a time and listen for any leaks by putting your ear against the tube.

Check the firmness of the attachment points of the steering console on an RIB. Do any storage compartments seem to allow water to enter?

Equipment included

As previously mentioned, one advantage of buying a second-hand boat is the equipment that's likely to be included with it.

If this includes a road trailer, it should fit the boat well, and needs to be checked carefully before use. Ideally it should be fully galvanised and rust-free. Rollers should be free running and an efficient winch should be mounted to help haul the boat onto the trailer. A problem with trailers used for boats is that they tend to be submerged in salty water when the wheel bearings are still warm from the journey, and as they cool, water is drawn into the bearings, leading to rapid corrosion. Particular attention needs to be paid to bearings. Do the wheels rotate freely? Are there any grinding noises from the bearings? If brakes are fitted, do they operate freely and efficiently? Is a working lighting board included? Are the tyres legal and in good condition?

A launching trolley is sometimes used for small boats stored near the water and should not be confused with a road trailer. The trolley is used only over short distances and to get the boat in and out of the water – definitely not to transport it by road towed behind a vehicle.

A small rowing dinghy called a tender may be included with a motor cruiser. This is used to get to a boat kept on an offshore mooring. When cruising and anchoring for an overnight stop you may want to tow the dinghy behind the cruiser so that you can use it to get ashore. Children often find that the fun they can have with a dinghy is one of the main attractions of family boat ownership. Obviously it will need oars and rowlocks.

The condition of other included equipment needs to be checked and a clear list of exactly what's included should be agreed. Preferably you should take a few photographs too – things can 'disappear' before you complete your purchase, and it helps to have proof of what was originally there.

Later chapters in this book provide information on such things as safety equipment and anchors, etc.

Look at the joints where the tubes on an inflatable boat have been attached to the hull and transom, and at the cones at the end of the tubes, to check for seams failing or any evidence of repaired damage.

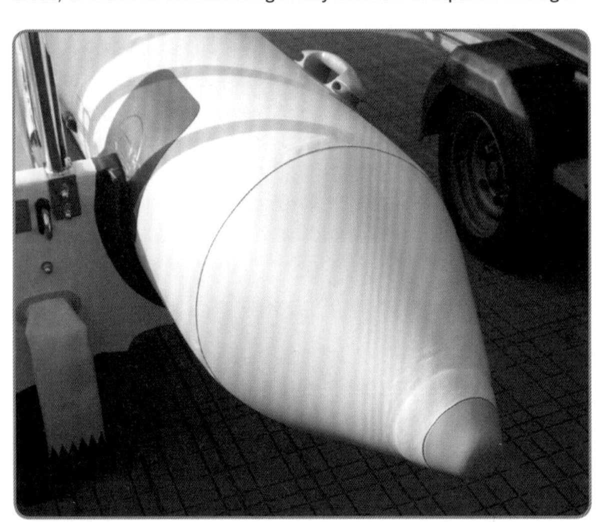

A boat with its own purpose-designed road trailer is ready for a buyer to tow away – after checking the trailer thoroughly.

This cruiser has a small sailing dinghy as a tender – an interesting combination for maximum enjoyment when afloat.

Negotiating price and purchase

Try not to show too much enthusiasm or excitement about the boat, however keen you are to buy it. The seller of a second-hand boat is unlikely to expect the full asking price unless a queue of potential purchasers are keen to thrust cash in his hand.

The above checks are likely to reveal some faults that will provide you with a basis for negotiation. Make the point that defects found will cost particular amounts of money to rectify, and ask for a reduction. The ability to pay cash promptly will also help to achieve a reduction. A compromise price can usually be agreed amicably.

Small to medium-sized boats aren't necessarily registered in any way like cars are, and aspects concerning this have been mentioned earlier under the heading 'Minimising risks'. However, there could be useful paperwork available from the seller, such as a voluntary registration certificate, copies of receipts from previous owners, insurance documents, Recreational Craft Directive paperwork (see above under 'Minimising risks'), harbour or waterway registration certificates, or local boat watch scheme documentation. It's worth asking for all of these. Check any hull identification number (HIN) that you can find on the boat against numbers on the paperwork, and get these numbers included on the receipt. Outboard motors have serial numbers, which should also be recorded.

A 'Bill of Sale' is available as a printable form on the Maritime and Coastguard Agency's website at http://www.mcga.gov.uk/c4mca/msf4705.pdf. This should be used to formalise the purchase and provide a receipt – especially where a boat is registered with the Pleasure Craft/Small Ships register. Keep all paperwork carefully so that it's available when you come to sell the boat in the future.

The RYA provides further advice on the paperwork involved in buying boats and has its own Bill of Sale available to members.

Safety inspection

In the case of boats to be used on inland waterways, see the section in Chapter 6 on the Boat Safety Scheme (BSS). A valid inspection certificate provided by an authorised inspector is needed for motor cruisers on inland waterways. The seller should have this available to show you if the boat is currently used on these waterways.

Motor Boat Manual

5 New boats

Boats out of the water provide an opportunity to see the shape of their hulls.

Buying new

If your budget allows, buying a new motor boat ensures instant pride in ownership through its appearance and up-to-date features. It should avoid the need for most of the inspections and surveys that are involved in finding a good second-hand boat, and will spare you having to deal with the faults that take time, effort and money to rectify. If any faults do appear, your warranty should cover them.

On the other hand, depreciation in price is rapid in the first few years of ownership compared with second-hand boats. These tend to hold their value, which can even increase if they're well maintained. So it's important to be sure the new boat is one that you'll want to own for a number of years.

Owning a new boat will make you feel particularly proud.

Many motor boats are likely to be available to a standard design, and often from stock already built. However, you may get into a situation where the boat you order needs to be built especially for you. It may seem obvious, but it's important under such circumstances to make sure you know exactly what you're ordering. Occasionally a salesman will be more inclined to sell you a design and specification he wants to sell rather than one you actually want and can afford.

Be sure you know whether the company you're ordering from is the builder of the boat or an agent/dealer. Also check that they're the company providing the warranty and are easily accessible – you don't want any problems if any claims need to be made on the warranty. Niggling faults can occur with a new boat and you'll want to deal with a company willing and able to respond promptly, and is preferably not too far away from where you'll be keeping the boat.

Avoid paying too much as a deposit or 'up-front' in the case of a new build; ideally you should pay less than 25 per cent on a boat that hasn't yet been built. Also, check the contract for reasonable arrangements for stage payments, and try to arrange for satisfactory sea trials of a motor cruiser before taking delivery and making the final payment. The British Marine Federation has a standard contract approved by the Royal Yachting Association and it's wise to check the contract against this, taking appropriate professional advice if there are any uncertainties. The BMF website at http://www.britishmarine.co.uk is helpful and provides many contact details.

The delivery date needs to be clearly established, and if possible you should take the opportunity to include penalty clauses in the event of delivery being delayed.

Boat shows

The boat shows have a magnetic draw for those with even the slightest interest in getting afloat. Whether buying new or second-hand, or simply fascinated by the huge range of boating equipment on display, they provide a great opportunity to learn how to have fun on the water.

As a boy, the annual London Earls Court Boat Show was a highlight of my year. My Uncle Maurice was involved in its organisation and was well known to the exhibitors. He got me in free of charge – along with some friends – and gave us the grand tour. We gazed with awe at the vast and colourful range of magnificent vessels and their equipment, displayed in surroundings that evoked the joys of summer afloat, even in the gloomy depths of winter.

Opportunities to try new boats afloat are often available at boat shows.

6 Running costs

A mooring in an estuary is usually much cheaper than in a marina.

Running costs need to be calculated before you buy a boat. Overall totals can range from an annual outlay of a few hundred pounds for a small open motor boat to a couple of thousand for a motor cruiser kept in a marina.

The expense involved in owning and using a motor boat largely depends on its size and how and where it's used. A boat kept at home and transported on a trailer for occasional use will be the cheapest. If it's transported frequently to slipways, charges for launching and parking for the car and trailer can add up to a significant sum. In this case it may save money and time to arrange and pay for storage beside the water. Larger motor boats will need to be kept on a mooring.

Whatever arrangements you make for keeping down the cost of storage and actually getting afloat, there are some costs that can't be avoided. These include insurance, navigation licences, maintenance, servicing, motor fuel, equipment replacement costs and, on inland waterways, the BSS inspection. Club membership fees may need to be added to this list.

Insurance

Everyone who owns a boat should have adequate insurance cover. Unlike car ownership, it's possible – though very unwise – to own a boat and to use it in some locations without insurance. However, there's a strong case for boat insurance to be made a legal requirement, and this could happen at any time.

In many locations byelaws and licensing regulations make insurance compulsory if you want to get afloat there, so always have your insurance documents with you. Boating clubs invariably require their members to be insured. Obviously this is in everyone's best interests. Boating accidents are rare compared with road traffic accidents, but if they happen you'd want the other party involved to have insurance, and you may need to rely on your own cover if hundreds of thousands of pounds of third party claims are made for injuries and damage.

Some organisations, such as boat owners' associations and clubs, have arrangements with particular insurers to provide discounts for their members. A further advantage of this is that in the rare event of a dispute over an insurance claim, the organisation may help negotiate with the company concerned, since the insurer is unlikely to want to risk damaging its reputation among that organisation's members.

Another tip is to ask your house or car insurer or broker if they do boat insurance. There are sometimes discounts on such schemes if you arrange it with a company with whom you already do business.

No-claims discounts can reduce premiums considerably.

Most insurance companies will want assurances that your boat is in good, safe condition. This can mean a professional survey is required for older boats, such as motor cruisers over 15 or 20 years old. It might be possible to avoid the need for a survey by negotiation – perhaps by getting a reputable boatyard to carry out an inspection or by arranging cheaper third party insurance. The problem with third party only insurance is the eventualities that it doesn't cover, such as the removal and disposal of a wreck if such a disaster should occur, as well as, of course, any damage to your boat.

The insurance premium will also be influenced by the location and security level of the mooring or storage for the boat and exposure to the risk of storms, vandalism, flooding or other damage. Remember to inform your insurance company if you decide to keep the boat in a different location.

If at any time you decide to take part in events which might involve extra risk, such as a race or an extended cruise beyond your normal area, it's essential to contact the insurance company to extend your cover to include these. Understandably, the insurance company will require extra

A secure storage compound for your boat will help you to gain insurance cover.

Considerable skill at close quarters is being demonstrated here, but extra insurance is needed when racing.

payment for the increased risks. Likewise, if you go abroad with your boat check that your policy will provide appropriate cover, or arrange for it to be extended.

Some policies are designed specifically for the use of a motor boat on inland waterways. If you plan to go into the sea or an estuary – perhaps to reach another inland waterway – it's vital to consult your insurance company and comply with their conditions in order for your cover to continue.

Shopping around for insurance has been made much easier by the Internet, and the best way to find out what's available in a rapidly changing market is to use a search engine. Some companies provide online forms to complete and provide an immediate online quote. Take care, though, to read their full details of coverage and conditions, either on the appropriate web page or in the paperwork you're sent in the post, before paying the premium.

Read the policy's requirements for maintenance carefully
In the past insurance companies have used the expression 'due diligence' to explain how boat owners are expected to take reasonable precautions to ensure the boat and its mooring are in safe, sound and reliable condition. More recently there has been a trend to change this to more specific and exacting requirements, including the requirement for mooring equipment to be professionally laid, inspected and maintained at regular intervals. A further recent development in some companies' insurance conditions has been to specify that the boat, along with equipment and repair materials, be used and serviced in line with the manufacturers' recommendations. Consequently the following chapters on practical tasks include frequent reminders to consult product manufacturers' instructions in order to be able to comply with insurance requirements. Your insurers may want some DIY work to be checked by a suitably qualified person before the boat is used.

Navigation licences

It's a legal requirement to register and licence a boat for navigation on inland waterways. Each area or river is administered by a particular authority. The main ones are British Waterways (www.britishwaterways.co.uk), which covers most canals and some rivers including the Severn, Trent and Yorkshire Ouse; and the Environment Agency (http://www.environment-agency.gov.uk), which licences boats on the Thames, the Medway and many East Anglian rivers with the exception of the Norfolk and Suffolk Broads,

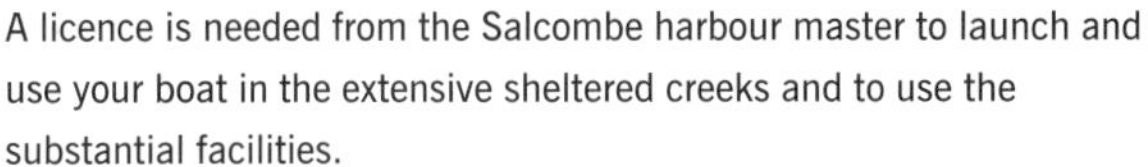

A licence is needed from the Salcombe harbour master to launch and use your boat in the extensive sheltered creeks and to use the substantial facilities.

which are run by The Broads Authority (http://www.broads-authority.gov.uk). Further information on licences can be found on the websites listed in the Appendix.

The situation on the coast varies greatly. No licence is needed for the open sea, but many of the sheltered locations where boats are likely to be launched are covered by a harbour authority. Normally a notice will be displayed beside slipways giving instructions on obtaining any necessary licence. This may be available from the harbour master, who'll collect harbour dues and fees for launching, provide keys to access facilities, and give valuable advice on safe boating in the area. As an example of the facilities that you might find, Salcombe Harbour in Devon has a supervised slipway, parking for boats, trailers and cars, visitors' moorings, short stay mooring pontoons, toilets and plenty of helpful information from the harbour master's office.

Enquiries to the local council or tourist office before you visit an area will determine the procedure you need to follow, including when and where you can get any necessary licences.

You'll usually need to produce an insurance certificate when buying a licence. See in addition the section below concerning the BSS certificate, which will also be requested when buying an inland navigation licence. The charge for a licence is based on the size and type of the boat. Many are annual licences, but if you're visiting an area for a shorter period a cheaper one-week or one-month licence may be available.

It's not worth risking going afloat without the necessary licence, as the authorities do patrol their areas by boat and by foot along the banks where boats are moored. Fines for not having a licence can be quite substantial.

Mooring costs

Mooring charges for a motor cruiser will depend very much on the location and facilities, and might range from around one or two hundred pounds a year on a swinging half-tide mooring in a remote East Coast creek, to several thousand pounds in a South Coast marina with luxurious facilities.

Many boats are hauled out for the winter to be laid up on hardstanding. A club may provide this facility cheaper than a boatyard or marina. Such storage charges can, of course, be avoided if the boat can be taken home on a trailer. More on rented moorings can be found in Chapter 7.

In some areas such as the Norfolk Broads the freehold or leasehold of a mooring may come up for sale. Prices have gone up in a similar way to house prices, and in response to demand, but if sufficient cash becomes available it might be worth considering such an investment if you're sure you want to make the area your base for boating. Although

A marina may cost more but you also get the use of its shore-based facilities.

outright purchase avoids the cost of renting a mooring, check whether there are still annual charges to be paid, such as rates, ground rent or mooring equipment maintenance. Bear in mind too that you'll have to pay any costs of repairs to the quay heading or access roads, although this might be covered by any increase in the property value over time.

Boat Safety Scheme inspection for inland waterways

The BSS was established in 1997 to improve safety on inland waterways. All boats with engines, and/or lighting, cooking, heating, refrigerating and other domestic appliances, need to have passed an examination by a BSS examiner before they can be put on inland waterways. Open boats propelled only by outboard motors or sails, or manually, don't need a BSS certificate.

Basically, then, certification applies mainly to motor cruisers with cabins rather than open boats. Unfortunately the regulations do change quite often. It's therefore best to check the exact rules that apply to your boat for a particular waterway to see if it requires a BSS certificate. This is usually made clear in the documentation when you apply for a navigation licence, and you'll be asked to produce a current BSS certificate before being issued with the licence.

The actual examination is rather like the vehicle MoT but has to be carried out every four years rather than annually. Another difference is that BSS examiners' fees vary considerably, so it's worth getting several quotes. Typical fees are between £100 and £150.

The examination checks that the risks of fire, explosion and pollution are minimised. A new boat should be built to meet the specifications. It should have the CE mark and documents showing that it complies with the Recreational Craft Directive. Check with the navigation authority for your waterway that this documentation will be sufficient for their regulations without a BSS examination. This should be the case and an examination is unlikely to be needed until the boat is four years old.

A BSS certificate is needed for cruisers on inland waterways.

If buying a second-hand boat on inland waterways, be sure to check it has a current BSS certificate or that the seller will arrange for a satisfactory BSS examination before purchase. A boat that has passed the examination previously is less likely to fail when re-examined, but faults could have developed which may require work to be done, for example on the fuel supply, gas fittings or the replacement of expired fire extinguishers. Any work on gas fittings must be carried out by a suitably qualified engineer and not by an amateur.

The full up-to-date *BSS Essential Guide* can be downloaded, and a list of examiners accessed, at http://www.boatsafetyscheme.com. A printed version can also be ordered. Additional safety advice is provided on the website.

Specialised marine products are available from chandlers.

DIY or maintenance by professionals

A major purpose of this book is to offer advice on the DIY tasks that can help you to keep down maintenance and repair costs. Much of such work is quite straightforward, but as with most DIY you need to ensure that safety is a top priority. In the case of boats, this means more than just ensuring you don't damage yourself or others whilst you work: you also need to be sure that your repairs will cope with the stresses of boating. Having said that, a major advantage of DIY repairs is the fact that you'll save the expense of labour charges, which can vary from around £25 per hour to more than twice that figure.

How you value your time has to be taken into consideration. The amount of time needed tends to vary according to the materials used in the boat's construction. Any wood on the boat will probably need more time spent on it than GRP. The amount of use a boat gets will inevitably have an influence on wear and damage, but bear in mind that unused boats also deteriorate.

If you enjoy DIY at home, you'll enjoy the work on your boat away from home, in a different environment, preparing for fun on the water. This can make the money-saving aspect even more rewarding.

Materials used for maintaining boats tend to be more expensive than DIY materials for home maintenance. This is often because a boat exists in a harsh and very wet environment, and the strains put on it by water, weather and use are considerable. Higher quality and tougher paints, fillers and equipment are needed, which cost more to produce. In the past this has been used in some cases to justify unreasonably high prices, but the ability to shop around on the Internet and buy via mail has led to far greater competition, and this has helped to make prices fairer.

It's sometimes suggested that certain household DIY materials such as cleaners, paints and so on could be used to keep costs down. However, though this might work using the best-quality products on a boat only used on inland waterways and not exposed to the worst of marine conditions, you could still end up having to pay for the true marine products if the experiment should prove unsuccessful.

If a job's too big, affects safety or is too time-consuming for an amateur to learn and use the necessary skills, you'll need to get the professionals involved. As with all situations where work is to be carried out for you, ask for recommendations from people who've used the services of the appropriate specialists, and ask several boatyards for estimates of the costs and/or their hourly charge for labour. Boat owners' association websites and general boating websites have forums where such topics are discussed. An example is the highly informative and entertaining Norfolk Broads discussion forum at http://www.the-norfolk-broads.co.uk.

Fuel and other consumables

Fuel costs vary enormously according to the size of boat, the size and type of engine and the use it gets. Although in the past cheaper red diesel was available in the UK for boating use, this is no longer the case, although a lower price may still apply when using diesel for heating purposes. When buying a boat, ask for details of its fuel consumption figures according to how it is used. Obviously, higher-powered engines generally use much more fuel per hour than lower-powered, slower running engines.

In the case of two-stroke outboard motors the cost of the oil that has to be added to the petrol is a consideration that needs to be taken into account.

All fuel-burning engines will need to be regularly topped up with engine and gearbox oil, and spare parts will need to be purchased for the engine and other parts of the boat, such as bulbs for navigation lights and interior lights. Bear in mind that 12V batteries, fire extinguishers and emergency distress flares have a limited lifespan and will eventually need to be replaced. See Chapter 18 for further information on equipment maintenance.

The cost of improvements and accessories is best controlled by the application of strong willpower when visiting chandlers or reading mail order catalogues!

7 Moorings, storage and transport

Storing a boat at home on a trailer keeps down the annual running costs.

The availability of moorings and storage spaces varies from location to location. In some areas it's necessary to go on a waiting list before securing one. In others one of the least popular moorings may be available initially, with the possibility of moving to a better one when vacancies occur. Elsewhere, moorings may be available immediately, particularly if new ones have just been laid or constructed, in a marina, boatyard or by the local boating club.

Moorings are often advertised in the same places as boats for sale, *eg* websites such as www.boatsandoutboards.co.uk and the classified sections of boating magazines.

A mooring may be available to take over when buying a second-hand boat, providing the owner of the mooring agrees. Check whether there's a hand-over fee and exactly what the regular charges are, including VAT and any extras for electricity, water and parking. If you plan to buy a new motor cruiser or buy one from a boatyard, ask what help they can give with finding a mooring before buying the boat.

Trailer boating

Most of the smaller motor boats and cruisers can be transported on trailers, making them suitable for storage at home, in a club's boat storage compound or in a rented storage facility on land. This assumes, of course, that you have a vehicle that's suitable for towing your boat.

Check the weight of the boat and trailer against the car manufacturer's specified towing weights, and the nose weight, where the trailer attaches to the car. Also bear in mind the cost of having a towing hitch and electrical connections fitted.

Trailers need to be fully roadworthy and need to conform to the regulations. The *Haynes Trailer Manual* covers this very fully. If in any doubt about the trailer or your ability to make it legal and roadworthy, local trailer specialists or car servicing garages will usually advise and carry out necessary work.

The National Trailer and Towing Association has helpful advice on using trailers and on the current regulations at http://www.ntta.co.uk/law/index.htm.

Towing a boat on a trailer needs to be done at a slower speed than normal and care needs to be taken on cornering. Once you get used to it, though, towing a boat is fairly straightforward and somewhat easier than towing a caravan, as you can see the wheels and most of the boat, whereas a caravan blocks much of your rear view.

The most vulnerable part of a boat-trailer is its wheel bearings. If it's necessary to submerge them when launching, allow them to cool completely before you do so. As mentioned earlier, hot wheel bearings submerged in salt water will draw the water into them as they suddenly cool, causing considerable damage.

Wherever you keep your boat, remember to secure it against theft. Hitch locks, wheel clamps and chains with padlocks all help deter thieves. Remove items such as an outboard motor before a thief does.

A boat-trailer provides a choice of storage and launching options.

Left, below and opposite: Finding space at home may be difficult, but the owners of these boats have managed it.

The use of this slipway is included in the parking charges for your car and trailer.

Notices beside a slipway usually explain the procedure for using it and the arrangements regarding car parking, etc.

Low-cost slipways and boating locations

Trailer boating is an effective way to minimise boating costs since it avoids mooring fees, although you have to get permission and pay to launch at supervised harbours and slipways. The harbour master will provide any necessary keys for barriers and provide valuable advice on boating safely in local waters.

Some public slipways are available to use without charge. Always get local information on tides, navigation, weather and safety before launching.

Although some slipways may be free and easily accessible, you'll still need parking for the car and the trailer. This needs to be checked out in advance, as there may be problems of congestion and overcrowding if you arrive later in the day during warm summer weather at weekends.

Details of many slipways, with location maps, are available at http://www.boatlaunch.co.uk. The book *The Good Launch Guide* can also be purchased from this website. Local tourist information offices and navigation authorities can also help with advice on finding launching sites – for example, for the Norfolk Broads try http://www.broads-authority.gov.uk/boating.

If you're a boating club member it may be possible to get permission to launch at other clubs. They often welcome visitors from other parts of the country and their facilities may be made available to you. However, you should contact them in advance to check whether you'll be welcome with a motor boat – some clubs are only for sailing boats.

Boating clubs may give visitors from other clubs permission to use their slipway.

Most slipways provide access to sheltered waters, but get local advice on tides and currents before launching.

Inland waterway bank-side moorings can be rented from navigation authorities, boating clubs or land owners.

Inland waterway moorings

Many inland waterway bank-side moorings are rented out by the navigation authorities that organise boat registration and issue licences. Their contact details are in the Appendix. The procedure usually involves joining a waiting list, although alternative methods can include bidding or tendering for a mooring that becomes available. Some waterway moorings can also be rented from boating clubs or from farmers and other landowners. These can be difficult to find and identify if you're not familiar with an area, but using websites that provide aerial photographs and detailed maps, such as Google Earth, can help.

Some websites advertising boats for sale also advertise vacant moorings for rent or sale. A list of such websites is given in Chapter 4.

Harbour moorings and marinas

Keeping a boat afloat when not in use is sometimes described as pouring money into a hole in the water. This is a very negative view from a minority who don't understand the appeal of having a boat afloat, ready to use whenever the mood takes you. How much you actually pay is linked to the facilities that go with this watery hole.

Marinas provide plenty of facilities, such as access to your boat via easily accessible walkways and floating pontoons, car parking, toilets, water taps, electricity and security. Obviously, however, you have to pay for this luxurious level of boat accommodation. The most expensive can run to thousands of pounds a year, depending on the length of your motor cruiser, fees being generally charged per metre per month or per year. Also, beware of VAT: is it included? And are there any extras, such as for electricity used?

By comparison, a basic mooring with few facilities on a jetty at a basic boatyard, or on a swinging mooring offshore, may cost no more than a few hundred pounds a year. But bear in mind a boat on an offshore swinging mooring will need a rowing boat to reach it, and this will also need a storage space on land. An alternative is an inflatable dinghy carried in your car.

A marina provides plenty of facilities, including water and electricity for each boat as here at the Pike and Eel Marina on the Great Ouse.

This marina at Essex Boatyards on the coast provides sheltered moorings with plenty of facilities, including fuel available from a floating pontoon.

Many boats are brought ashore at the end of the boating season and kept on hardstanding at a boatyard, marina or club during the winter. Depending on the way their charges are calculated, this may be included in the usual mooring

Swinging moorings offshore are usually much cheaper than a marina but not as easily accessible.

A tender is needed to reach a mooring such as this.

A bank-side mooring may be available quite cheaply on a canal or river. Such a remote location may be secluded and tranquil, but enquire about any risks resulting from the lack of security measures. The local police may help with such enquiries.

fee or it may involve an extra storage payment. Taking the boat home on a trailer is a cheaper alternative. This process of laying up for the winter provides better protection for the boat from winds and weather damage and provides an opportunity for maintenance, painting and the application of antifouling paint before launching in the spring.

Maintenance of moorings

Insurance companies will want to know exactly where you'll moor or keep your boat, since the level of risk will affect the annual premium. If you keep it on an offshore swinging mooring they'll want to know that the mooring equipment is regularly and properly maintained. More on this can be found in Chapter 14.

Boat storage on land near the water

Boatyards and marinas have storage areas where boats can be kept for a monthly or yearly fee. A rapidly increasing facility at many locations, helping to overcome a shortage of mooring space, involves a park-and-launch area for boats, with the facility for an owner to telephone the boatyard and ask for the boat to be launched when it's needed. After use the boat is taken out of the water by the boatyard or marina staff. Obviously there are charges for this, but it can work out to be similar to or even cheaper than the cost of keeping the boat afloat in a marina.

Some campsites, caravan sites and caravan storage facilities are also prepared to store boats on trailers. This can be a cheaper alternative if near to a launching site. It can also be an option if there's no space to store a boat at home. Check that the boat can be kept away from children on the site, who may regard it as playground equipment.

Sometimes a co-operative farmer near the coast or waterway may find room for a boat in a barn for a small fee. Farmers are being encouraged to diversify and vary their business activities...

Boating clubs – cheaper than marinas

Boating clubs provide a much cheaper opportunity to keep a boat near the water. Clubs are generally non-profit-making organisations, mainly organised and run by elected committee members. The ones with the lowest membership and boat storage charges rely on voluntary work by their members to maintain facilities.

Lifting out for laying up.

This mooring buoy had broken adrift because of chain wear and corrosion, which demonstrates the importance of regular mooring maintenance.

Lifting and storage on land advertised at a boat show.

Boat parking and launching on request.

A significant number of clubs are for sailing boats only. This is usually made clear in the club's name. They often specialise in racing sailing dinghies and sail cruisers and don't have the space or facilities to cater for motor boats. However, it's worth enquiring whether they might welcome some motor boats. The rescue boats used during sailing races are, after all, motor boats.

Clubs more likely to welcome motor boats are those that call themselves 'Yacht clubs', 'Cruising clubs' or, of course, 'Motor Boat clubs'. Some clubs welcoming all types of boat are associated with marinas or harbours.

If you join a club and use its facilities frequently you need to be prepared to play a part in the voluntary work mentioned earlier – usually by joining working parties or a rota of volunteers for various tasks. This need not be regarded as a chore. Involvement with a club becomes an enjoyable way of life for many.

As well as community spirit, a club will have the all-important car park, clubhouse, bank-side or pontoon moorings, and rowing dinghies or a crewed motor launch to reach more remote moored cruisers. Low-cost moorings for cruisers may be available through the club, although there could be a waiting list.

The membership fees of many clubs provide remarkably good value for money compared with the commercial alternatives.

Above, left and below: The Rochester Cruising Club is pleasantly located between the castle and the tidal river, where there are well-organised moorings for members.

Motor Boat Manual

8 Introduction to motor boating

The boat's engine power should overcome the effects of current and wind, providing you allow for these variables.

The brief introduction provided here will help you get started with motor boating if you're new to the experience.

It's often possible to try a boat and get some tuition in boat-handling at boat shows.

Preparation

Reading a book certainly helps to prepare you for boating but you'll need practical help too, so try to get some experience as crew in your chosen type of motor boat. Boating clubs may provide opportunities and boat dealers will often take prospective customers afloat in new demonstration boats or second-hand boats to show them how it's done. There may also be opportunities to get afloat and receive some initial instruction at some boat shows, such as the Southampton Boat Show.

Hiring a boat for cruising on an inland waterway will help you to gain initial boat handling skills, but check with the hire company just how much instruction will be provided before you set off. Some boatyards have been known to let people take charge of large motor cruisers with very little instruction and preparation, so if you've no experience be sure to explain clearly in advance that you'll need substantial help. It's wise to choose a boat hire company that definitely provides substantial instruction for beginners.

There are plenty of boatyards and organisations that provide hire boats, but one club with an unusual approach, particularly suitable for beginners and those who want to try using several different kinds of motor cruiser, is the Boatline Quayside Club on the Norfolk Broads. Membership provides thorough tuition and the opportunity to book motor cruisers for short or long periods of time at quite short notice. The scheme provides an introduction to motor boating and many of the advantages of boat ownership. Members may then either go on to buy their own boat with a good knowledge of what's involved, or else continue their membership in a way that provides them with a type of share in boat ownership. Full details can be found at http://www.boatlineuk.com/.

Unlike many other countries, the UK has the tradition of allowing anyone to go afloat in charge of a boat without qualifications or certificates. This freedom is greatly valued but could be removed if too many people take the risk of going afloat with no idea of what they're doing and get into difficulties. The Royal Yachting Association has established a range of qualifications and approves course providers. Examples include basic short helmsman and boat handling courses, engine maintenance, and a five-day coastal skipper course for those wanting to cruise by night and day. A list and full details can be found at http://www.rya.org.uk and http://www.ryatraining.org/leisure/motorcruising.

For those wanting to extend their cruising knowledge and skills, some clubs and other organisations offer the

Some of the boats available to members of the Boatline Quayside Club.

chance to go on a cruise in company with other boats and with experienced and qualified boat owners. For example, the RYA occasionally organises such an event. Details are at http://www.rya.org.uk/NewsAndEvents/events/cruises/Pages/motorcruise.aspx. Another website with information on courses is http://www.powerboat-training.co.uk. Most training establishments are approved by the RYA but it's wise to check that this is the case before booking.

A fee obviously has to be paid to the course provider, but bear in mind that the knowledge gained will not only help you enjoy boating but will also help you avoid the expense of repairing a boat damaged through lack of the necessary skills. You could combine learning with a holiday abroad on a boating activity holiday.

Watching other people using and handling their boats is further good preparation for doing the same with your own. You'll see plenty of examples of what to do and, possibly, what not to do.

Not like driving a car

Some people think that because a boat has a steering wheel and levers to change gear and speed, it can be 'driven' like a car. However, whereas a car steers with its front wheels on solid ground, a boat steers as if these 'wheels' for steering are at the back. It also moves as if it's on ice rather than being firmly attached to the surface. It has no brake pedal or lever, and the wind blows it around while currents move the water under it. But don't let this put you off – you have an engine to help you overcome these forces, and mastery of them can be gained. Using the necessary skills effectively is part of the pleasure of motor boating.

Make sure you're aware of what forces are operating at any given time. The strengths and directions of both wind and current can be seen and reacted to. As you get used to how a boat behaves, your responses will become second nature.

A further point to understand is that a boat's response to the steering takes time. There's consequently a big temptation to over-steer, so that you end up constantly correcting this and zigzagging across the water. Instead, particularly at slow speeds, you should steer gently, a little at a time, and bring the wheel back to centre before the turn is complete. At higher speeds sudden turns can be dangerous, throwing people and equipment out of the boat.

Along with the practical skills involved with boating, you need to know about the effects of tides, currents, wind direction, weather and other hazards in the appropriate area. The local harbour master, boating club, experienced local boat owners and up-to-date marine maps and charts will all help with this information. Wind can affect a motor boat more than some beginners realise.

Check the weather forecast – wind directions and particularly wind strengths can change quickly, or fog can develop. Plenty of forecasts are available through various media such as the Internet, local and national radio and television. In particular the Meteorological Office and the BBC provide detailed forecasts via their websites at http://www.metoffice.gov.uk/weather and http://www.bbc.co.uk/weather/coast. Many other websites also provide forecasts for boating, and the coastguard broadcasts forecasts updated every few hours to VHF radios.

Awareness of the effects of wind and currents is important, especially when passing under bridges and passing obstacles or other boats.

Obviously you'll need to dress appropriately before preparing the boat. Remember that it's almost always significantly colder out on the water than on land and that you'll need non-slip footwear. The most important item to wear is your lifejacket, having first checked that it's in good condition.

Always make sure someone reliable knows where and when you're going out in a boat and what time you expect to return. They can then take appropriate action, including contacting the coastguard, if you haven't returned and may be in difficulties. Obviously, you need to let them know when you've returned. Chapter 18 includes details on communication equipment and distress flares, etc.

A lifejacket or buoyancy aid is essential. Wear suitable warm and waterproof clothing as well, though – unlike the dummies shown here...

Get to know your boat

As well as learning the general principles of boat handling, you need to find out how your particular boat, or one of the type you intend to buy, behaves on the water. This is an interesting and quite enjoyable experience, but should only be undertaken after you've gained the necessary boat handling skills. Preferably it should also be done with the assistance of someone who's already familiar with the type of boat.

Take the boat to a quiet spot free of hazards, in an estuary, harbour or inland waterway. Keep a good lookout for other boats at all times. Do what you can to let any onlookers, such as the harbour master, know that you'll be practising manoeuvres, otherwise they may think you're in trouble!

Try experimenting with steering at slow speeds. See what happens when you put the engine in neutral and when the wind takes hold of the boat. Depending on the type of engine and drive, the boat is likely to drift with its stern towards the wind because of the drag caused by the propeller, outboard motor or stern drive. Although there are no brakes, the boat can be slowed and stopped by heading into the current or wind and reducing speed. Obviously, using reverse cancels much forward motion and is the closest you can get to an emergency stop in a car, but reversing will also result in loss of steering. It's much better to be moving slightly against the wind or current in order to keep better control.

At slow speeds, the rotation of the propeller tends to pull most types of boat slightly to one side as well as pushing it forwards. This can be useful when manoeuvring in a very narrow channel or a small space in a marina. Turning a stationary boat in its own length is possible with many boats if you turn the steering wheel hard over and then just give a very short burst on the throttle. This pushes the stern sideways before any forward movement starts. If you then turn the wheel hard over the opposite way and do the same in reverse any forward momentum will be stopped and a further push will be given, turning the stern further in the same direction.

Before you venture further afield, find a quiet area of water where you can safely get to know how your boat handles.

Using the rudder and short bursts on the throttle, it's possible to turn a boat without much forward motion.

Boat handling

You need to keep in mind the general points already covered when reading this section, which is designed to prepare you for practical tuition sessions in boat handling with someone either qualified or appropriately experienced. The crew will also need appropriate preparation and instruction. Some inexperienced skippers try to give orders to unprepared crew who don't know what he's talking (or shouting) about – with disastrous consequences and damaged relationships!

Moving off from the mooring

Preparing and starting the motor is covered in Chapter 17.

With the motor warmed up and running in neutral, reduce the number of mooring lines attached to the pontoon or bank so that you have only the fore and aft lines secured. Have fenders in place in case of any minor collisions. If currents or winds are not affecting the boat, it's often possible to simply untie it, push its bow away from the bank with the boathook and simply motor away slowly. However, it's often necessary to steer sharply to one side to avoid obstacles such as other moored boats. If this is done too quickly the stern will swing in towards the bank and hit the pontoon or quayside. Carefully placed fenders are a precaution against resulting scrapes.

With a strong tide, river current or wind the procedure is more difficult, but these natural forces can be used to your advantage. If the wind or current is coming from ahead, first remove the stern line and then motor forwards slowly in order to slacken the bow mooring line. Get the crew to untie the bow line and push the boat away from the bank with the boathook pushed against a firm and safe point. Once the boat is turning away from the bank the current or wind

Speed should be reduced to ensure that wash causes no problems for other boats.

will probably help to move it away somewhat faster than expected, so be prepared for this.

An alternative is to undo the bow line and let the wind or current swing the boat out, with the stern held in place by its mooring line until you're ready to motor away. Then remove the stern line and go.

Where there's open water and no restrictions speed can be increased.

Similar manoeuvres to swing the boat out in a controlled way according to the strength and direction of wind and current can be carefully planned in advance. In some confined situations it's best to keep the bow line fastened and swing the stern out by turning the wheel away from the bank and using reverse thrust on the engine. The bow line can then be released and the boat can be motored and steered forward and away from the mooring.

Handling the boat whilst cruising will depend very much on the type and size of boat, engine and drive system. This is where hands-on tuition and experience with someone knowledgeable is important. Bear in mind that most inland waterways, estuaries and harbours have speed limits and take care to ensure that the wash (the waves caused by your boat) doesn't affect other boats or threaten to damage the riverbank.

The rule of the waterways is that you travel on the right. This is, of course, the opposite to the rule that governs driving on the UK's roads. When approaching an oncoming boat you both move to the right to pass. But there are exceptions – large vessels will need to keep to a deep water channel, for instance – and caution and common sense must always prevail.

If you're boating at sea or contemplating a sea passage you'll need to know much more about navigation, procedures to avoid collisions, and boat handling. These topics are covered in the important motor boating courses referred to earlier and in books on navigation such as those listed in the Appendix.

Returning to the mooring

Always prepare in advance for the approach to the pontoon, quay or bank by having the fenders in place and the mooring lines secured and coiled ready for use. Check the direction of wind, tide or current and the movements of nearby boats.

The most important point to remember is to head *into* the wind or the current, whichever is the stronger, in order to slow the boat down whilst retaining forward motion and

Have fenders and mooring lines prepared before approaching the bank diagonally against the current or wind.

Excessive movement of a moored boat can be stopped by using 'springs'. These are extra mooring lines run diagonally to the bow and stern as shown in this photograph.

A dinghy will be needed to reach an offshore swinging mooring.

control over the steering. If you approach *with* the wind or current rather than against it, you'll find your boat moving much too fast to stop where you want it to, and will probably hit something. This is the most common mistake made by people who hire motor boats on inland waterways without adequate tuition.

Approach the pontoon slowly at an angle of 45° or less. When you reach the pontoon, steer alongside and use reverse to stop the boat whilst the crew quickly secure the bow line to prevent the wind or current from swinging the boat out again. The other mooring lines can then be secured and adjusted to allow for changes in water level. In a tidal area it's essential to allow enough slack in the mooring lines for the range of tidal rise and fall, unless you're moored to a floating pontoon which does this automatically. Some inexperienced boat owners have returned to find their boat suspended by short mooring lines from a harbour wall at low tide. Water levels on rivers also rise and fall, so ask for local advice on the amount of slack to allow.

More information on ropes, knots and anchoring and mooring equipment is provided in later chapters.

Swinging moorings

In the case of a motor cruiser on an offshore swinging mooring you'll need to use a tender – a dinghy – to reach the boat, either by rowing or by using an outboard motor. This can be the most hazardous part of a boating session. All too often the dinghies seen going to and from moored motor cruisers are dangerously overloaded. It only takes an unexpectedly big wave, the wash from a thoughtless passing boat owner, or sudden movement by an occupant, to swamp and sink an overloaded dinghy.

It's much safer to make more than one journey to the cruiser if there's a risk of overloading the tender. Stepping into and out of the dinghy – particularly to and from the cruiser – needs to be done slowly and cautiously. This is where many mishaps occur.

As well as securely tying the dinghy to the cruiser at both ends, someone should hold it steady, and those left in the dinghy should be prepared for the change in weight distribution, since the dinghy can tip up dangerously if all the remaining weight is at one end. Obviously, lifejackets must be worn at all times.

Once on the cruiser, attach the dingy to the mooring buoy unless you're going to tow it behind the boat. Remove any covers or open the canopy. The engine should be run sufficiently to warm up to its efficient operating temperature before moving off. Take care to look all round for other boats and hazards before leaving the mooring and at all times whilst boating. Keeping a good lookout is essential.

Returning to the mooring

As described previously, the best approach is against the tide or the wind, depending on which force is the stronger. This will help to slow you to a stop whilst still retaining the ability to steer.

Hazards you need to be aware of can be both large and small, so keep a good lookout all round.

This motorsailer is approaching a mooring buoy with the tender attached to it. A boathook is used to reach the line attached to the buoy.

You could send a crew member to the bows with a boathook to catch the mooring buoy's pick-up line and secure the boat, but it can also be done from the safety of the cockpit. Before approaching the mooring, or before setting off, run a rope from the bows back to the cockpit on the outside of all stanchions and other obstacles and secure it. This rope can then be threaded through the ring on the mooring buoy as you come up to it. Put the motor in neutral, and as the boat drifts backwards the buoy will slide along the rope to the bows. When you're ready it can be secured there. This reduces the problems that can occur if the crew and/or helmsman are not experienced in picking up a mooring.

Practising boat handling in quiet conditions is worthwhile. If you miss the mooring buoy first time it doesn't matter – just go round and do it again. You can always tell onlookers that you were just practising your approach!

Safety

It's probably true to say that your road journey to the boating location is more hazardous than the risks involved in going afloat in suitable conditions. For probably 80 per cent of the time spent boating in sheltered inland and coastal waters in suitable weather, there's very little risk of accident. However, you do need to be fully prepared for the unexpected, such as a sudden change in the weather, submerged hazards, mistakes made by others and your own miscalculations.

The Royal National Lifeboat Institute and HM Coastguard are well known for carrying out rescues, but they're also very active in promoting safety, and the following advice is based on their recommendations. For the RNLI's full range of safety information, visit their websites at http://www.rnli.org.uk and select the 'sea and beach safety' link. For HM Coastguard, go to http://www.mcga.gov.uk and select 'safety information' and other relevant topics concerning risks, etc.

Both organisations publish leaflets on safety and the RNLI provides a booklet *Sea Safety – The Complete Guide* with an interactive CD ROM. This information is free of charge, but remember that the RNLI is a charity dependent on contributions and that lifeboat crews are volunteers. Everyone involved with boating should join one of their membership schemes and contribute on a regular basis.

The RNLI offers free 'Sea Check' safety inspection to boat owners. Carried out by trained volunteers, this is a way of providing friendly and helpful advice to improve the safety of your boat.

The Inland Waterways Association also has plenty of helpful advice and information on its website at http://www.waterways.org.uk/Waterways/UsefulInformation. *The Boater's Handbook* which can be downloaded from this site provides safety information for inland waterways along with details on how to operate locks and navigate canals.

The Boat Safety Scheme, already mentioned in Chapter 6, requires compulsory safety inspection and certification every four years for boats with cabins on inland waters. The

Five fingers safety tips from an RNLI display.

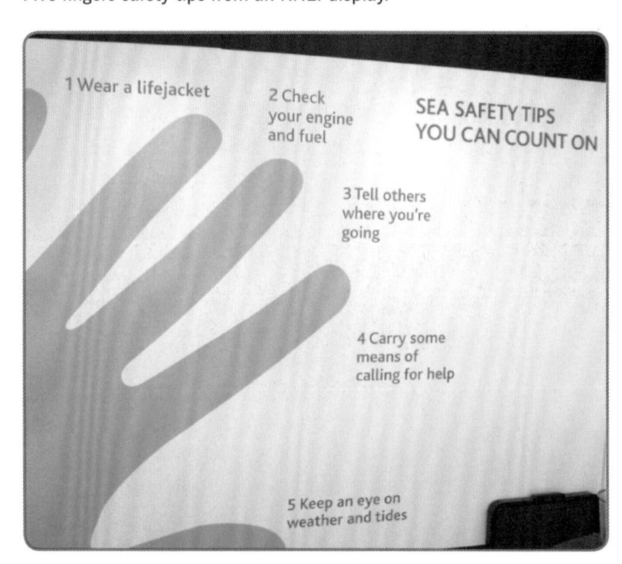

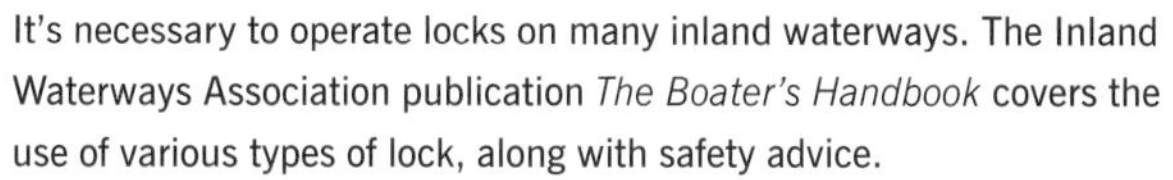
It's necessary to operate locks on many inland waterways. The Inland Waterways Association publication *The Boater's Handbook* covers the use of various types of lock, along with safety advice.

BSS website provides excellent safety points for all boats whether for inland or maritime use.

All the excellent and thorough safety advice available from the RNLI, the Coastguard and inland waterways organisations could fill much of this book, so it's essential that you consult their websites and/or their printed publications as part of the learning process before going afloat.

The most important piece of advice from the RNLI is that you should always wear a lifejacket. This isn't a legal requirement like wearing a seat belt in a car is – except in Ireland – so the decision whether to wear a lifejacket in the cabin and cockpit of a cruiser is, of course, one for the individual to make. As can be seen in some of the photos in this book, some people decide to risk not wearing one when boating in calm conditions or on inland waterways and they have a right to make that choice. But as the RNLI says, a lifejacket can only save you if you're wearing it – and people have been known to fall overboard even in the calmest of conditions.

Detailed information on buoyancy aids and lifejackets is in Chapter 18.

Rules of the road

Under sail –

- Port tack gives way to starboard tack.
- Windward yacht keeps clear of starboard tack.

Under power –

- A yacht under power gives way to a yacht under sail.
- Vessels under power approaching head on should turn to starboard.

General rules –

- An overtaking boat must always keep clear.
- The skipper is responsible for maintaining a good lookout at all times in order to carry out the above and avoid hazards.
- Vessels of less than 20m length should not impede vessels having to keep to a narrow deep-water channel or vessels using a traffic separation scheme.

The Royal Yachting Association publishes *The Complete Regulations for the Prevention of Collisions at Sea*, which covers all eventualities for those carrying out more ambitious cruising.

Of course, common sense must prevail. Some boat owners may not know the above rules, so always be cautious and ready to take avoiding action if necessary.

Open boat cruising

You don't necessarily need a motor cruiser with a cabin to stay on your boat overnight for an extended boating session in suitable weather. Any large and stable open boat can carry the necessary camping equipment. You then have the choice of finding a remote beach or bank-side location for camping or sleeping in the boat under a tent or canopy. However, it may be necessary to improve the floor of the boat with boards to make a flatter surface for airbeds and to protect the hull.

Small to medium-sized motor cruisers – boats with berths

Small motor cruisers can be quite comfortable for two people. A cruiser with a little extra length can provide a quite surprising amount of additional room in its increased 'beam', or width, sufficient to accommodate a family of four or more for a holiday afloat.

Canopies and covers can be used to provide shelter on an otherwise open boat, as here on electrically-powered river boats. They can even provide overnight camping accommodation.

Whether to take small children on a boating holiday is a difficult decision. Even if well-behaved they can be unpredictable and get bored easily, so take plenty to keep them occupied so that they're not tempted to 'explore' where they shouldn't. Ways of improving their safety include not allowing them on deck, having a secure cockpit canopy and installing safety netting all round the boat. Obviously, they should also wear lifejackets carefully chosen to fit and support them without slipping off over the head. Again, the RNLI's advice on this is thorough.

Inside the cabin, with limited space, it's vital to have your storage organised and to keep clothing and equipment tidy. The crew need to take care with the limited water supply, and the 12V electricity supply will also be restricted when cruising. Remind everyone that it's not like using the taps and electricity supply at home.

Since you may be cruising where spray and waves could enter the boat, it's wise to keep sleeping bags and clothing in plastic bags, or plastic boxes with clip-on lids, whether in lockers or not. It's surprising how spray, condensation and drips can penetrate the cabin of even the best-designed and maintained boat.

Netting will provide additional safety if you're planning to keep children on board.

More on using motor boats and their equipment will be found in the later chapters on maintenance and repair.

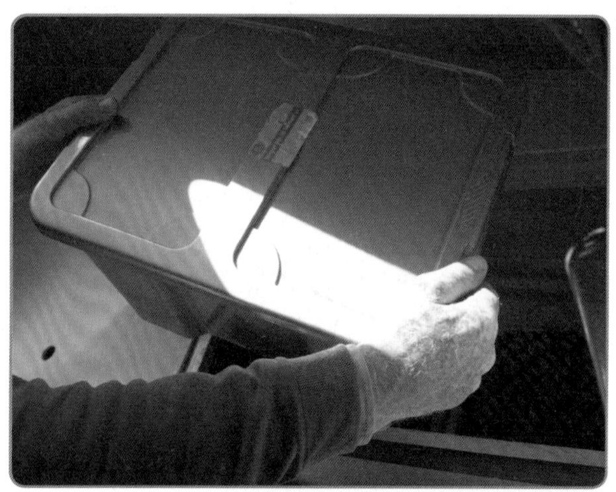

The lockers under the bunks in this boat owned by Ian Davies have been equipped with cut-down plastic vegetable crates. These raise items clear of any accumulating bilge water and provide a level surface for waterproof plastic storage boxes with clip-on lids.

9 Simple and basic maintenance/repairs

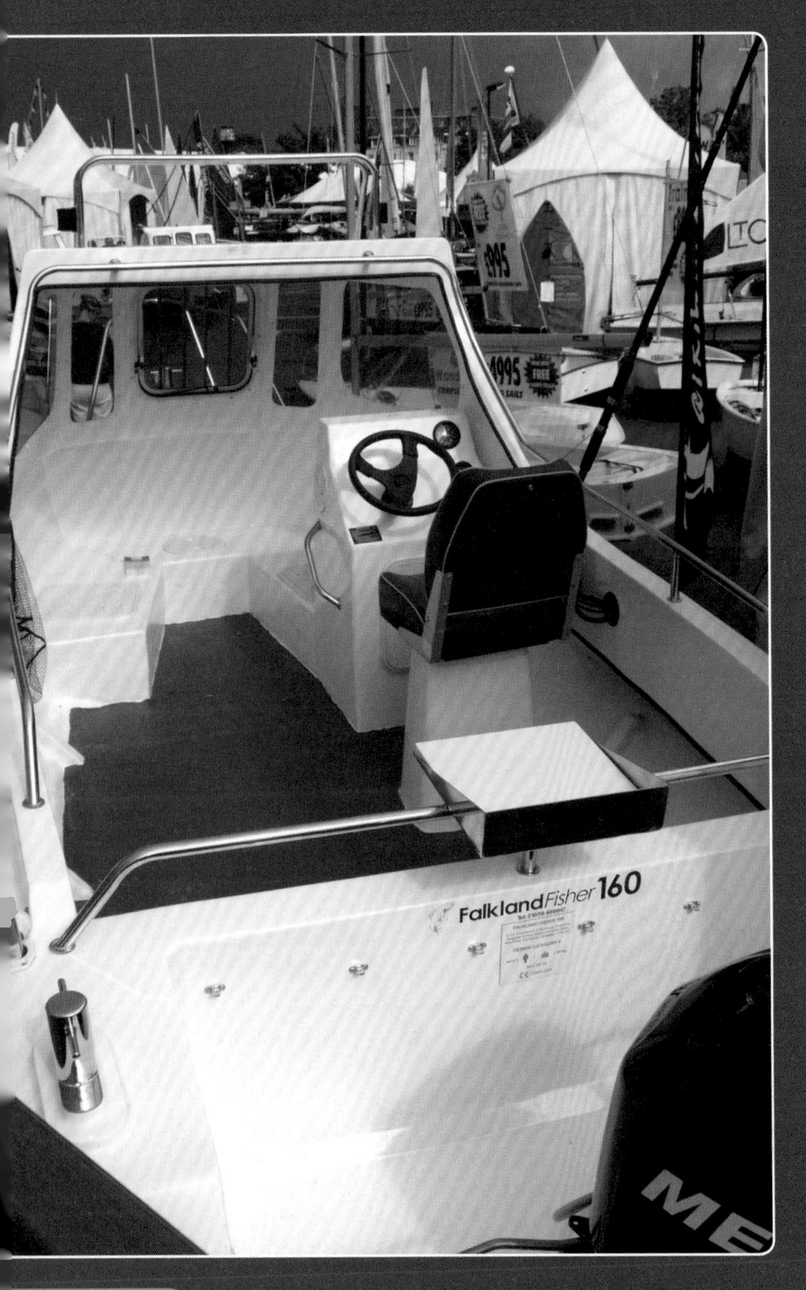

A new GRP boat can be kept in showroom condition with simple cleaning and basic maintenance procedures.

Anyone capable of basic DIY can do many of the tasks necessary to keep a motor boat in good condition, and most of the tools you'd use at home can be used on a boat. As explained in Chapter 1, most of the practical advice in this book is about straightforward maintenance tasks and basic repairs rather than modifications or the installation of extra equipment.

Above and opposite: A new boat can be kept in good condition quite easily with regular maintenance. Older boats will need more effort and it may not be realistic to try for 'as new' condition if you want time for boating as well.

Perfectionist or pragmatist?

Boat owners tend to fall into three categories. The first is the perfectionist, who always has a beautifully clean and superbly maintained boat. After all the time spent keeping their boat in this 'as new' condition, a perfectionist may not have much time left over to actually use it. But if pride in having the smartest boat around is his way of getting the most pleasure from the boating experience, that's fair enough – provided he's not critical of those who prefer to shift the balance in favour of actually using their boat.

The second category is the pragmatist, who wants his boat to be well maintained, as safe as possible and reasonably smart most of the time. A boating session will take preference over polishing when the weather is great for enjoying the boat.

The third category includes those who only work on their boat when things start to fall apart. Cleaning is rarely done and safety issues threaten the enjoyment of boating. Obviously, becoming a member of this third category is to be avoided: neglected boats tend to sink.

A neglected boat may eventually sink.

The second category may well be the most appealing, and the tasks described later in this book are intended to strike a balance between maintaining your boat to perfectionist standard and still finding plenty of time to enjoy using it.

Safety aspects

The safety rules that apply to the DIY work you do at home also apply to working on boats, but with some additional considerations. Obviously, if you do the work afloat on a motor cruiser you have to take care not to end up getting very wet, either by losing your balance or by damaging the hull below the waterline. The safest situation in which to work is, of course, on land, with the boat securely set up so that it won't tip over or collapse on top of you or others. Ladders and platforms need to be securely fixed.

All tools, equipment and materials come with instructions on the packaging or in an enclosed leaflet, and can also be found on the manufacturer's website. These instructions should be read carefully, even though the health and safety details often include the irritatingly obvious. In amongst the patronising comments like 'take care not to cut yourself with sharp objects' are less obvious and important cautions you need to know about. It's not only for

Hazards are indicated on this cleaning product container, but it's also important to read the health and safety instructions often supplied in the small print on labels, leaflets and company websites.

safety – some people take the misguided attitude, 'If all else fails read the instructions,' but misusing and wasting expensive repair materials, and incorrectly fitting costly equipment, constitutes a wealth risk as well as a health risk.

As mentioned previously in connection with insurance, the conditions and requirements for insurance cover have been getting stricter concerning the quality of boat maintenance. Policy clauses now place more emphasis on following the manufacturers' instructions provided with boats, equipment and maintenance materials. Reminders of this will therefore be found repeated in the following chapters.

Special chemicals used with marine quality products can be toxic, so instructions should be followed very carefully.

Suitable facemasks, overalls, eye protection, gloves and ear protection need to be worn even though they can be irritating and uncomfortable. The chemicals in boat repair materials are often stronger and more harmful than corresponding household DIY products. Toxic fumes and dust from using and sanding epoxy resins are examples, and antifouling paint obviously has to contain harmful poisons to deal with the organisms that like your boat as much as you do.

To protect the environment from the above types of pollutant, place a tarpaulin where it will catch shavings, dust, spillage, drips and any other effluent from work on your boat. All such waste should then be disposed of carefully and appropriately. Boatyards, marinas and clubs are increasingly installing facilities for this. Plenty of helpful advice on environmental issues for boat owners can be found at http://www.thegreenblue.org.uk.

DIY or not?

All electrical, gas, fuel and safety installations should be carried out or inspected by properly qualified engineers before use. An appropriately qualified Corgi-registered engineer *must* carry out gas installations and should be asked to do regular inspections.

You need to ensure that any other repairs you carry out can cope with the pressures of motor boating, waves, currents and the actions of the crew. One way to be sure of this is to arrange for it to be checked by professionals. If you do the work in or near a boatyard with co-operative staff this may be easy to arrange. They'll also be available to take over if you find some tasks are beyond your ability.

Where to do the work

Some boatyards allow DIY work on their premises when you keep your boat on their area of hardstanding. In return for appropriate charges, they'll make available the necessary electricity, water supply and possibly shelter and heating inside the boatyard buildings. This has the advantage, as mentioned above, of specialists being nearby who can advise you and, if necessary, carry out any tasks you may find too difficult. If you can establish this ideal arrangement with a boatyard you'll find it very reassuring, and you can still keep costs down by doing most of the work yourself.

If you have the space, taking the boat home on a trailer means you can work on it whenever it's convenient – although there can be distractions, such as the garden that's been neglected whilst you've been boating. A garage or workshop can be used, or a tent-type cover can be erected over the boat. This not only provides you with dry working conditions but also the possibility of introducing suitable safe heating.

Some boatyards allow DIY work on their premises, where experts may be available to offer advice and provide materials.

A cover or tent over the boat provides necessary protection.

This is significant, because most paints, resins and fillers need a minimum temperature of 10°C to set or cure, and this can be a problem out in the open during winter. However, heating which involves a naked flame needs to be kept well away from inflammable fumes given off by many repair products. Suitable containers filled with hot water may sufficiently warm a small, enclosed space round a repair without any risk of fire.

Practice makes perfect

If you're not an expert at working with quite expensive paints, varnish, fillers, resins and other materials used in boat repair, don't start applying the advice in this book without first practising where a mistake won't matter. For example, try varnishing a piece of scrap wood, painting the inside of a locker, or applying filler, glues, resins and the like out of sight where a bit of extra strengthening might be a good idea but isn't vital, such as inside a storage compartment.

Before going into detail on maintenance and repair, the following chapter provides a brief insight into how many types of motor boat are built using some modern materials.

Materials and equipment for boat maintenance, repairs and improvement are available from chandlers, along with advice. Many also have websites so that you can order by mail.

10 Motor boat construction, self-build and materials

Top: The Scintilla motor cruiser, which can be built from a kit of parts.

Left: A newly-built Viking 20 cruiser.

Wood was the traditional boat-building material for centuries, and many books have been written on the building, maintenance and restoration of wooden boats. Here, however, we're concerned with the materials and methods that have been used more recently, as well as some of the basic aspects of boat construction.

GRP boats

'GRP' means glass reinforced plastic, often referred to simply as fibreglass. Although later parts of this chapter outline the possibilities for amateur boat building using some materials, GRP construction requires special moulds and controlled workshop conditions along with substantial knowledge and experience of boat building. The following should, however, provide a basic understanding of GRP construction. The photographs were taken during the construction of Viking motor cruisers, with the assistance of David Taylor of Riverside Marine and Leisure Ltd (http://www.boatsaleuk.com).

A mould of the shape of the hull is cleaned, polished and coated with layers of gel coat resin. Sheets of fibreglass matting are then laid onto it and saturated with resin.

The fibreglass matting used in construction.

Fibreglass lay-up is applied to the inside of the hull mould, saturated with resin and rolled flat.

The deck mouldings and interior mouldings are produced in the same way, using appropriate moulds.

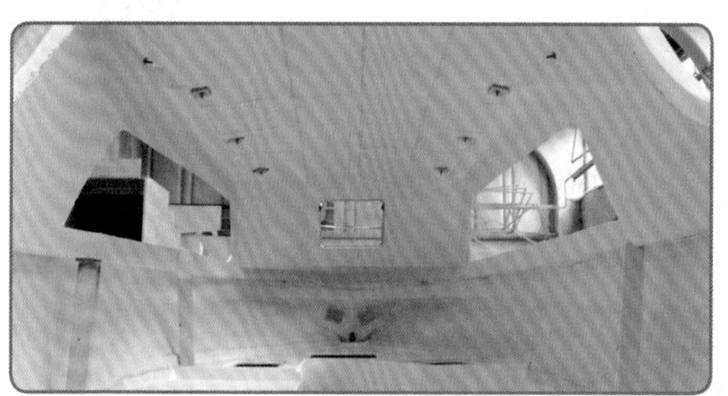

The deck and other components are fastened and sealed together and the boat takes shape.

Plywood bulkheads and all necessary fittings are installed.

The cockpit canopy supports and cover are added.

Interior furnishings, upholstery and equipment are installed in the cabin.

A completed Viking motor cruiser ready for a new owner at the Pike and Eel Marina on the Great Ouse.

The European Recreational Craft Directive and self-build

The European Recreational Craft Directive applies to self-built boats if they're sold within five years of being built. As you can't be sure whether you'll sell the boat in that time, it's important to be familiar with the Directive's rules and requirements.

A future buyer will want to see the necessary documentation and there are heavy fines for anyone convicted of selling a qualifying boat built since June 1998 without the necessary evidence of compliance. As mentioned in earlier chapters, the regulations change from time to time, so be sure to check the latest rules and procedures for compliance. These are available online at http://www.berr.gov.uk. Put 'Recreational Craft Directive' in the search box. Suppliers of kits and partly-built boats will give advice on the regulations and may do much of the work towards compliance for you. Be sure to ask about this before you order the kit.

As with many of the Bruce Roberts designs, the boat shown here can be constructed in steel or in aluminium. The following photographs of the Coastworker, kindly supplied by Bruce Roberts, show some of the stages in construction.

Steel, aluminium, wood and self-build

Though the majority of motor boats are made of GRP, a considerable number are constructed from steel while some use wood or aluminium. The following photographs depicting various stages of the construction process are of motor cruisers being built from plans designed by Bruce Roberts, which can be used by enthusiasts for their own self-build projects. The full range of Bruce's plans and much information on self-build projects can be found on his website at http://www.bruceroberts.com.

Those who are skilled in working with metals and have, or are willing to learn, the appropriate welding and other skills may be interested in self-building using these materials, but even if you're not, the following pictures will still provide some useful insights into further aspects of boat building. This section will prove useful when you're inspecting a boat for purchase or when you're working on the repair and maintenance of such boats.

Ribs and stringers are assembled and the aluminium or steel sheets are attached to them.

The hull is turned over for work to continue on the interior.

These five photographs show further stages in the building of a hull, this time constructed in steel.

Self-build with marine ply and epoxy resin

Plenty of designs exist for amateur boat building projects using marine plywood. Though a large number are for sailing boats, many of these can, of course, be used with a motor as well as sails. Plans, specifications, kits and instructions for building such wooden boats can be purchased from suppliers. Some plans are available for small motor cruisers to be constructed in marine plywood.

Kits

Building from a kit of parts can save a large amount compared with the cost of a newly built boat. Synthetic resins include the polyester type commonly used for GRP boats or epoxy resins which have greater adhesive and waterproof properties and are often used in building wooden boats, as in the examples below. The basic method of use is to mix the resin and the curing agent or hardener supplied with it, according to the instructions provided by the manufacturer. The speed at which it solidifies usually depends on the temperature, the humidity and the ratio of the quantities mixed together. Various resin products are available, providing a range of glues and fillers.

The following picture sequence shows the construction of kit boats mainly using marine plywood, epoxy resin and various appropriate types of wood by Simon Tomlinson and Max Campbell of Whisper Boats. A range of boat-building kits, known in Australia as the 'Scruffie', are available from Whisper Boats (http://www.whisperboats.co.uk). These include the Scintilla motor cruiser and the Secret, which can be used as either a motor boat or as a sail cruiser.

Completion of partly-built motor boats

Another way to save money on a new boat is to buy one that's been only partly built and then complete it yourself, thus saving on the labour costs involved with a fully completed boat. This provides an alternative for those who lack the time or inclination to build from plans or a kit. It also means that there's the possibility of having a GRP hull.

Plenty of boat builders can be asked if a partly completed boat can be supplied instead of a fully completed version. There may already be several levels of completion available and priced but not necessarily publicised.

Equipment not included

In calculating the overall cost of kit boats and self-completion projects, remember to calculate the amount needed for equipment that's not included, such as an outboard or inboard motor, steering equipment, anchors, ropes, bunk cushions and cockpit cover.

These photographs were kindly supplied by Max Campbell and Simon Tomlinson.

Boat-building kits are supplied with a great many hardwood parts, pre-cut to shape. They're shown here in the shipping crate.

The boats are built 'right way up' by adding components to the ready-made keel assembly, seen here on the left.

The ply components are supplied pre-cut, with small tabs left that the builder has to cut through to separate them. The sheet shown here has two full-width frames, one half-width frame, and one side of the anchor well floor.

The ply frames have slots pre-cut in them that correspond with slots cut in the fore-and-aft components. The frames fit into slots pre-cut in the keel, very quickly forming the shape of the boat.

Here, deck stringers and the foredeck support beam meet. Wherever two ply components slot together they're bonded with a fillet joint made with epoxy resin.

After the top skin panels are fitted with the boat 'right way up', it's turned over and the bottom panels are fitted. The hull is then faired with epoxy filler. Fibreglass sheathing adds structural strength and abrasion resistance, and the epoxy resin is immune to the problems of osmosis that are possible with most resins used in GRP boat production.

The cabin has been built and veneered using silky oak, an Australian timber. These veneers are 4 to 5mm thick and add to the structural strength.

The Secret kit boat can be used as a motor launch or as a motorsailer.

11

Motor Boat Manual

The hull and decks

Cleaning, polishing and preservation

Though fibreglass boats are sometimes referred to as 'maintenance free' they still need cleaning and polishing. Surface dirt can be washed off with water and a mop. A hosepipe or pressure washer can be used, but take care to ensure that water isn't forced into air vents or through other gaps such as joints round hatch covers. In addition be aware that the sealant round windows and fittings can be damaged by high-pressure water jets.

More persistent dirt and stains will require use of cleaning fluids. Take care with these too, and be sure to rinse them off immediately, since there's a risk of some commonly used chemicals etching into the gelcoat surface if left to dry on it.

Green algae grow on GRP surfaces quite rapidly in warm and damp conditions. This can be wiped off smooth surfaces but is difficult to remove from non-slip deck surfaces, even with vigorous scrubbing. Various products can be used to remove it, but one which actually kills such growths, makes removal much easier and helps prevent re-growth is 'Simply Gone'. This is advertised as harmless when left on boat surfaces. It's sold as a concentrated liquid, which is diluted according to instructions provided, and then sprayed or brushed onto the algae and left for a few days to kill it. The algae turn black. They're then easily removed and may even get washed off by rain without scrubbing. If not available locally it can be ordered from the website at http://www.simplygone.com.

Particularly persistent stains occur along and just above the waterline. A product called 'Y-10 Stain Absorbent Gel' removes these stains and will shift rust stains from the deck. It contains poisonous oxalic acid, so, as when using

A fibreglass boat's surfaces aren't entirely maintenance-free. They need to be kept in good condition with cleaning and polishing.

Right: 'Simply Gone' removes algae.

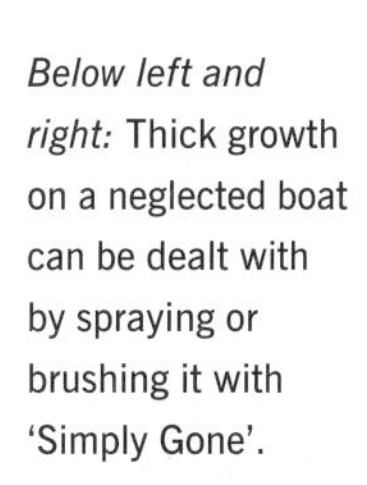

Below left and right: Thick growth on a neglected boat can be dealt with by spraying or brushing it with 'Simply Gone'.

Special products for removing rust stains and yellow waterline stains.

Brush Y-10 onto the stain.

Leave for a few minutes.

Agitate the gel with the brush.

Rinse off thoroughly.

all chemicals, wear suitable gloves. You simply brush it onto waterline stains and rust stains, leave it for a few minutes and the stains fade away before your very eyes, without scrubbing – though a little agitation with the brush might be necessary to spread the gel and remove all signs of staining. Rinse it off thoroughly after use. Although it's formulated not to damage GRP or painted surfaces it's not a good idea to leave acid on the gelcoat.

Oxidation

The sides of the hull above the waterline and GRP decks will lose their shiny surface and discolour as the boat ages. Sunlight is the main cause of this, along with abrasion, dirt and salt water.

A small motor boat taken out on a trailer can be rinsed with freshwater after every use. The application of a suitable wax polish helps to protect the

Cleaning and polishing restored and preserved the reflective shine on the hull of this 25-year-old boat formerly owned by the author. This process not only makes the boat look smart but protects its surfaces from oxidation.

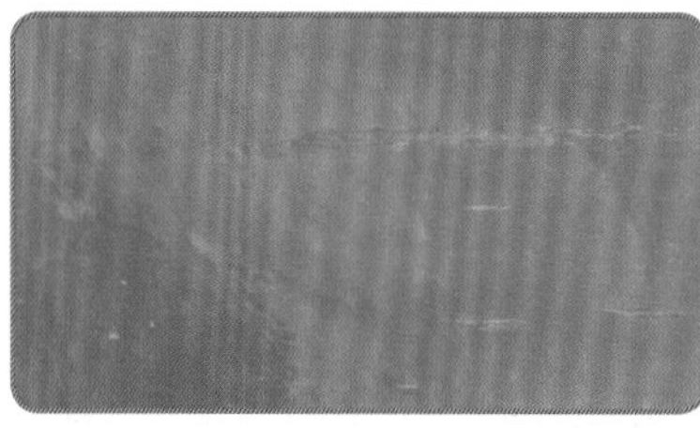

Oxidation and scratches on an old boat.

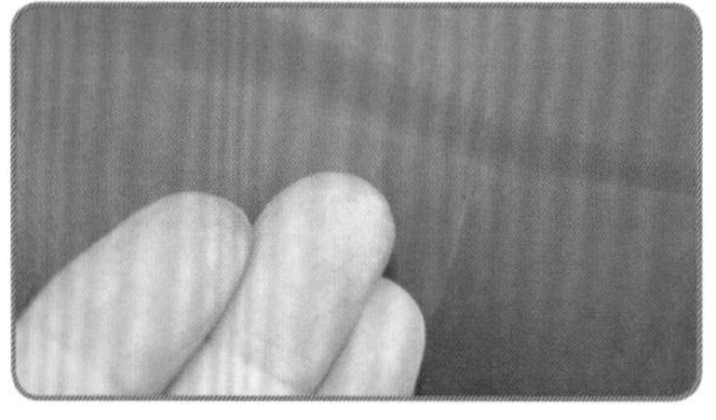

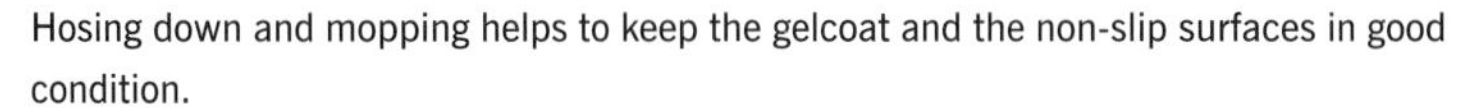

Hosing down and mopping helps to keep the gelcoat and the non-slip surfaces in good condition.

Oxidation causes a chalky powder to form, which comes off on your fingers.

gelcoat and gives it a good shine. It also reduces drag and helps increase a boat's speed through the water. Covering the trailed boat when not in use helps to protect it from the sun. Obviously, rinsing and covering can't be done as easily with a motor cruiser on a mooring, so the boat needs to be polished to protect it and to restore its shiny surface.

As the boat ages, oxidation will eventually cause the gelcoat to roughen slightly and coloured surfaces will become cloudy-looking. Mild to moderate oxidation shows as dullness which polish won't remove; there's no reflection in the surface at this stage. Severe oxidation is indicated by a chalky powder that can be wiped off the gelcoat with your fingers.

When polishing will no longer bring back the original shine it's possible to restore it with oxidation remover. Various grades of remover are available. As they remove a thin layer of the gelcoat, be sure you don't use an abrasive restorer that's stronger than necessary. The instructions on the remover will indicate how to use it and whether it should be rubbed until it disappears or should be left to dry before being rubbed off. Check the cloth you use for build-up of the surface material being removed and change to a clean cloth frequently in order to prevent scratching.

This process takes considerable energy and you may want to do one side of the boat at a time, leaving you the opportunity and remaining energy to polish the newly restored gelcoat. It's quite important to get polish onto the new shiny surface as soon as possible in order to preserve it. Electrically-powered polishers can be used, but be careful to keep the rotating head moving to avoid building

Products for restoring the surface of gelcoat.

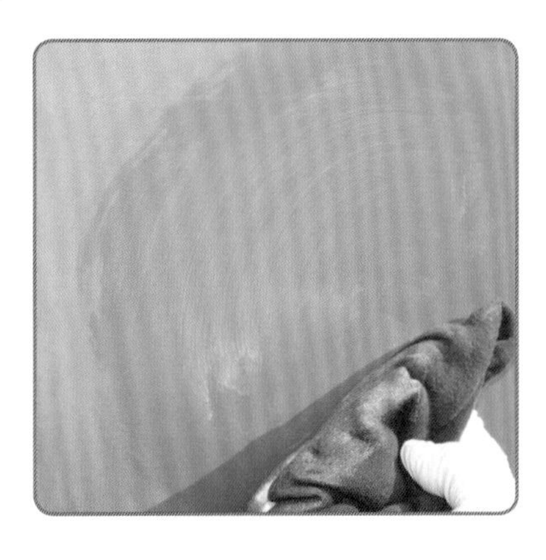

Application of rubbing compound with a circular motion to remove oxidation.

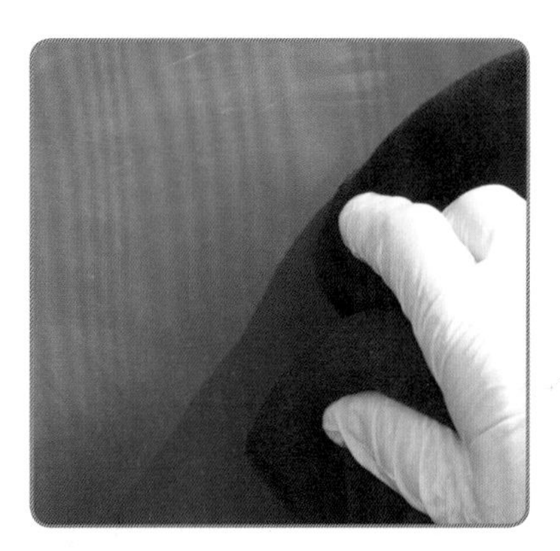

Buffing with a cloth to remove the whitened surface.

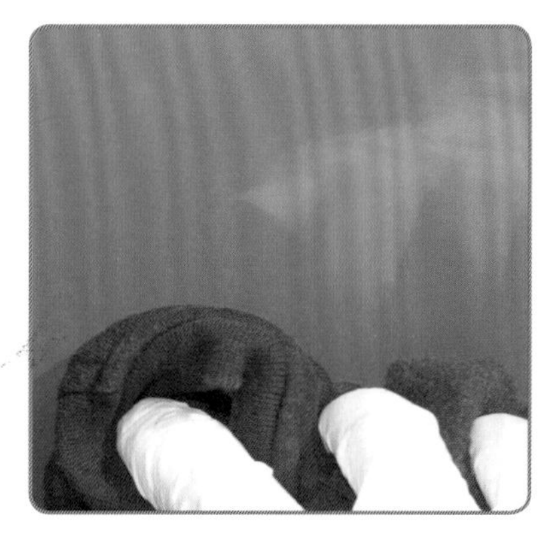

Finish with wax polish to restore a good protective shine.

Polish protects against further oxidation.

up heat through friction, as heat could damage the gelcoat.

Although hard work, this process of removing oxidation is more rewarding than many, as you're likely to see your boat return to its former shiny self.

When polishing, avoid getting polish on the non-slip surfaces where you tread. These are best kept clean by scrubbing with water and a little cleaning fluid. Polish on these surfaces will cause your feet to slide around the boat faster than the rest of you, with unfortunate consequences…

Boat polishes should delay or even prevent the build-up of oxidation again. This is quite important because each time an abrasive product is used to remove oxidation, a thin layer of gelcoat is removed. Obviously, therefore, as the gelcoat is quite thin to start with the process shouldn't be repeated too often.

To paint or not to paint

Instead of restoring and polishing, the gelcoat can be painted. On an old boat, however, you should first try the process of surface restoration described above on a small area to see if it will work, before you decide to cover the hull with paint. Eventually, though, an old boat's gelcoat will no longer respond to this process. There may be too many scuffmarks, scratches and gelcoat repairs to get a worthwhile finish. This is when painting the gelcoat becomes necessary in order to improve the appearance and provide protection to the ageing GRP.

Painting GRP

As with all painting jobs, careful preparation and priming/undercoating of the surface is the key to success. This may well take up 80 per cent of the overall time involved. Before commencing work, read the health and safety data sheets which all paint manufacturers publish and which can also usually be found on their websites.

Choice of paint

A two-part polyurethane paint is usually recommended for the best results on the area of the hull above the waterline, referred to as the 'topsides'. When choosing the colour you can, of course opt for one that appeals to you and matches or complements other colours on the boat, such as the canopy or upholstery. However, a practical point to consider is the possibility of the paint getting scratched. Although this type of paint is tough, the layer is thin and can get worn with time. Touching-up will help, but if you apply a colour which contrasts with the underlying gelcoat finish scratches and worn areas will become very obvious.

The following websites provide plenty of help on choosing paints and varnishes:

- http://www.blakespaints.com
- http://www.yachtpaint.com
- http://www.boatpaint.co.uk

Preparation

Mask all fittings and remove nameplates or lettering, the latter by sanding or peeling it off. Remove any remaining adhesive.

Bare gelcoat needs careful cleaning and preparation to remove all dirt and traces of wax and silicone polish. Use a product such as International Super Cleaner. Wash the whole hull with a sponge, rinse with fresh water and allow to dry.

Scratches and any other blemishes can be filled at this stage, or after the first coat of paint, using a filler such as epoxy. Wear suitable gloves when handling the filler.

Wash and rinse the surface thoroughly.

White spirit helps to remove grease and dirt.

It's important to wear eye protection and a suitable mask or respirator before doing any sanding work. Make sure the mask fits tightly to filter out all the toxic dust and fumes.

Using 240 grade sandpaper, sand the areas to be filled. Clean away all dust. Mix the filler according to the instructions on the product and apply it with a suitable spreader or pallet knife. When it's set hard sand it back to a smooth finish.

Mix the filler with the appropriate amount of hardener.

Overall sanding is next. An electric random orbital sander could be used but sanding gelcoat isn't like sanding solid wood, where going a little too deep doesn't matter. You could go through the gelcoat into the fibreglass underneath if too much pressure is applied. It's therefore safer to sand lightly by hand over the whole area.

Remove all dust with a brush or vacuum cleaner and wash and dry the surface again as before. Check for any

With this make of filler the colour changes to an even grey when it's completely mixed.

After scraping the filler into scratches, sand off the excess.

It's necessary to wash the surface whenever any dirt or sanding dust remains on it. Large areas can be washed with spray from a pressure washer.

Matching gelcoat filler can be applied to form the final surface of any repaired areas that won't be painted.

Any stick-on lettering or decoration should be peeled or carefully scraped off.

Sanding the whole area before painting can be done with an electric random speed orbital sander, but gently and carefully in order to avoid penetrating the gelcoat. But if the gelcoat is thin and there's a risk of breaking through you should do it by hand.

remaining scratches and fill them, repeating the process already described.

Mask the waterline with tape, ready for applying the primer/undercoat. Note that masking tape needs to be chosen carefully. The cheaper types need to be removed promptly, otherwise the adhesive clings too firmly to the hull and makes it difficult to remove smoothly and neatly. Look for tape like 3M 'Long Mask' that can be left on until the job is finished. Details of a tape's suitability for different types of painting job should be on the packaging.

The undercoat

The ideal temperature for most paints is 10 to 20°C, with little or no wind, relative humidity below 70 per cent and no risk of rain, mist, frost or dew whilst it's drying. You may want to wet the ground around the boat to settle any dust that could get blown onto the paint.

It's possible to paint the topcoat straight onto the prepared gelcoat, but a perfectionist requiring the best finish will want to apply an appropriate undercoat first. Two layers of undercoat will prevent patchiness and give a good depth of colour. More filling and sanding could be necessary if scratches are still visible.

In the case of a two-part polyurethane paint system, which gives the most durable finish, the corresponding two-part undercoat needs to be mixed according to the instructions. Stir and then measure out the appropriate amount of each of the two liquids – base and curing agent – and mix them in a clean metal paint kettle or bucket. Allow any bubbles to disperse by leaving the paint for ten minutes, placed away from the boat. During this time you should give the surface a final wipe to remove any dust.

Disasters have been known to happen when a helper has grabbed the base paint and brushed it on without first adding the curing liquid. To avoid this, make sure that any helpers know the procedure to be followed with the paints being used.

Start with a paint roller to apply the undercoat in places where a join with later application won't notice – at the edge of the transom, or at the point of the bows. Cover a section of the hull and then use the tip of a wide brush to remove any roller stipple and spread the paint evenly with

With two-part paints, gently stir the paint and pour an appropriate quantity into a paint kettle.

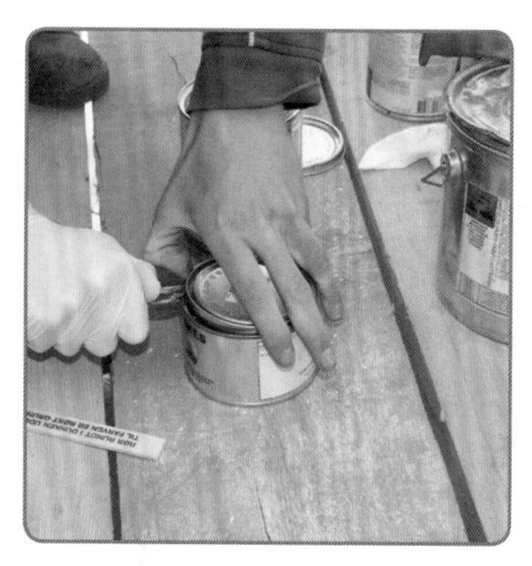

Open the tin of curing agent – the catalyst which causes the paint to cure or set and dry.

Add the appropriate amount of curing agent to the paint.

Stir the two together thoroughly.

According to the instructions on the tin an appropriate thinner can be added.

Depending on the actual paint system being used, a primer coat can be applied before other layers.

downward strokes of the brush. Runs in the paint should be avoided by taking care with the amount applied, but check for any runs that have occurred and brush them out now, before they set.

Move on to the next section of the hull and repeat the process. Where there the inevitable roller overlap occurs, use your brush to smooth the paint with light downward strokes. Repeat the process along the whole of the hull and leave it to dry overnight. Actual drying times depend on the temperature, and are usually shown on the paint can or an accompanying leaflet. Remember that it gets colder at night and this could slow the process.

Start to apply the paint at an edge where the join with a later application won't notice.

When using a brush, diagonal criss-cross strokes followed by downward strokes will help to ensure thorough coverage.

Left: Suspend the brush in a container of cleaning fluid appropriate to the type of paint

Right: Lightly sand the surface between each coat.

Clean the brush and suspend it in a container of the cleaning fluid recommended for the type of paint you're using. It's best to discard the roller, as they can be difficult to clean properly and it will probably set hard.

A second coat of undercoat is recommended, using the same procedure as described above. When set, this provides sufficient thickness to sand lightly, dust down and get a really smooth surface for the topcoat.

The topcoat

Now for the final 20 per cent of the job. Stir the base paint tin first and then mix the appropriate quantities of base and curing agent liquids, stirring them together thoroughly. Take care to read the instructions regarding the amount of each to be used – don't assume the proportions are the same as for the undercoat. Leave the mixture in a covered metal bucket for ten minutes for bubbles to disperse.

Have the appropriate thinner to hand in case you need to add a little of it to the mixture or to clean up any spills. Give the hull a final dusting.

Apply the paint with roller and brush in the same way as the undercoat. When using the brush, hold it at an angle of 45° to the surface in order to minimise brush marks.

This type of paint dries quickly, and delays can result in a hard dry edge forming. It therefore helps to have two people involved, the first to apply the paint with the roller and the second to follow on quickly with the brush while the paint is still wet.

If the brush feels like it's dragging on the surface the paint needs a little thinning, but no more than 10 per cent. This can happen when the air is dry and warm.

Leave the paint to dry overnight. Sand it with 400-grade paper to remove any sags or dirt and then lightly sand over the whole area. Dust it thoroughly.

Prepare and apply the final coat as previously. When it's set, pull off the masking tape carefully and replace any lettering that you previously removed. It's best to leave the paint for a week to harden fully before you move the boat.

The superb shiny finish will need occasional washing and polishing at the start of the boating season as described earlier in this chapter.

Repainting and maintaining a steel or aluminium narrowboat is beyond the scope of this book, but is covered thoroughly in *Narrow Boats – Care and Maintenance* by Nick Billingham, published by the Crowood Press.

Painting the bilges

The bilges, down in the lowest part of the hull, will inevitably accumulate some water. Although it's best to keep them as dry as possible to minimise the risk of rot in a wooden boat and osmosis in a GRP boat, you won't achieve

Remove all traces of dust with a tack rag.

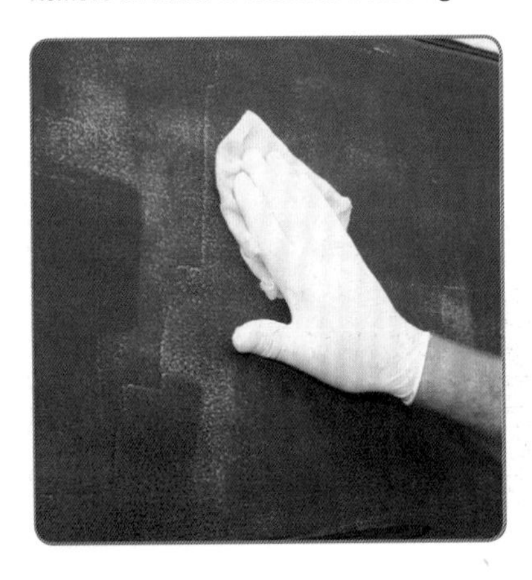

Applying the top coat.

Polishing the painted surface after it's fully hardened will help it to keep its shine.

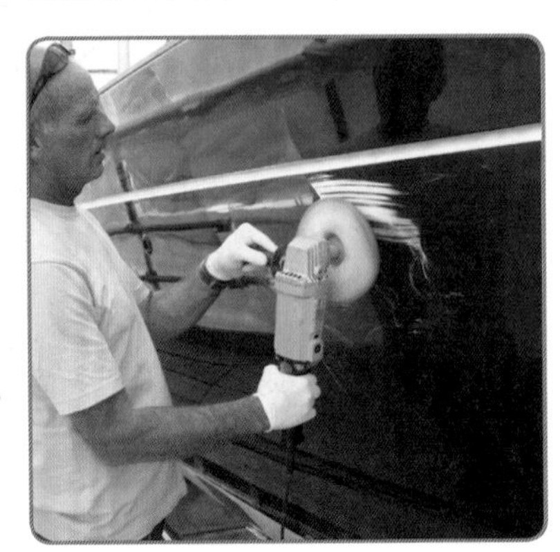

Painting other surfaces

The principles of painting with most paints on most surfaces are similar to those outlined above for painting gelcoat. Consequently they aren't repeated here.

If repainting a previously painted GRP hull, don't use the two-part paint described above as there will be adhesion problems. Instead you should use a conventional one-part system, but otherwise follow the same procedure – omitting, obviously, the paint mixing process. The existing paint needs to be sound and thoroughly prepared by careful cleaning and sanding. If it isn't sound it will have to be removed, otherwise painting over it will be a waste of time.

One-part paints are normally used on wood, as they cope better with flexing. On bare wood a suitable primer should be applied before the undercoats.

Inside the boat, hard types of varnish can be used if preferred, to resist the inevitable knocks and scrapes.

Steel keels, rudders or skegs may be galvanised and require no treatment. However, they may need to have rust removed and be treated with appropriate rust-curing paint before being covered with paint designed specifically for use on steel below the waterline.

permanent dryness. Painting will help to keep any water and less pleasant liquids away from the wood and plastic.

First the bilges need to be thoroughly cleaned and old flaking paint removed, along with all traces of oil and grease – not a pleasant job, but it will help to get rid of any odours that rise from below, and once they're painted, bilges are much easier to clean.

Before painting, dry out the bilges completely. The use of absorbent materials help. Some expensive products are available for this, but disposable nappies can be almost as effective. Old leftover paint is often used to paint bilges, but because the liquids and oils that leak into this area can be quite damaging special paints are available for the purpose, such as Danboline.

Painting the bilges isn't a pleasant job but suitable paint will help protect the hull from accumulating dirt, oil and other liquids.

Antifouling paint

Small motor boats and cruisers kept ashore or taken out of the water on a trailer after each use can either have the underwater area of their hulls painted as described above or their unpainted gelcoat polished and then hosed down. However, motor cruisers kept in the water on moorings will need antifouling paint applied to the underwater area to prevent the build-up of weed, slime and barnacles. These would otherwise consider the hull an ideal home. Antifouling paint is designed to deter them, since fouling of the hull roughens its surface and causes drag, which slows the boat.

Wooden boats also benefit from antifouling protection against attack from wood-boring marine creatures. An alternative is to scrub the hull regularly, but how many owners want to spend good boating time on this chore every month or two?

A neglected boat that's been left to accumulate marine growth is likely to have a covering of slime, weed and barnacles. However, even with antifouling paint on the hull, some growth will take hold in places. The amount will depend on the water conditions, including temperature, light penetration and the speed of the water flowing past the hull.

When working with antifouling paint you need to bear in mind that it contains poisons. It's therefore particularly important to avoid contact with it and with any paint removed by any method. Read the instructions on the tin for a guide to the full precautions to be taken, which should include wearing protective clothing, goggles, mask and gloves. Inadequate protection leads to permanent health damage.

Any growth revealed when the boat is hauled out of the water should be cleaned off immediately while it's still wet. Leaving it to dry results in some types of fouling setting as hard as concrete. Removing it with a hose and scrubbing brush or pressure washer is preferable to laborious scraping later. If a boatyard is arranging the lifting out of your motor cruiser when you're not there it's best to ask them to wash the hull too.

Slime, weed and barnacles accumulate on the hull and should be washed and scraped off whilst still wet.

A pressure washer can be used to remove much of the fouling.

A range of antifouling paints is available to suit different conditions and uses of boat.

The choice of antifouling paint depends on where the boat is used. Fresh water contains different species wanting to attach themselves to your hull compared with sea water. The paint also needs to perform appropriately. Poisons in the paint are designed to deter growths. The softer antifoulings also gradually dissolve, shedding thin layers of paint so that any growths leave with them as they erode in the flowing water.

Harder versions last longer and include some that can be polished clean. On small cruisers likely to be hauled out every winter, the softer eroding paints are more commonly used. This type is cheaper and easier to apply each spring before launching.

Usually the paint should be applied no more than a week or two before launching the boat. Obviously it needs to have dried before launching but many types also need to have contact with the water, within times specified by the manufacturer, in order to be effective.

Mask the waterline with masking tape. If there are 'sacrificial anodes' attached to the hull (see page 116), mask them with tape, as painting them will negate their effectiveness.

If you keep the tin of paint indoors before use, it will be easier to apply than if it's below room temperature. This type of paint is different from others in some ways as it contains heavy ingredients. A little thinning – by 10 per cent or less – helps when spreading the paint. Use the thinner recommended on the tin.

Stir the paint very thoroughly and frequently during use, since otherwise its heavy substances will settle to the bottom. A roller is normally used to apply it, as this covers the large area involved quickly. Alternatively a large and wide brush could be used. Two coats of paint are usually recommended, with an extra coat where turbulence wears the paint and growth tends to accumulate, such as on angular edges of the hull, along the waterline and on the keel and rudder.

Overpainting with antifouling

Most of these paints can be applied over existing antifouling but it pays to check with the paint companies' websites and publications for specific details. If you've just bought a boat try to find out what was used by the previous owner. If you don't know, a coat of the appropriate primer paint should be applied first. Obviously the existing surface needs to be sound to be able to accept a new coat, otherwise removal of the old paint will be necessary. When removing antifouling

Good health and safety protection is being worn here whilst using antifouling paint.

If there's a thick build-up of old antifouling paint it may all have to be removed.

A new coat of antifouling paint ready to repel growths on the hull.

paint, take the precautions described earlier. *Never* dry sand antifouling – the dust is highly toxic.

A combination of hosing or pressure washing and scraping can be used to remove old antifouling, although use of an appropriate paint stripper suitable for GRP makes the job much easier. International Interstrip is one example. A thick layer of stripper may need to be left on the paint for some time before being washed off, taking the paint with it. Disposal of the poisonous slurry resulting from antifouling removal needs to be done carefully. Many marinas and boatyards have settling tanks to collect such waste in their DIY areas, along with suitable disposal procedures.

Non-slip deck paint

A wet shiny paint surface is dangerous to walk on even with proper deck shoes. Non-slip surfaces are needed on deck if you want to stay upright when moving about, and these will need to be cleaned to preserve their effectiveness. Cleaning non-slip surfaces is actually the hardest part of boat cleaning, as they have to be scrubbed to extract dirt from the rough surface. It's worth doing, though, to make sure the surface remains non-slip.

Where it's desirable to improve or extend the areas of non-slip surface, International Paint's anti-slip additive can be mixed with paint of whatever colour you wish to use on the decks. Alternatively their Interdeck one-part polyurethane paint already contains a slip resistant additive.

Various grits are also available to add to paint, or you can sprinkle fine sand onto a fresh coat of paint. When it's dry, paint another coat on top of the sand. This provides an effective rough surface, although it can be damaging if your skin comes into contact with it.

A less abrasive surface can be achieved by sprinkling salt or sugar onto a coat of paint. After the paint has dried, dissolve the sugar or salt by washing with water. This leaves a slightly rough surface.

Non-slip material is also available that can be stuck on the deck in patches or strips. Unfortunately it's rather expensive, and may tend to come unstuck after a few years.

GRP damage repair

GRP is able to take wear and use quite well, depending on the quality of the original build. Inevitably, of course, with normal use there will be the occasional bump and scrape, however careful you are.

Decisions on damage

Scrapes and small holes can be suitable for DIY repair. More substantial damage above the waterline could also be tackled, providing you include sufficient reinforcing to achieve the necessary strength. Repairs to holes below the waterline are another matter and you need to be absolutely sure the repair won't let you down – below the waves. Either get this type of repair checked by someone suitably qualified before going afloat, or have it done professionally.

Repair materials

Scratches in the gelcoat can be filled with a colour-matched two-part filler, often sold as a gelcoat pigment kit. Car body filler has often been used on boats in error: for repairs to

Non-slip deck surfaces need to be scrubbed in order to stay non-slip.

Slip-resistant paint.

In the interests of safety, larger scale damage – particularly damage below the waterline – is best repaired by the professionals.

Repairs to holes in the deck

The following picture sequence describes how GRP repairs can be carried out to holes in a deck such as might result from a fitting being removed. The repair illustrated was carried out by Essex Boatyards Ltd.

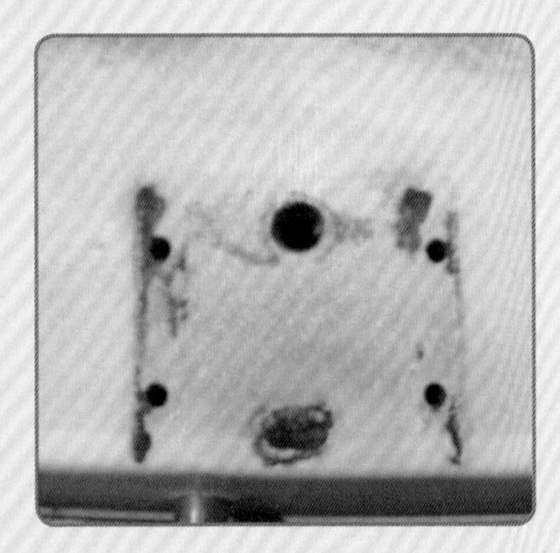

These holes were in the non-slip area of the deck.

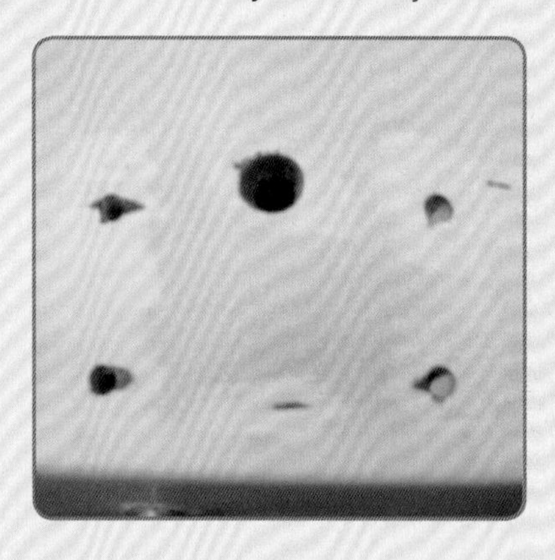

Clean the area very thoroughly using acetone. Wear suitable gloves and be aware that acetone is highly inflammable.

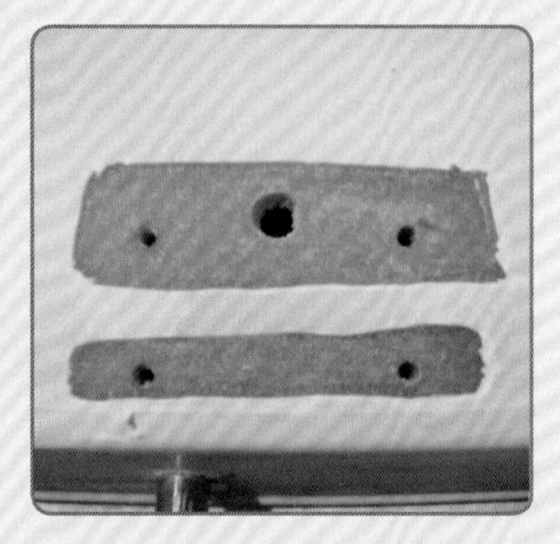

Lightly grind the area using a 40-grade grit soft-backed pad grinding disc to expose clean GRP to work up from.

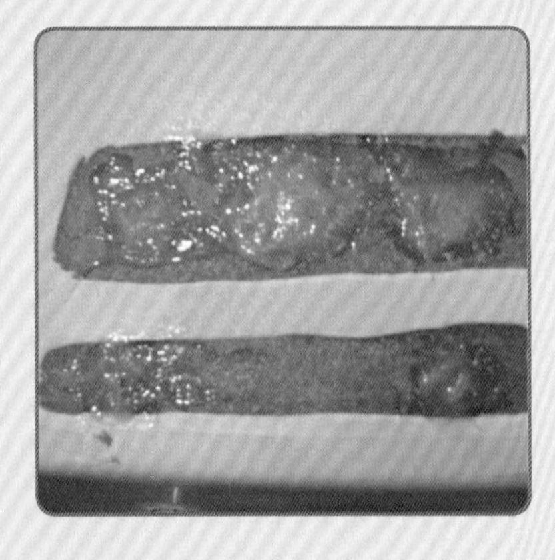

Fill the holes with a reinforced polyester resin. Chopped strand fibreglass mat can be cut into very small pieces and added to resin to reinforce it.

Once dry, grind back the filler until faired off.

Cover with one or preferably two layers of chopped strand mat saturated with resin. This stops circular cracking, which can later appear in the gelcoat around old repairs. Once dry, the matting can be faired off so that it's smooth and flat.

Apply two coats of matching gelcoat with a brush or spatula. A match can be obtained by mixing coloured gel pastes or ordering the correct colour gel from the manufacturer.

A non-slip surface can be achieved by stippling with a stiff brush. If the non-slip deck pattern is repetitive a mould could be made from another area of deck to create a former to press into the wet gelcoat.

Be sure to use marine-grade fillers in repairs.

boats, a *marine-grade* product has to be used. Marine fillers are easy to use and are sold in chandlers.

Deep scratches, cracks, gouges and holes need building up with something stronger such as epoxy filler or polyester resin reinforced with fibreglass, as in the original construction.

The basic method of use is to mix the resin and the hardener in the proportions indicated in the instructions supplied with the product. This is then applied and allowed to dry before sanding smooth.

Salt and dirt should be removed before any repairs are attempted, and all working areas and surfaces must be completely dry and clean before application. Wear protective gloves and a suitable mask to prevent the inhalation of dust. Good ventilation is also necessary, as toxic fumes are given off. The temperature should ideally be about 15 to 20°C.

Cellophane, cling film, Mylar tape or other similar types of smooth sheet plastic that won't stick to it can be used to cover the applied filler in order to achieve a reasonably smooth finish which will need less sanding.

Try removing superficial scratches as described previously rather than going straight for the filling option. If this isn't successful use the following technique.

Scratches and minor blemishes

Matching gelcoat filler should be mixed and a thin layer applied, ensuring it enters all scratches and irregularities. Add more filler as necessary to the required thickness and leave to harden.

Sand the repair until smooth, using wet and dry abrasive paper with plenty of water to avoid clogging. Use coarse paper first followed by a fine abrasive paper. If any irregularities remain, fill them with a further application of filler and sand it smooth when it's set hard. When you're satisfied, apply rubbing compound and then wax polish the repair.

Wherever possible, with most repairs, the inside of the hull should be reinforced with a layer or two of glass fibre

Mix the appropriate quantities of gelcoat filler.

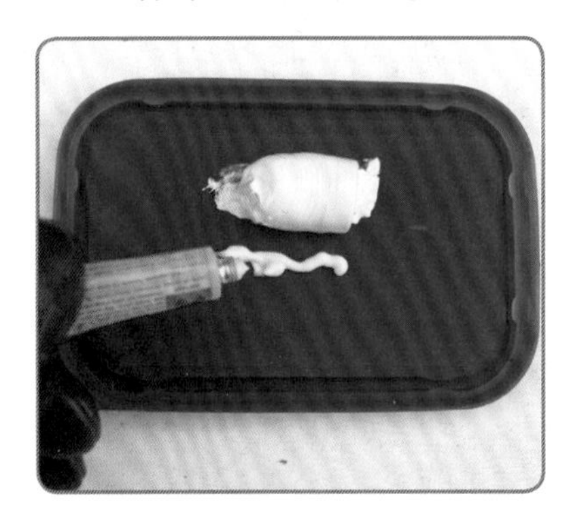

After working a small amount of the filler into the scratches, spread more on and smooth it off.

Chopped strand fibreglass mat is the most commonly used material for reinforcing repairs, thoroughly 'wetted out' with synthetic resins. Woven tape and matting are also available.

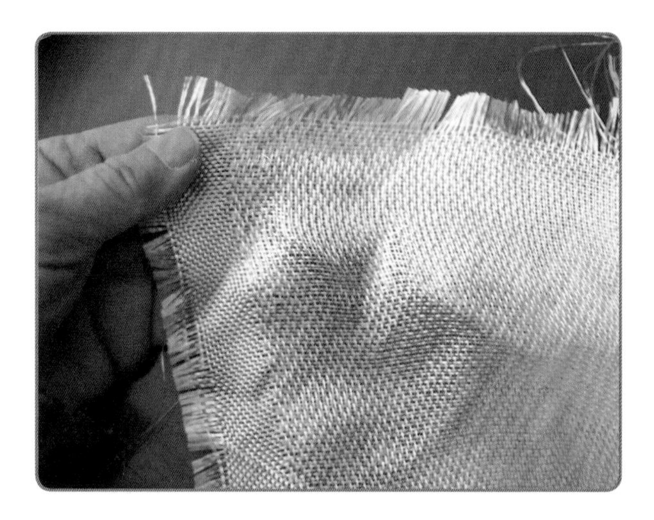

matting impregnated with resin. Larger repairs to holes have to be bridged and reinforced with such matting on both sides, thoroughly saturated with resin.

Osmosis again

Osmosis and blistering have already been mentioned in Chapter 4, so hopefully you'll have avoided buying a boat with serious blisters in the gelcoat.

The best way to avoid blistering is to keep a GRP boat away from water! However, there's now an increased tendency for boats to be kept afloat all year round in sheltered, secure marinas, which means that it's less likely they'll be lifted out and laid up ashore during the winter. But in fact it's better to give the hull a chance to dry out from time to time. Most small motor boats kept out of the water on trailers when not in use will avoid osmosis problems, and providing rainwater isn't allowed to accumulate in the hull they shouldn't suffer from blistering.

Motor cruisers kept on moorings are another matter. They may develop blisters as water penetrates the gelcoat, which isn't completely waterproof. Special paints have been developed to protect the hull from osmosis but even they won't necessarily provide a total protection for the lifetime of the boat. One precaution that can be taken is to keep the bilges as dry as possible, since wet bilges increase the risk of water penetration.

As explained earlier, blistering occurs when water penetrates the top layer of the gelcoat and combines with chemicals that prevent it from getting out again. The resulting pressure build-up can result in blisters.

It's essential to wear eye and skin protection if you decide to investigate a blister. If penetrated, the acid inside the blister is likely to spurt out into your eyes with harmful consequences.

The advice of apparent experts on osmosis varies greatly. Taking a rather cynical view, those who profit from the costly treatment of a hull with osmosis sometimes emphasise the urgent need to have the gelcoat stripped away and replaced. Others involved with selling boats that betray signs of osmosis may tend to give the impression that all boats have the problem to some degree, and it's just a minor cosmetic problem that can be ignored.

If a boat develops a rash of dozens of blisters the drastic treatment of complete gelcoat removal and replacement with appropriate coatings may be the necessary course of action. On a small second-hand motor cruiser, however, this could cost more than the boat's worth. The blisters may affect the resale value of the boat, but if they're few and only superficial they may not necessarily affect the strength of the hull. Seek independent expert opinion from a surveyor on the best course of action, depending on whether the structural integrity and strength of the hull really is being affected.

In the case of a few small blisters, each no bigger than a 10p piece, there are several courses of action you can take. One would be to do nothing, but not to ignore it: check whether the blisters get bigger or more numerous over time or stay the same. An older, well-built, solid boat may not develop more or larger blisters during your ownership of it.

Another option is to cut or grind open each blister, remove the chemicals by washing them out repeatedly with hot water and dry the area very thoroughly. With all work on GRP it's important to remove all moisture before applying any filler, but in this case it's even more important in order to prevent new blisters forming. Leaving the area to dry thoroughly under cover for several months is recommended. The blister can then be filled with an appropriate filler. Epoxy fillers are often recommended for this purpose, followed by paint that provides further protection against water penetration. The filling procedure is the same as that for repairs detailed earlier.

Hugo du Plessis, author of *Fibreglass Boats*, now in its fourth edition, is a recognised expert on fibreglass boat construction. He recommends filling for most mild cases of blistering, rather than costly complete gelcoat replacement, which should be a last resort. His book goes into great detail and is an excellent source of further information on all matters concerning GRP construction and maintenance.

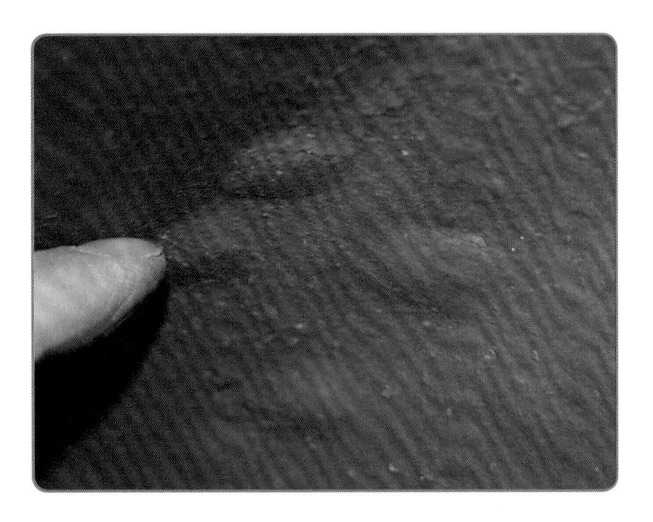

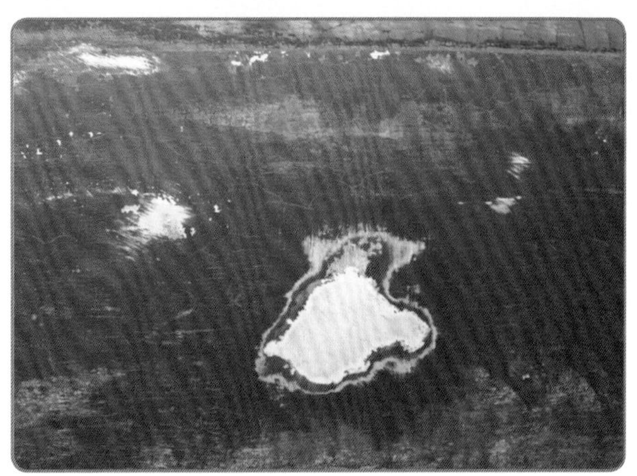

Blisters can be opened, cleaned, thoroughly dried, and then filled with a marine-grade filler. The surface can then be finished with paint or matching gelcoat.

Maintenance of wood and plywood

The emphasis here is on boats which have GRP hulls. However, the care and maintenance of plywood and some woodwork is relevant to motor boats that are partly built from or fitted out using these materials.

Although wood was overtaken by GRP as the main material for leisure boats in the mid-20th century, some motor boats have continued to be built using marine ply and other timbers treated with epoxy resins, as illustrated in the self-build section of Chapter 5. These make the wooden boat much more waterproof on a long-term basis and can therefore compete, to a certain extent, with the advantages of GRP. An epoxy-treated boat should need much less maintenance than an untreated, traditionally painted and varnished wooden boat. Even so, the epoxy finish has to be protected from sunlight by paint or a suitable protective varnish.

The most important consideration is to keep all woodwork, including the wooden parts on a GRP hull, covered with a protective film of paint, varnish or other preservative coating. This can be maintained by touching-up with the appropriate product as soon as any damage or wear occurs. Full replacement of the protection can then be carried out at the end of the boating season.

The salt in sea water gives it an antiseptic quality that makes it less likely to cause wood to rot than fresh water. In fact it's fresh water from rain that does the most damage, along with weathering – the effects of sunlight and the expansion and contraction caused by heating from the sun and wetting and drying.

Wherever water can accumulate and persist, rot is likely

Many boats made of GRP or steel also have parts made of wood – such as rubbing strips, handrails, cockpit bulkheads and interiors – that need to be maintained.

Weathering from sunlight and rain attacks unprotected wood. In this case it has also caused the plywood to delaminate.

Neglected varnish spoils the appearance of woodwork.

to set in. In the case of unprotected plywood it also causes the resins binding the layers of wood to fail. The resulting delamination is difficult to treat on a boat and will usually mean replacement is necessary in order to maintain a safe level of strength.

Painting wood

Some GRP motor cruisers have woodwork that needs to be painted, and many motor cruisers have some woodwork in need of varnish or wood sealer. The preparation of wood for painting, and application of traditional paints, or one-part paints, is very similar to that needed for varnishing. This is described below.

Two-part polyurethane paints, requiring the mixing of base paint and hardener before use, are not as flexible as one-part paints. As explained earlier, they're good for painting GRP, but one-part paints can cope better with the more flexible surface and varying moisture content of wood. Two-part paints should not be used to overpaint existing areas of one-part paint.

Appropriate primers and undercoats should be used with all paints. The manufacturers' instructions on their tins and leaflets provide appropriate advice for each type.

Painting the gelcoat of a GRP boat was covered earlier on pages 94 to 98, which should be read for additional advice that can also be applied to the painting of wood.

Weathered wood can be sanded carefully by hand with 120-grade paper and then cleaned with white spirit before applying Burgess wood sealer.

Varnish and alternatives

Shiny varnished wood looks beautiful when in good condition, but the problem with this beauty is its fragility. Even a little varnished woodwork can improve the appearance of an otherwise ordinary boat, but neglected varnish has quite the opposite effect.

However, peeling varnish and discoloured wood can be avoided. The main preventative measure is to touch-up every little scratch and scuff before water gets a chance to enter and lift much more of the varnish. Then you need to

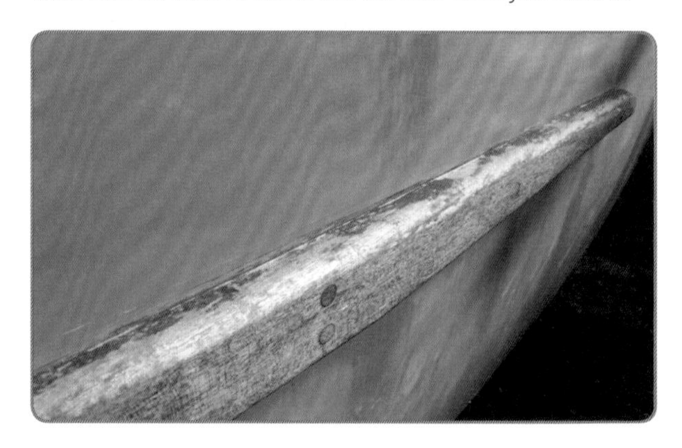

Varnished horizontal surfaces deteriorate more rapidly because they receive more intense sunlight.

Marine wood sealer is more effective than varnish on teak. The finish it provides isn't as shiny as varnish but is easier to maintain.

A belt sander can remove old varnish rapidly from the flat surfaces of solid wood.

Removing varnish from awkward surfaces.

give the varnished areas a new coat at least once a year. This commitment is required for most types of varnish.

If you don't want to do this, strip the varnish off as described below and either paint the woodwork or apply sealer or oil-based preservative such as Burgess wood sealer. A new coat of wood sealer can then easily be applied each year. Oily wood, such as teak, is often more successfully treated with sealer than with varnish.

Assuming that you want to persevere with glossy varnished woodwork such as rubbing strips, hatch covers and grab rails, the following description takes you through the process of stripping back to bare wood and applying the necessary coats.

It's important to wear a suitable mask or respirator before any of the following work. Make sure it fits tightly to filter out harmful dust and fumes.

On flat solid wood, varnish can be removed quickly by the careful use of an electric belt sander, detail sander or various types of scraper. Take care not to gouge the wood and always sand along the grain – not across it – to avoid scratches showing in the varnish later. Finish with medium, then fine, abrasive paper to get a smooth surface.

On plywood, the process of stripping varnish is more delicate. The top layer of the plywood provides the attractive wood grain. Unfortunately, however, it's

usually very thin, and overenthusiastic scraping or sanding can penetrate the top layer to reveal the ugly contrasting layer below.

A confusingly large range of varnishes exists. Some, such as the two-part varnishes, are harder than others and may last longer. Many are intended for the wooden boat enthusiast who knows exactly how he wants his varnish to perform. The problem with the more sophisticated harder varnishes is the difficulty of touching them up and removing them completely at some time in the future. You may therefore want to choose the straightforward traditional original-style or one-part varnish. This can be touched-up, over-coated and later removed more easily than many harder varnishes. Remember that sunlight

Sanding needs to be carefully finished to get a smooth scratch-free surface.

Take care not to remove the top layer of plywood.

Use a cloth dampened with white spirit or a tack rag to remove all traces of dust from the surface of the wood.

Varnish should be gently stirred, not shaken.

Pour some into a container before you start varnishing.

damages varnish, so check the varnish you choose has ultraviolet inhibitors.

Use a cloth or brush to remove dust. A vacuum cleaner is also useful here. Use of a 'tack rag' is often recommended to remove dust before applying coats of varnish or paint. These are cloths impregnated with suitable substances to lift dust. However, if you use them you should only use light strokes, as there's a risk that some of the chemicals in the rag could be spread onto the wood, reducing adhesion of the varnish.

If varnishing outside, check the weather forecast: you need dry weather, preferably with little or no wind, which could blow dust onto the wet varnish. Don't varnish when fog or dew might form and ruin the finish as it tries to dry. Unfortunately, bright hot sunlight can also be a problem, since it makes the varnish dry more rapidly than it should, and this can cause blistering.

Never shake a tin of varnish, as this can cause vast numbers of troublesome bubbles. For the same reason stir it only gently. Don't apply varnish straight from the can. Pour a small amount into a clean container and then put the lid back on the varnish tin. This protects the bulk of your varnish from contamination.

The traditional way to seal and prime bare wood is to thin the varnish with about 15 per cent white spirit or according to the instructions on the tin. Alternatively, you can buy special clear wood sealer to use before the varnish, but this can cost three times as much as using thinned varnish and doesn't automatically achieve better results.

Use a good quality brush. With a new brush it's worth checking for loose bristles before you start – even the best brushes seem to lose the odd bristle, dragged out by the very sticky varnish. Apply the thinned varnish sparingly and fairly quickly. The wood will change colour as most of the thinned varnish soaks into it.

Leave this first coat to dry overnight and then sand lightly to smooth any roughness and to key the next coat. Remove any dust and apply a full coat of unthinned varnish. Take care not to apply too much at once and watch for sags and runs if you overdo it. They need to be brushed out promptly before the varnish gets tacky.

To achieve a gloss finish and good protection for the wood apply at least two more coats, leaving each to dry overnight. For a mirror finish you may need a total of six coats, though this will depend on your enthusiasm and patience.

After replacing the lid on the varnish can firmly, slowly

Remove any loose bristles before using the brush.

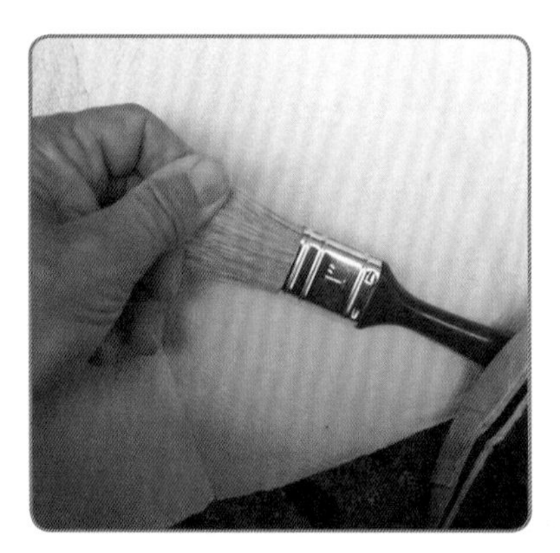

Brushing a layer of thinned varnish will change the colour of the wood as it soaks in.

Remove any sags or runs before the varnish starts to set.

A superb mirror finish can be achieved with sufficient coats of varnish.

turn the can upside down to seal the lid and avoid a skin forming on the remaining varnish.

Epoxy repairs to wood

If you've damaged the wooden decks on a GRP boat or are determined to repair an old wooden boat, modern epoxy products have been produced to make repairing and strengthening your boat much easier. Don't be tempted to use cheaper alternatives such as car body filler; this can't cope with the marine environment and disastrous leaks could ensue if it's used to repair the hull.

Epoxy products come with detailed instructions, and the website of manufacturer West System at http://www.wessex-resins.com contains much additional helpful information on wooden boat restoration. The same company also produces publications such as *Wooden Boat Restoration and Repair.*

West System Epoxy products.

Inflatable boat repairs

Before you repair an inflatable boat you need to be sure what type of material was used in its construction, since it's important to use the right adhesive and valves. This should be made clear in the boat's handbook or on labelling on the boat itself. If it isn't, check with the dealer or manufacturer of your particular boat.

Synthetic rubber: Hypalon and Neoprene

The synthetic rubber coatings used on polyester or nylon fabric include Hypalon on the outer surface and Neoprene on the inner. These are durable and possess excellent air-retaining qualities. The glued seams are usually very strong and the fabric itself tends to fail before the seams deteriorate. When it's sanded Hypalon appears matt and produces dust, whereas uPVC scratches and shows no change of colour.

Plastic coatings: uPVC

This type of coating increases the strength and tear-resistance of polyester or nylon fabric. It comes in a larger range of colours than Hypalon, which is mainly dark grey or black.

The procedures involved in applying patches, glue and replacement valves depend on the actual boat and the repair materials you're using. In the interests of safety, and to ensure the reliability of your repairs, the instructions provided with these products should be followed carefully.

Repair materials, emergency repair kits, glues and some types of replacement valve can usually be obtained from chandlers. If there's no local supplier, Polymarine provides a specialist inflatable boat and RIB repair materials and spare parts mail order service at http://www.polymarine.com. The 'Advice and Technical Information Sheet' on their website also contains seven pages of detailed instructions on repairs and valve replacement, along with other inflatable boat technical matters.

As inflatable boats age the material from which they're constructed can eventually deteriorate, becoming porous as a result of numerous slight leaks which are difficult to find and seal. A product which helps to extend the life of ageing inflatables is 'Sealflex'. This is a flexible acrylic latex sealant that's introduced into the inflatable via the valve. The boat is then inflated and tumbled to circulate the sealant, which sticks to the inside and cures to form a waterproof membrane.

12 Fittings and their maintenance

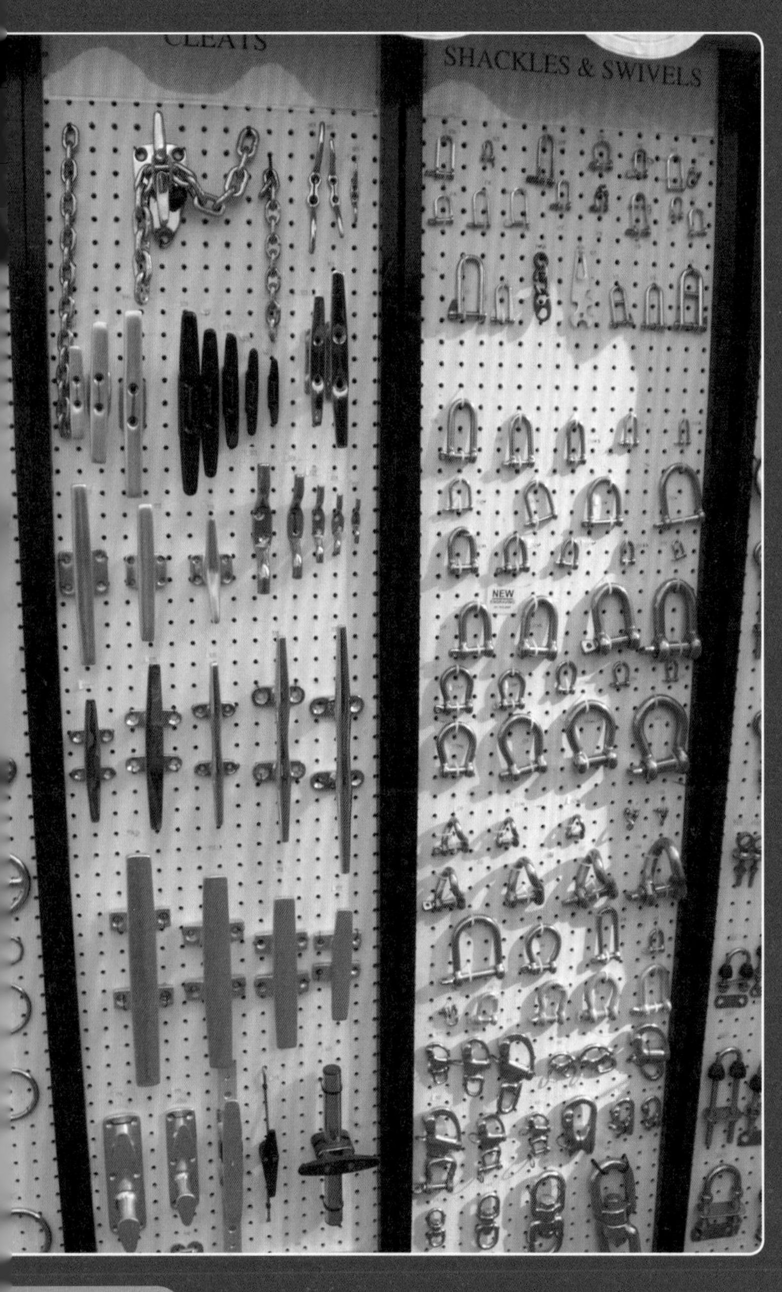

Stainless steel boat fittings at a Boat Show display.

Drainage

Spray, rain and wave splashes inevitably result in some water accumulating in the hull of an open motor boat. Many have some way of draining water from the hull when ashore. This may be a simple drain plug at the stern, which is unscrewed when ashore. The screw-in plug should be attached with a short cord so that it doesn't get lost. To avoid embarrassing flooding of the boat, don't forget to replace it before relaunching! In order to avoid leaks the fitting the plug screws into should itself be checked to ensure it's securely attached and sealed to the hull.

Self-bailers are devices that drain water out of a boat as it moves forward. They are also sometimes called 'one-way drain systems'. Open boats such as inflatables and RIBs often have them in the transom (the panel at the stern to which the outboard motor is mounted).

Self-bailers can get blocked with weed and grit so clean them regularly. An old toothbrush and water pressure from a hose can be used for this. If the bailer is leaking it may have to be unbolted and re-seated in sealing compound or a new rubber gasket. It's best to have some new bolts ready in case the old ones need to be replaced. Service kits for self-bailers, which include seals, washers and screws or bolts, can be purchased at chandlers. Identify the type and make to be sure of buying the right kit.

As a safety precaution, have a good-sized bucket, scoop bailer and hand-pump secured somewhere accessible inside the boat to deal with large volumes of water quickly. A sponge can deal with the remaining drops.

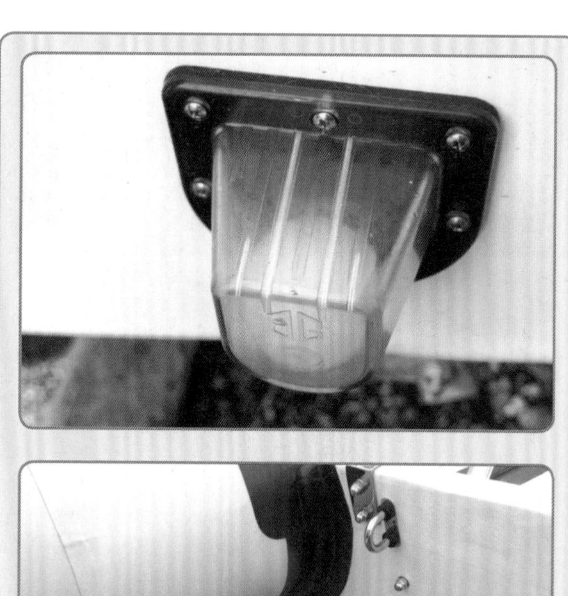

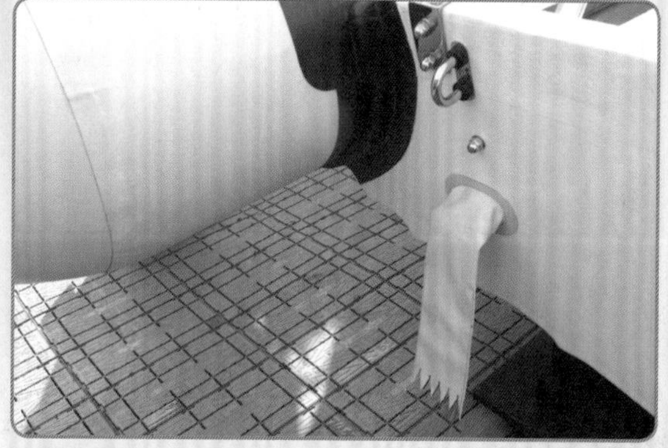

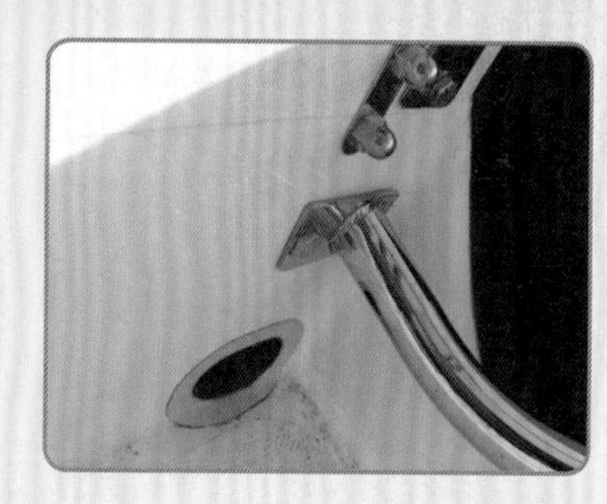

Self-bailers of various types drain water from the hull and need to be kept clear of anything that might block them.

A scoop bailer, bucket and sponge should be tied securely in the boat ready for bailing, particularly in an open boat likely to receive spray and rain.

Lubricate the thread on the screw-in covers on buoyancy chambers.

Buoyancy

Buoyancy chambers are built into some boats so that they don't sink if they get swamped with water. Open boats usually have some type of buoyancy. In the case of RIBs and inflatable boats the inflated chambers provide it. Hatch covers can be removed to access and check the chambers on some GRP boats. On others, under-floor and under-deck chambers are filled with foam plastic.

Some buoyancy chambers can be used for storage, but remember that this will reduce the effectiveness of the buoyancy to some extent, so don't overdo it.

Mounting points for outboard motors need to be checked.

Outboard motor mount

An outboard motor can cause substantial stress on the transom and may need reinforcement by means of a strong back fitted to its inside. Check the condition of the plywood pad where the motor clamp is bolted onto the transom and reinforce or replace it if it shows signs of disintegration. Adjustable outboard motor mounts are fitted to many boats. These are common on motor boats with inboard engines, in order to mount an auxiliary outboard motor in case the main engine fails. They need to be securely attached and the mechanism for raising and lowering the motor should be lubricated regularly.

Rubbing strips

Rubbing strips and bands on the hull and on the gunwales are there to take the scrapes that would otherwise damage the hull. Consequently they may themselves need to be repaired from time to time so they can continue to protect the hull. It may be possible to cut out and replace part of a

An adjustable outboard motor mount should be lubricated to ensure that it can be raised and lowered smoothly.

Wooden rubbing strips get worn and need to be replaced using screws and waterproof glue on this type of boat.

Many rubbing strips are made of rubber. Most types can be replaced by screwing them onto the boat or sliding them onto a metal mounting plate.

rubbing strip without replacing the whole length, although complete replacement is likely to be necessary eventually on a well-used motor boat.

Rubber fendering strips and combined rubber and aluminium strips are used as rubbing strips (also called rubbing strakes) on many motor boats. Exact replacements are often difficult to find locally but can be mail-ordered online from http://www.sealsdirect.co.uk and http://www.wilks.co.uk.

Deck fittings

Most good quality fittings will take plenty of wear and use providing they're designed for the strains put on them. The majority are made of stainless steel, which resists rust because a protective layer forms on its surface encouraged by oxygen. However, if air can't reach a sealed part of a stainless steel fitting it can still rust, particularly in crevices, where salt water accelerates any deterioration. So don't expect stainless steel fittings to last indefinitely. They'll also wear, and will need to be replaced eventually. The main weak point, though, is where equipment is attached to the hull or deck.

Fittings will loosen over time and sealant will harden, lose its adhesion and crack. All fittings should therefore be checked regularly to make sure they aren't loose. Do this by gripping with your hand and twisting. There should be no movement. If there is, tighten the screws or bolts. If this doesn't work, unscrew them and either fill the holes, re-drill them and screw the fitting back, or use thicker screws or bolts.

Stainless steel can deteriorate and the fixing points need to be checked.

Any new fittings shouldn't simply be screwed or bolted onto the fibreglass but should have a backing plate of marine plywood or preferably metal.

In order to provide maximum strength this handrail is bolted through the cabin roof and a metal reinforcing plate underneath it.

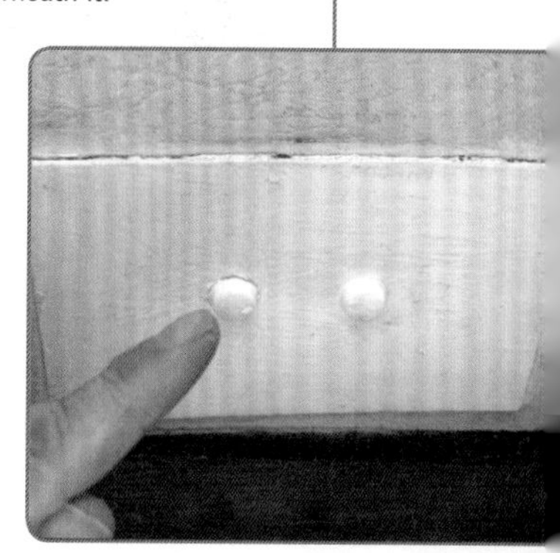

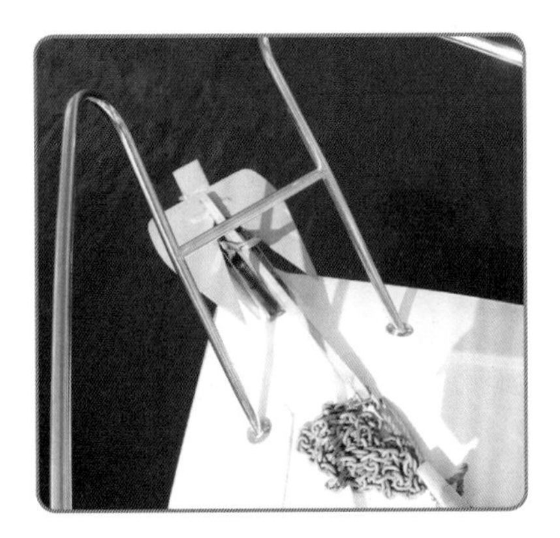

Fittings designed to secure and guide ropes, chains and anchors must be tightly fixed to the deck, with no movement.

Some fittings that go through the deck include fillers for fuel and water and fishing rod supports. Check that these are secure and don't allow water or fuel to leak into the boat.

Mounting points should already be strengthened sufficiently to take the load put on the fitting, but if there are any signs of stress or cracking, extra reinforcement with metal backing plates may be necessary. Some reinforcement with epoxy resin will help if cracking has already started in the area around such fittings.

Failed sealant round a fitting usually makes replacement or refitting necessary, with new fastenings – usually bolts rather than screws – and sealant.

There must always be substantial backing plates to spread the load, which can be very great and has been known to rip out an insecure fitting – such as a cleat holding a mooring rope – and send it flying dangerously across the deck. Obviously, further harm is then caused by the loss of the securing point, which may have held vital mooring lines in place. Where stanchions and their lifelines or rails take the force of stopping someone falling overboard, secure attachment is vital.

Bolts go through the fitting, the deck and the thick, preferably metal, backing plate, before sealant, washers and nuts are attached and tightened inside the boat. On some boats plywood backing plates have been installed. Leaks through the boltholes can cause these to rot and the whole fitting to become dangerously loose. Streaks on the inside of the hull, caused by leaks from the deck running down through tiny gaps around loose fittings, help to show when refitting is needed. Stress cracks in the gelcoat may also develop, showing where refitting and reinforcement is needed to ensure the fitting is safely secured.

Sealants

The range of sealants available can be rather confusing. Polyurethane sealant has strong adhesive properties, so if you want to stick and seal a joint this is a good choice. Sikaflex 291 is a particularly popular general-purpose sealant of this type. Its disadvantage is that it sticks quite firmly and it may be difficult to remove the fitting in the future and to eliminate all traces of it.

Silicone-type sealants can be removed more readily and are good at forming a flexible gasket, but they're not strongly adhesive in the way that polyurethane sealants are. Silicone should not be used below the waterline or where it's expected to provide a strong bond. However, it does make a good insulating barrier between different metals and strongly resists most chemicals.

Captain Tolley's Creeping Crack Cure – a sealant for stopping leaks through hairline cracks – is useful for sealing leaking decks and windows, as will be explained in more detail in Chapter 15, which includes work on window frames.

Sikaflex 291 is a widely used adhesive sealant.

Silicone rubber sealant forms a flexible gasket.

Replacing a deck or hull fitting

The procedure described below applies to most deck fittings such as cleats, stanchions and stem head rollers. Obviously it's easier to do this work ashore but it may have to be done afloat. With all work on a boat afloat on a mooring, there's an amazing tendency for loose items to find a way to fall overboard, so take care to hold on to the fitting as you undo its fastenings – ideally tie it to something in order to stop it taking a dive over the side.

Penetrating and releasing fluid can be used to help release the nuts and bolts holding fittings. Have someone hold one end of each bolt firmly with a spanner or pliers while you undo the other end if it's below the deck, otherwise the loose bolt may simply swivel as you try to undo the nuts.

Once the fitting is removed, scrape and clean all adhering sealant thoroughly from the base, the thread of the bolts, and the deck. Both surfaces have to be completely clean and dry. This can be a difficult part of the process, as the remaining sealant can cling on amazingly firmly, despite the fact that some of it has failed. Acetone or a thinner appropriate to the sealant can be used to remove remaining traces. Wear gloves when using such chemicals in order to avoid removing skin as well as old sealant. Bear in mind that these and other such chemicals are highly flammable.

If the bolts are not permanently attached to the fitting, it's best to buy new bolts and nuts of the correct size.

Replacing a fitting such as a mooring cleat on the deck requires a backing plate of thick aluminium. This should be cut larger than the base of the cleat – as large as will fit in the space available under the deck. File the sharp edges and corners off the plate.

Place the fitting on the plate and mark the position of the holes. With a punch and hammer, make an indentation in the centre of one of the marked holes, and with the plate held in a vice drill a small pilot hole in the dent made. Next, drill a hole of an appropriate size to take the bolt.

Place the fitting on the deck and push a bolt through the hole. Get a helper to hold the plate up onto the bolt under the deck and screw the nut on from below. The positions of the remaining holes can then be marked and drilled.

Before bolting down the fitting, remove it and apply a substantial amount of sealant to its base, the holes and the upper surface of the plate. Enough has to be applied for it to squeeze out from under the base as you screw it down. The fitting can now be bolted in place, lightly bedding it down in the sealant until it begins to squeeze out. Don't over-tighten at this stage, otherwise all the sealant could be squeezed out. Let the sealant partially set and then tighten the bolts fully. Remove the excess sealant from the fitting above and below the deck.

Cleaning and lubrication

All moving parts such as a stem head roller for the mooring rope and chain, and the adjustable outboard bracket mentioned earlier, should, from time to time, be washed with fresh water and a little detergent to remove salt and dirt. They should then be dried and lubricated.

Use a Teflon-based lubricant or a quick-drying lubricant such as McLube, which, though comparatively expensive, is claimed to last approximately ten times longer than any other type. Such lubricants resist being washed out by water and help to prevent water penetration. Dry types of lubricant are also preferable as they're less likely to attract and accumulate dirt.

Special water-resistant and long lasting lubricants are available.

Leaking through-hull fittings will need to be unscrewed and re-bedded in a sealant suitable for underwater use, using new screws or bolts.

Hull fittings on motor cruisers

Motor cruisers vary in the way they've been equipped, and much of the above information will apply to most boats. However, the bigger and more luxuriously equipped the motor cruiser, the more fittings will be attached to the hull, including through-hull fittings for toilet intake and discharge, shower and galley sump pumps and engine cooling water.

These holes in the hull need to be checked and maintained frequently, as faults will lead to leaks and are a major cause of boats sinking. This is emphasised by the fact that many insurance companies insist that all inlet pipes below the waterline are fastened to the hull fitting with at least two stainless steel worm-drive jubilee clips.

Electrolysis

Through-hull fittings and all metal fittings below the waterline are often damaged by a process called electrolysis. When different metals are near each other and immersed in water – particularly in sea water – they form an electric cell. As an electric current flows, the baser of the metals, as listed on the galvanic series table, is gradually eaten away.

Some boats have fittings made from a variety of metals below the waterline. Zinc is a base metal lower on the galvanic table than these metals, so lumps of zinc called 'sacrificial anodes' are attached to the hull near the metal fittings, beside propeller shafts and to the underwater casing of outboard motors. Because the zinc gets attacked by electrolysis before the other more 'noble' metals, it protects them from corrosion.

Zinc anodes should be replaced when half of their original bulk has been eaten away. They should never be painted over, as this would stop the protective process. Take care to reconnect any wires to a new anode as these will be needed to make the anode fully effective.

Checking hull fittings

Even when anodes are regularly replaced, the hull screws or bolts holding the hull fittings can deteriorate and should still

A zinc anode half worn away and ready for replacement.

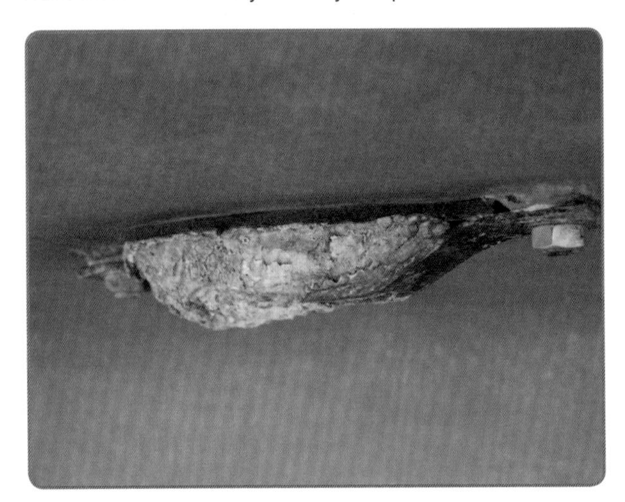

New anodes to replace the worn one in the previous photograph.

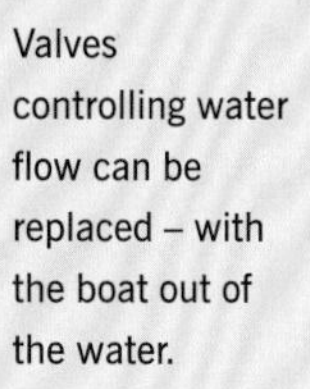

Valves controlling water flow can be replaced – with the boat out of the water.

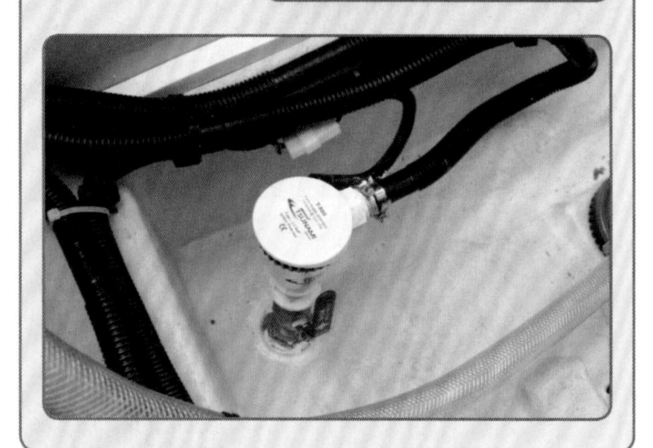

Corrosion and leaks from keel fittings indicate that removal and refitting with new bolts is necessary.

be checked for looseness and replaced if necessary. Leakage into the boat shows the sealant or gasket between the fitting and the hull has disintegrated, and the fitting will need to be removed and re-bedded in sealant. As usual with all work on the underwater area of the hull, involve the expertise or advice of professionals if you have the slightest doubt about doing this safely enough to prevent leaks.

As indicated above, inside the hull the pipes need to be very securely attached to the through-hull fittings. Any leaks here may just require the two jubilee clips to be tightened a little, renewed one at a time, or have an extra clip attached to stop the leak.

Seacocks are the taps or valves used to turn off water from the hull fittings. Open and close them regularly to prevent them from becoming seized up. They also benefit from lubrication.

Keels

The keel or skeg suspended under many types of motor boat or motorsailer improve directional stability and protect the rudder and propeller. They also often provide the necessary weight to keep a boat as upright as possible. Their structure varies: many GRP boats have lead or iron keels encased in the GRP, while wooden cruisers and some made of GRP have their keels bolted on.

Corrosion and leaks from the vicinity of the keel indicate problems with the bolts and the seal between the keel and the hull. The bolts can corrode over time. Removing them will be difficult if they're badly corroded, and this isn't a simple repair task. As it's below the waterline, removing and refitting a heavy keel is best left to the professionals who have the necessary tools and equipment to do the job safely. They'll take the keel off and re-bed it in sealant, refastening it with new bolts.

Motor Boat Manual

13 Steering equipment maintenance

A selection of steering wheels.

If steering equipment works it can get neglected, but it's worth checking it every couple of months or whenever you can get at it to make sure it doesn't let you down.

Rudder

Considerable strain is placed on the rudder bearings, which inevitably wear and eventually need replacement. The propeller constantly pushes water against the rudder and this buffeting helps to loosen the fittings. The bearings should be checked every year by holding the bottom of the rudder and attempting to move it backwards and forwards and from side to side. If looseness is revealed, undo the appropriate screws or bolts and replace the bearings. If the rudder is large, heavy and difficult to detach it would be best to get a boatyard to tackle removal and bearing replacement.

Where the rudder is attached to the transom, it pivots on 'pintles' (the pins) and 'gudgeons' (the fitting on the transom that the pins fit into). These fittings should be regularly lubricated. They will need to be replaced if there is excessive movement.

It may be possible to purchase rudder fitting replacements from a chandlers, but it could prove necessary to have them made by a local engineering workshop. Alternatively you might be able to find suitable replacements second-hand. Try a boat jumble or a chandler selling second-hand fittings. Obviously, you need to be sure that they're strong enough to use as replacements.

Many motor boats don't have a rudder because the steering is provided by the controls of the outboard motor. However, the problem with this can be that there's little steering control at low speeds. A way to overcome this problem is to attach a rudder to the outboard motor leg. Such rudder attachments include the Rudderguide from

Steering position on a typical small motor cruiser.

In this case steering is provided by turning the outboard motor, rather than by a rudder.

Various types of rudders are shown here along with their rudder bearings, which eventually wear and need replacing if looseness is detected.

14

Motor Boat Manual

Anchoring and mooring equipment

Cut lengths of rope can often be purchased cheaply at boat shows and boat jumbles.

Some new boat owners planning to explore inland waterways think that they need only a few mooring ropes to tie up to bank-side bollards or rings. Unfortunately, however, engine failure on a river can mean an anchor is suddenly an essential item. In fact it's important to be fully equipped for every eventuality, since it might prove necessary to anchor your boat against the force of a strong current or wind or to secure it in places where bank-side mooring posts, bollards or rings aren't available.

Adequate mooring and anchoring equipment is, of course, essential in tidal waters, and such equipment is the only way to stop a boat if the engine fails.

Ropes

Although it might seem strange to some people, handling ropes of different types can provide a pleasant sensation, which conjures up memories of seafaring traditions and visions of being in control of a beautiful vessel slicing through the waves. The variety of ropes is quite fascinating and each has its particular uses.

Types and uses

Ropes made of natural fibres are unlikely to be used as they don't have the durability or strength of the synthetic fibres that are most commonly used on modern motor boats.

Three-strand rope is twisted together, which makes it fairly easy to splice. However, it's not as comfortable to handle frequently as the smoother and softer braided and plaited ropes. Consequently the latter types are preferable for ropes that have to be handled a lot.

Polyester rope such as Dacron is braided and in addition has an inner core of braided rope. It is consequently referred to as 'braid-on-braid'. It combines uniform flexibility with great strength, is low stretch, has good UV light resistance and sinks in water. It's also rather costly and tends to be used on sailing boats (to control the sails) rather than on motor boats.

Nylon rope is particularly strong but stretches considerably. It's usually available as a three-strand rope with each strand containing many twisted filaments. The consequent stretch characteristic makes it very suitable for mooring lines and anchor warps, where it can absorb the shock of a sudden pull. It also has good UV resistance and sinks in water.

Polypropylene rope is quite cheap but has poor UV resistance, meaning that it deteriorates more rapidly than other types. It's often used for mooring lines, but it needs to be checked and replaced quite often, and nylon is a much better and more reliable choice. Its main advantage is that it floats and can therefore be effective for rescue lines, which need to be visible on the surface.

Three-strand rope.

Braid-on-braid with the inner core exposed.

Polypropylene rope is cheap but eventually deteriorates in sunlight.

Nylon guard-rail netting.

Nylon guard-rail netting is easily fitted to the stanchions and guard rails or wires on a motor cruiser. This helps to prevent loose items and people – particularly children – from disappearing overboard.

Rope maintenance

Looking after your ropes prolongs their life, reducing the rate at which the fibres break down and helping to stop them from breaking.

The ultraviolet light in sunlight gradually degrades ropes. This is unavoidable in most cases, but if possible you should try to keep them out of direct sunlight when they're not being used.

Ropes should be washed occasionally using lukewarm soapy water. This removes salt deposits and grit, which can cause wear. A pressure washer is sometimes recommended, but considering that they can take the surface off a concrete driveway there's a risk that the rope could be damaged by grit being forced into it.

Using a washing machine on a cool setting has also been advocated, but an almighty tangle will ensue unless you first place the coiled rope in a suitable cloth bag, such as a pillowcase. There's also the risk that a large, wet rope could be too heavy for the washing machine, damaging it and your relationship with other members of the household.

Ropes stiff with dirt and salt will need soaking for a day or two in soapy water, which should be agitated occasionally. Thorough rinsing may have to be followed by another soaking. Scrubbing with a plastic scrubbing pad helps to remove stubborn dirt.

Ropes that have become stiff with salt will also benefit from being soaked in a bucket of water with a cup of fabric conditioner added. After rinsing and drying the rope should be much more flexible and more pleasant to hold – and to smell!

You should stop ropes fraying by securing the ends as described below, and you should carefully coil all ropes when not in use. This helps to stop kinks forming, which can weaken a rope.

Check rope regularly for wear and abrasion damage. Try to alter the position of contact with fittings from time to time in order to spread the wear on the rope. To stop wear and fraying, you can thread plastic hose onto a rope at the points where it passes through or over fittings such as a roller.

Safety aspects

The safe use of ropes requires care and commonsense:

- In order to avoid entanglement and injury, don't stand in a coil of rope.
- Avoid standing in the line of recoil where a rope or cable might backlash if it breaks.
- Always check and test that knots and splices are secure.
- A rope with a heavy load should not be controlled directly by your bare hands. Take two or more turns round a cleat, winch or post to reduce the strain on your body.
- Don't wind a rope round your hand where there's a risk you could suddenly be pulled off balance before being able to let go.
- Be aware that knots weaken the rope, reducing its strength, depending on the type of knot, by between 20 and 50 per cent, or even as much as 70 per cent if the knot is poorly tied.

Ropes should be coiled carefully when not in use.

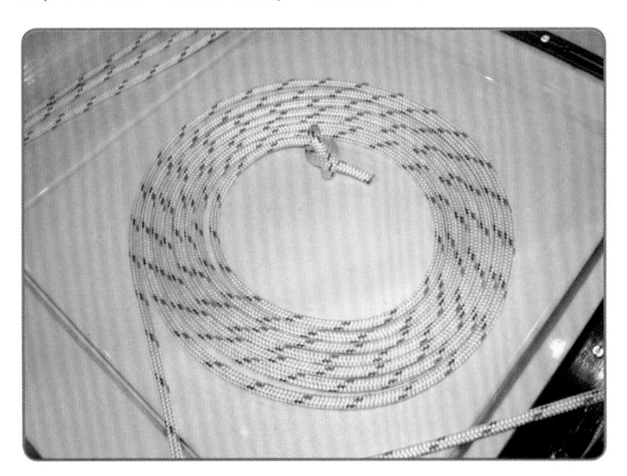

Watch out for fraying rope where it comes into contact with fittings.

Left: 'Dip-it Whip-it' seals rope ends.

Right: Plastic adhesive tape can be used temporarily to stop a rope fraying.

Sealing rope ends
The traditional way to stop ropes unravelling and fraying at the ends is to use twine winding or 'whipping'. Whether you want to spend a lot of time winding thread round rope ends depends on your dexterity and determination, but there are alternatives.

Synthetic rope ends can be fused with a flame from a gas lighter, after first taking the necessary safety precautions to avoid a conflagration. Obviously, you shouldn't touch the rope with your fingers until it's had plenty of time to cool, but you'll need to smooth the melted edges with something non-flammable, otherwise a nasty sharp edge could form as the solidifying end cools. Heat-shrink sleeving, available from some marine equipment suppliers, can also be used.

A safer method is to use a liquid called 'Dip-it Whip-it'. You simply dip the end of the rope into the glue-like liquid and let it dry.

An even simpler method only really suitable for the temporary securing of a rope end is to bind it with plastic tape of the insulating variety.

Knots and splices

Wherever possible, it's best to use splices to make loops instead of knots. Splices reduce the strength of the rope much less than knots. Ropes can be purchased with eye splices already provided at one or both ends.

Whole books have been written on tying knots. However, since ropes provided with splices are in widespread use only a few knots need be learned.

The excellent website accessible at http://www.animatedknots.com provides animated stage by stage demonstrations of how to tie the knots and splices mentioned below, along with a huge range of other knots. It also offers much advice on the use of each knot.

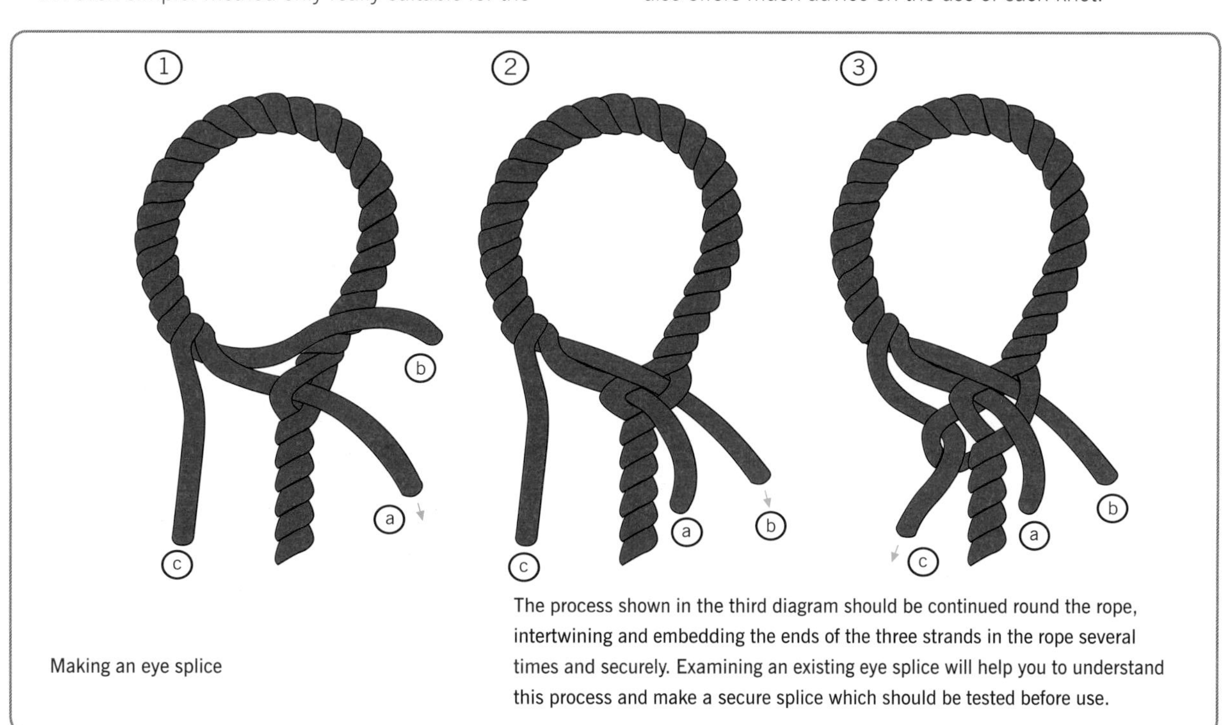

Making an eye splice

The process shown in the third diagram should be continued round the rope, intertwining and embedding the ends of the three strands in the rope several times and securely. Examining an existing eye splice will help you to understand this process and make a secure splice which should be tested before use.

Types of knot

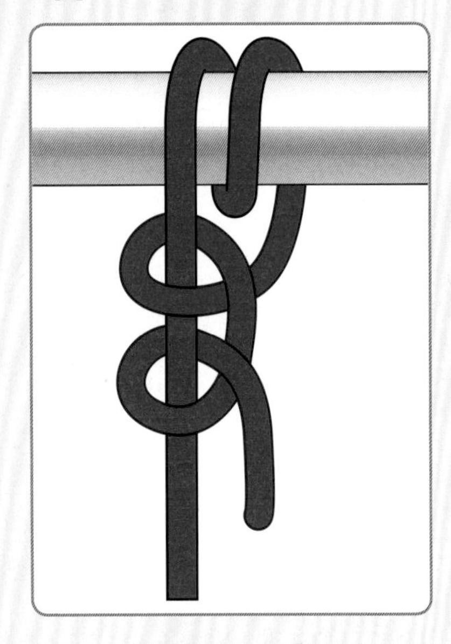

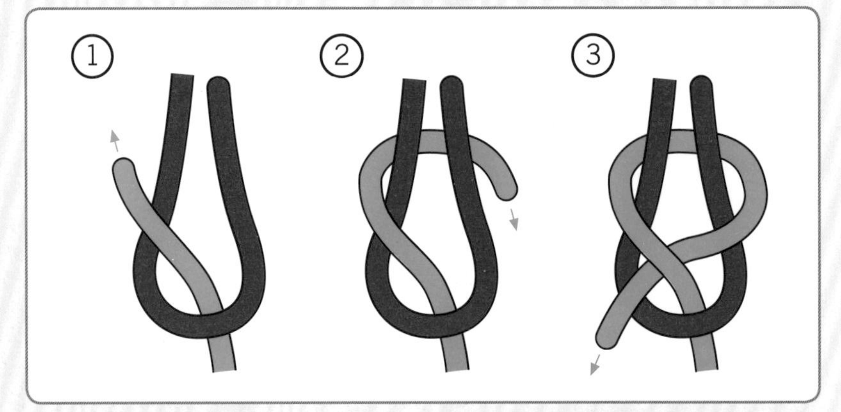

Left: A round turn and two half hitches is very good for tying mooring lines to posts and for many other purposes. Though a clove hitch is sometimes suggested for this it isn't actually suitable, as it can slip in response to a sudden pull.

Above: The sheet bend is used for joining two ropes, particularly where they're of different thicknesses. It's considered by knot experts to be more secure than the reef knot.

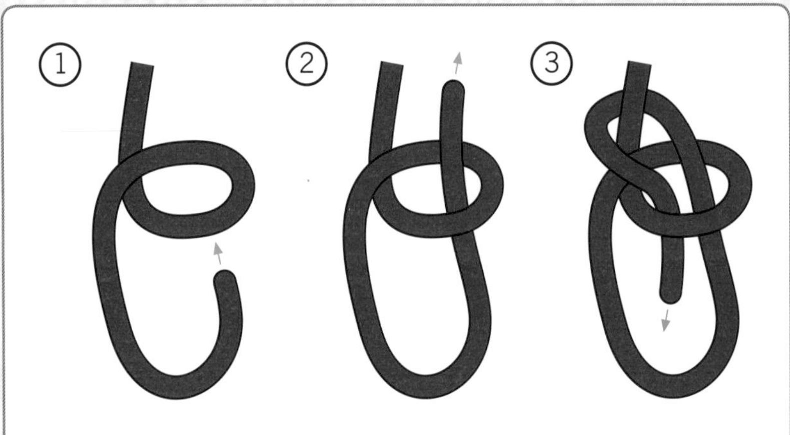

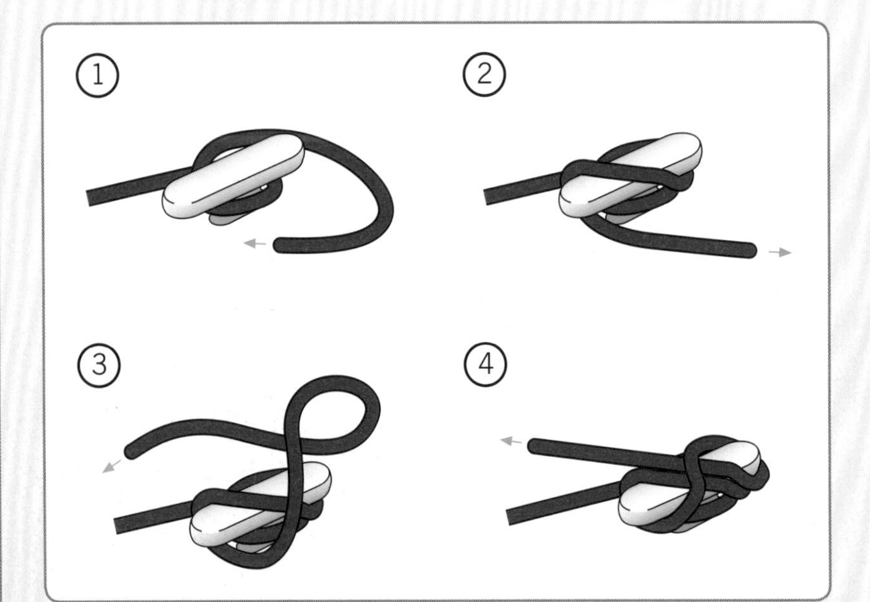

Above left: The bowline is useful for making loops and can be used for securing a mooring line, but bear in mind that it can't be undone when a load is pulling on it. An advantage is that it can be tied with one hand, which may be useful in an emergency.

Above: A figure-of-eight knot is a stopper knot. You tie it in the end of a rope to stop it running out through an eye.

Left: The cleat hitch is used to fasten a rope to a cleat.

Chain is sold by the metre.

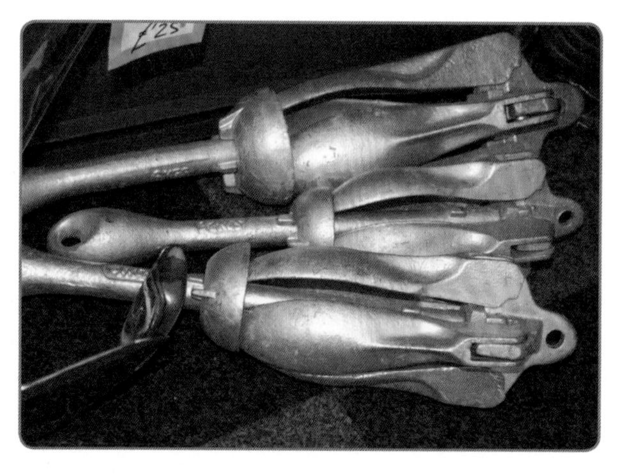

Folding grapnel anchors suitable for use as a 'lunch hook'.

Anchors, chain and rope

The size and weight of anchor depends on the size of the boat and the where it's to be used. The actual choice will depend on how you use your boat. For sheltered creeks in calm conditions a simple system using a folding grapnel anchor may be sufficient for brief stops. On inland waterways such as the Norfolk Broads a mudweight or rond anchor could be suitable. But if you intend at any time to venture out of very sheltered waters, and particularly if you plan to anchor overnight in a tidal harbour, river or estuary, it's most important to have equipment that matches the boat and conditions; otherwise you could drift onto the shore or rocks and be wrecked whilst asleep.

The 'rode' is the chain and rope used with an anchor. A length of chain should always be shackled to the anchor and attached to the rope. The chain's weight is vital in holding the anchor down so that it gains and keeps a firm grip on the riverbed or seabed. It also resists abrasion far better than rope. Recommendations for the length of chain vary from two to a very cautious five times the length of the boat. It may depend on the total weight you can cope with when lifting the combined chain and anchor.

The rope rode should be a type that stretches to absorb the sudden shocks and pulls of a boat riding the waves. Nylon is ideal for this. The length of rope, referred to as the 'warp' or 'scope', attached to the chain should be a minimum of three times the depth of the water in calm sheltered conditions. The longer the length, the more secure the anchor is. Length should be increased to at least five times the water depth in windy conditions, and a strong wind will require eight times the depth – although the proximity of other boats and obstacles needs to be taken into consideration, of course. The actual length carried on the boat should, therefore, be much more than the length you anticipate using according to the depths in which you expect to anchor. Remember to include the rise of the tide in your calculations.

The chandler who sells the equipment will provide advice on its selection relevant to the area where you'll be anchoring.

A 'belt and braces' approach is to have two anchors and a rode for each. The second one can be used at an angle to the other if there are ground-holding problems or the possibility of a sudden increase in wind or waves. An anchor sometimes referred to as a 'lunch hook' is a small folding grapnel type to use for an hour or two in a sheltered creek while you stop for lunch, or any other reason.

Recommendations for the weight of anchor for a particular length of boat vary considerably. A traditional non-metric expression has been one pound (0.45kg) in weight for each one foot (0.3m) of boat length, though recommendations for more recently developed types of anchor may be for a little less weight – as, for example, a Bruce anchor used in firm sand.

However, carrying an anchor heavier than the minimum recommended – providing you can lift it off the seabed – provides a reassuring safety margin. Chain diameter (the thickness of the steel used in making each link) is normally 6mm for a small open boat and 8mm for a small motor cruiser of up to 7.5m overall length. The chain link size for larger boats of about 10m to 18m should be increased to 10–14mm. The 6mm and 8mm chains should have nylon

The Bruce anchor.

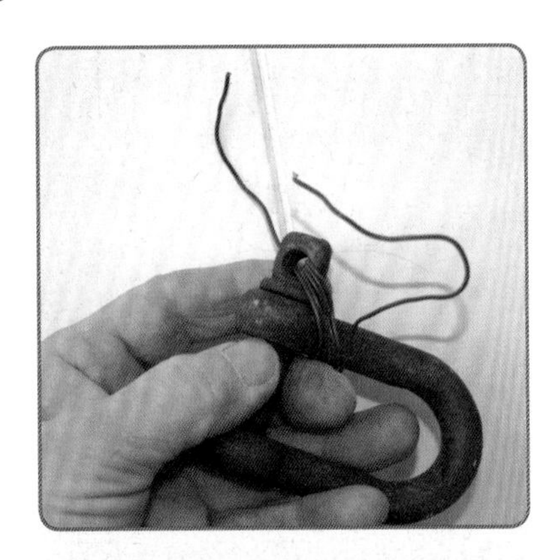

The shackle being 'moused' to stop it unscrewing.

rope of 10mm and 14mm diameter respectively, going up to 18–22mm rope for 10–14mm links. Shackles slightly larger than the chain size should be used and they should be 'moused', meaning the shackle should be bound with wire to stop it coming unscrewed.

The local harbour master should be consulted about anchoring and about suitable locations where it's permitted and safe to do so. It's always preferable to anchor in sand or firm mud. The anchor can then dig well in.

Anchoring technique is one of the subjects covered in motor boating courses. If you're in any doubt about anchoring for an overnight stay, particularly if increasing winds or waves are likely during your stay, plan in advance to arrive at a marina or harbour well before dark.

Anchors used on rocky or weed-covered seabed can get stuck and become difficult to retrieve. On many types of anchor, a suitable length of 'trip line' can be attached to the crown of the anchor and a float on the surface. If the anchor gets stuck, this trip line can be used to lift it clear of the obstruction.

More on the substantial topic of anchors, anchoring and mooring equipment and the actual process of anchoring can be found at the following websites and in books listed in the Appendix:

http://www.motorboatsmonthly.co.uk
http://marinestore.co.uk
http://www.jimmygreen.co.uk

Types of anchor

Many new and quite expensive types of anchor have been developed claiming all kinds of advantages for those who cruise far and wide in larger motor cruisers. However, the ones described below are a few of the tried and tested traditional types.

Mudweight
On inland waterways where there are no strong currents, such as the canals and the actual broads of the Norfolk Broads waterways, a mudweight can be used. In fact, this device should be used instead of an anchor on canals, as an anchor can damage the canal's clay bed and allow water to leak into the ground below.

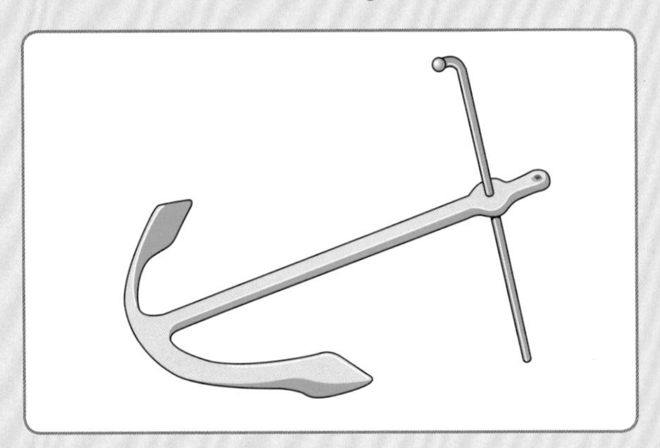

Fisherman
The fisherman anchor has been used for centuries and is still to be found on some boats. It can be effective on rocks or in seaweed but is cumbersome, and can become entangled with its chain. It needs the folding stock to be pegged in place so that the sharp points called flukes dig into the seabed; but the uppermost fluke can damage your boat as the tide goes out. If you get one with a second-hand boat, consider replacing it with one of the following.

Danforth
This anchor has good holding power and folds flat when stored. Take care when handling it, as fingers can get trapped when the flukes swivel.

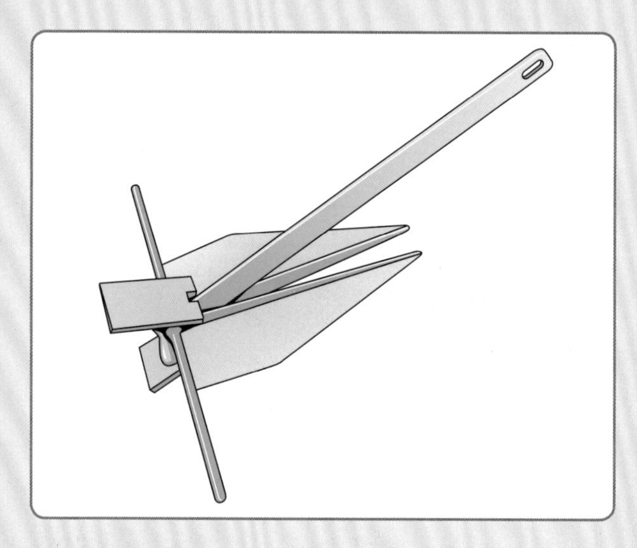

A selection of anchors for sale, some with chain and warp attached.

CQR or plough
This type 'ploughs' into the seabed and also holds well. It can be kept conveniently in a stem head roller over the bow of the boat.

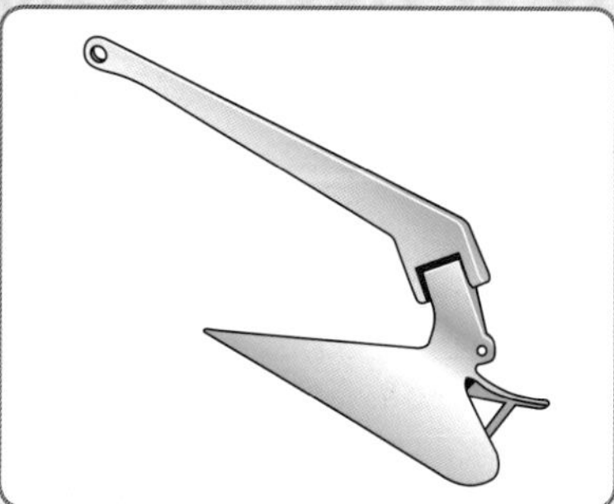

Mooring

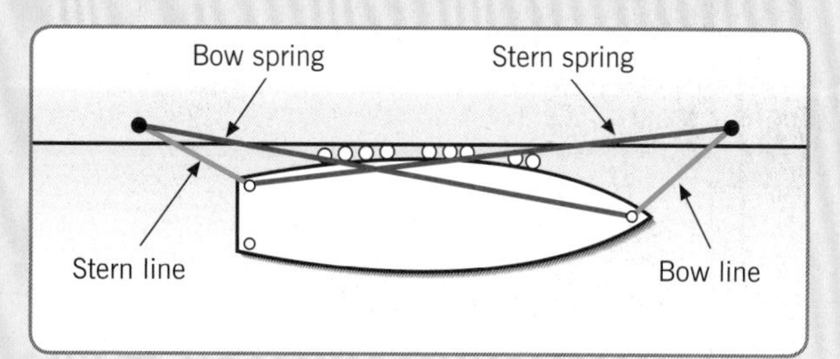

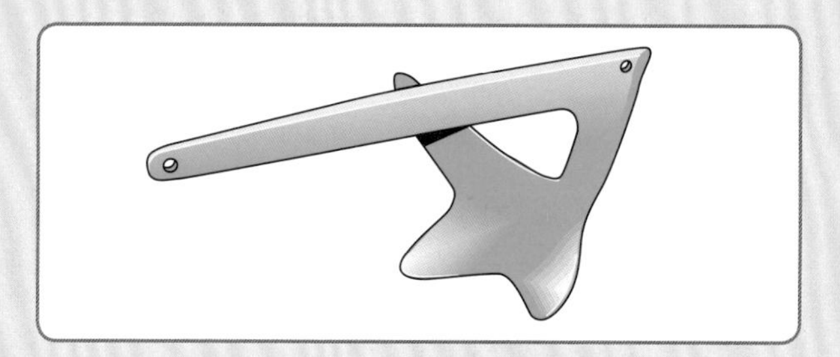

Bruce
The Bruce anchor has particularly good holding power in relation to its weight and stores well on a stem head roller.

Grapnel
The folding grapnel anchor is cheap and convenient for use as a 'lunch hook' on a day boat or dinghy but doesn't hold as well as the above types. It can be reasonably effective in rocky areas but may then get wedged and become difficult to remove.

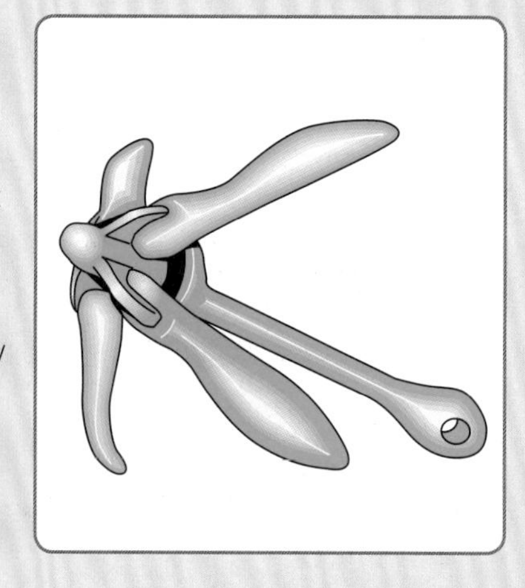

Warps
Warps are the ropes used for tying the boat to mooring points. Ideally you should have two for the bow and two for the stern so that two of them can be used as 'springs', as shown in the diagram, to stop the boat swinging and moving excessively when tied up. Unless you're mooring against a pontoon that rises and falls, the mooring warps need to be long enough to allow for the rise and fall of the tide, the range of which is indicated on tide tables. Some inexperienced boat owners have returned to their boat to find it suspended from the harbour wall by ropes that were too short for the fall of the tide. Don't forget that most rivers are affected by tides for some distance from their estuaries and that river levels also rise and fall, partly in response to variations in rainfall.

On inland waterways, in situations where there are no rings, bollards or posts available, mooring spikes, strong steel 'pins' or L-shaped anchors called rond anchors are used. These are tied to the end of the warps and pushed into the ground on the bank. It can be difficult to hold the boat and try to get a rond anchor into the ground at the same time, and it's much easier if someone on the bank holds the boat by the ropes until you're sure you have the anchors firmly in place.

Never throw any type of anchor. Rond anchors thrown onto the bank have a nasty tendency to bounce back and hit the boat or you.

This mooring shackle has seriously worn and corroded to the point of failure.

This corroded length of mooring chain shows wear at the points where chain links meet.

Fenders

Remember to have fenders in place before approaching a pontoon or riverside mooring in order to cushion contact with the timber, concrete or steel quay. There is more on fenders in Chapter 18.

Mooring tackle maintenance

In the case of permanently fixed mooring equipment – such as swinging moorings out in an estuary – regular maintenance is essential, as they sustain wear through use, abrasion with the seabed and corrosion. Insurance companies usually specify that such mooring equipment is regularly checked and maintained by qualified and experienced specialists. This should not be ignored. If a boat breaks free from a mooring, the first questions will be about mooring maintenance before a claim will even be considered.

Where a mooring is rented, get confirmation that regular professional maintenance is carried out. If you purchase the right to moor or gain a mooring through a boating club, maintenance issues should be agreed in writing and accepted by your insurance company. In the past many moorings were laid by amateurs using all kinds of weights, but greater awareness of safety issues and stricter insurance requirements have emphasised the risks involved with this.

The above should not stop you from checking aspects of the mooring tackle yourself, in addition to the professional maintenance, if you can reach it safely. Using a boat hook from a secure position on your boat, the chain and shackles that are fixed to the mooring buoy can be lifted. Although they may be substantial, the friction caused by waves, wind and boat movement gradually wears the shackles and chain links, reducing their diameter and strength.

Check that the screw-in pins on shackles are tight and 'moused' over (bound with wire to stop them unscrewing, as illustrated earlier). If you replace a shackle you must use one of the same size and type, or stronger, and of the same metal as the original. Using a different type of metal, such as stainless steel, enables electrolytic processes to cause a reaction between them, which will weaken the fittings.

In the case of a mooring exposed at low tide on firm sand or gravel, it may be possible to inspect the ground tackle for wear. Take great care to check that soft sand or deep mud won't trap you if you attempt to do this. One unfortunate boat owner attempting to check his mooring became stuck up to his waist in deep sticky mud, and a helicopter, lifeboat and fire appliances were involved in his rescue in front of a

On some drying moorings it may be possible to inspect the mooring tackle at low tide unless the soft mud is hazardous.

hundred onlookers out for a Sunday stroll. They were greatly entertained when he was dragged ashore and hosed down. Although his pride was hurt more than his body, he was lucky. In a more remote situation he could have faced a rising tide with no one to raise the alarm.

Chafing is the main enemy of mooring ropes. Where they rub against a stem head roller, or any other surface, fit a protective sleeve of flexible plastic pipe, a leather covering or something similar.

Picking up a vacant mooring for anything more than a brief stop instead of anchoring may be risky, if it hasn't been adequately maintained. It's best to seek confirmation of its reliability from the harbour master or some other reliable authority. Permission is likely to be necessary in any case, as the mooring owner could return and want to use the mooring you're attached to.

The condition of mooring posts or rings on harbour walls or riverbanks is much easier to check, but remember that rot or corrosion could be occurring below the surface. Try to attach the boat to several such posts or rings.

A protective sleeve of plastic pipe helps prevent mooring ropes from chafing.

Check the condition of any mooring posts you tie up to.

Picking up the mooring

This has already been covered in Chapter 8, but you might want to consider the following tips to make it easier. Firstly you could try using a 'Moorfast' mooring hook in place of a boat hook. And secondly you could attach a small pick-up buoy to the mooring rope, with a good-sized loop forming a grab handle. This small buoy is then fixed to base of the main mooring buoy, and becomes the target for your boat hook. It can be brought aboard and a loop on the rope slipped over the cleat, or samson post, in the bow.

The Moorfast mooring hook threads a rope through a ring or round a cleat and brings it back aboard with a simple push and pull action.

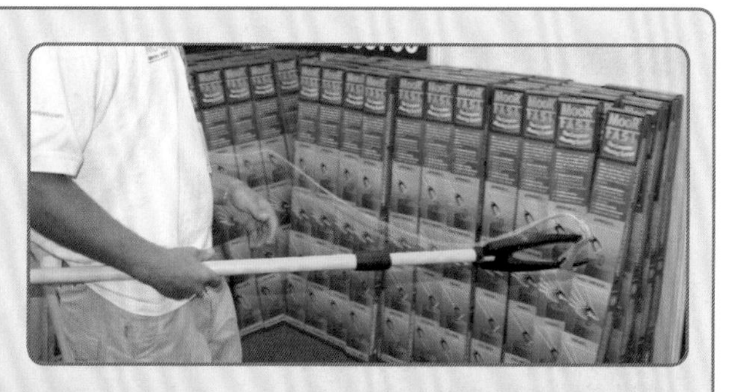

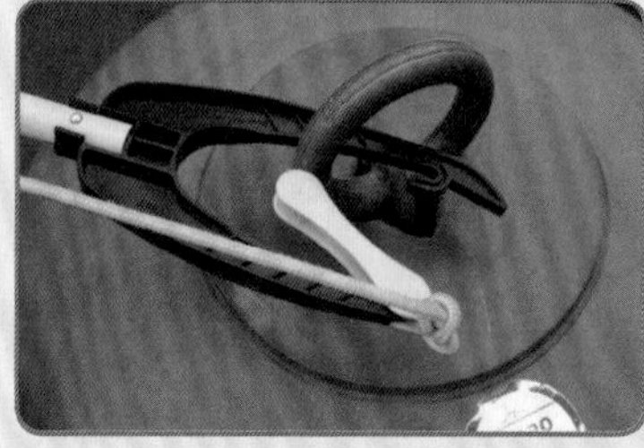

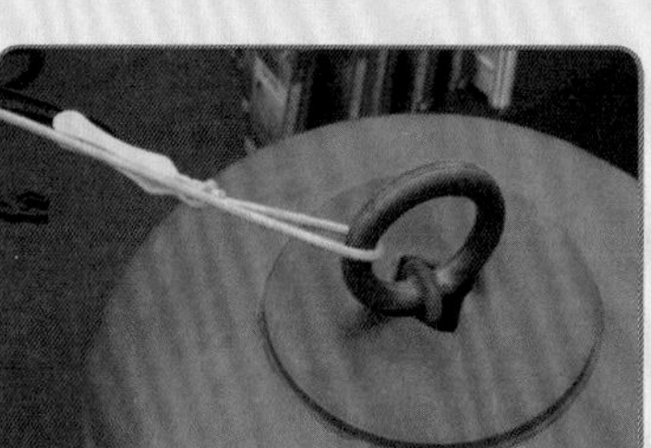

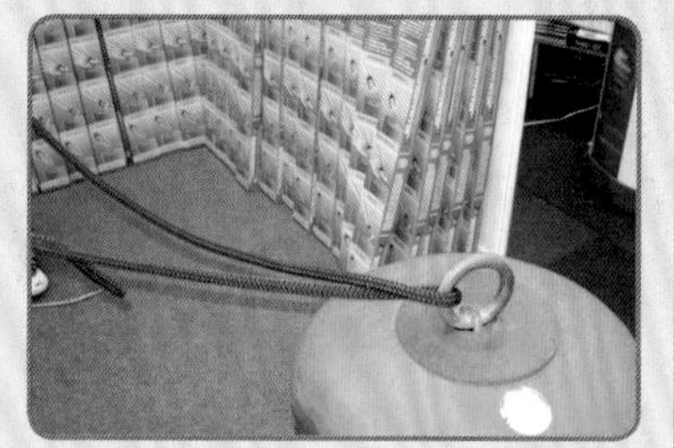

Winter precautions

In the winter, when the motor cruiser has been brought ashore, the common precaution where ice may form or other processes may damage a mooring out in an estuary is to replace the main mooring buoy with a small float and line, which provides a marker. You should certainly avoid dropping the mooring chain to the seabed without some sort of marker, as it will be very difficult to find the mooring next season. A precaution against this possibility is to use GPS equipment to get an exact fix on the position of the mooring ground tackle and to establish its position with reference to several permanent landmarks.

If the mooring buoy is lost and not exposed at low tide, professional help from a diver will be needed to find the ground tackle and reconnect the buoy. If it's exposed at low tide, be wary of sinking into soft mud and sand when looking for it.

15 The cabin

A smart and well-maintained cabin interior.

Leaking window seals

Window seals are a common source of leaks into the cabin of a motor cruiser. The sealant has to cope with the different rates of expansion of the various materials used in the window, the frame and the surrounding cabin sides. It starts off flexible enough to cope but over several years will lose this flexibility, become brittle and start to crack away from the surfaces to which it was originally stuck.

Water from rain and spray enters the cracks, and freeze-and-thaw action in winter can then cause more damage to the sealant. The remedy most often recommended is to remove the window and replace the sealant. This is a messy and time-consuming job, and during the boating season you may not want to spend valuable boating time removing and resealing windows. It may have to be done eventually, but there is a way to delay this whilst still solving the problem of drips coming through onto bunks and bedding: 'Captain Tolley's Creeping Crack Cure'.

Though it may sound a bit like an old-fashioned medicine-show remedy, this is, in fact, an ingenious liquid invented to cure leaks into the cabin on the Captain's own boat. The product was launched at the Southampton Boat Show in 1986. Captain Tolley's website at http://www.captaintolley.com/ is very informative and includes plenty of testimonials from much drier, happy customers.

Crack Cure is applied to the joints around a window where there are cracks less than 1mm wide. Although it can work in damp conditions, it should, ideally, be used when the joint is as dry as possible, in order to avoid water diluting it and reducing its effectiveness. It should also be applied when the temperature is between 5 and 27°C. It's a very runny, penetrating fluid and you have to be careful to control the rate of flow. Because it's so good at flowing it penetrates even the thinnest of cracks, often invisible to the naked eye. As the fluid disappears down any cracks, it actually helps to find the source of a leak.

After the first application, let it dry, and then apply more fluid to the point of the leak. Repeat this process every 30 minutes until the white fluid no longer drains away into the crack. In this way the sealant will have built up layers inside the crack, progressively sealing it against leakage. Wipe away any excess with a damp cloth before it dries.

Although it's recommended for cracks up to 1mm wide, Crack Cure can actually glue together debris in leaking cracks making a surprisingly long-lasting waterproof repair.

Since some of the fluid might leak through and out the other side of the crack with the first applications, you need to be ready to mop it up. It therefore helps to have someone on the other side of the leak to remove any surplus. A further application after allowing it to dry fully for 24 hours ensures the crack is completely sealed. Although the liquid is white when wet, it dries transparent and can be painted if required.

It's best to use Crack Cure on the window seals and other joints as part of your annual boat maintenance, providing prevention rather than cure. Bear in mind, though, that leaks from fittings that take considerable strains or bear a load indicate possible corrosion of bolts and fittings, which could be weakening them. In this situation, replacement would be better and safer than just sealing the leaks.

Captain Tolley's Creeping Crack Cure bottle is gently squeezed so that the liquid flows into cracks around the window frame.

Any excess should be wiped away with a damp cloth.

The Crack Cure can also be used where deck fittings are leaking water into the cabin.

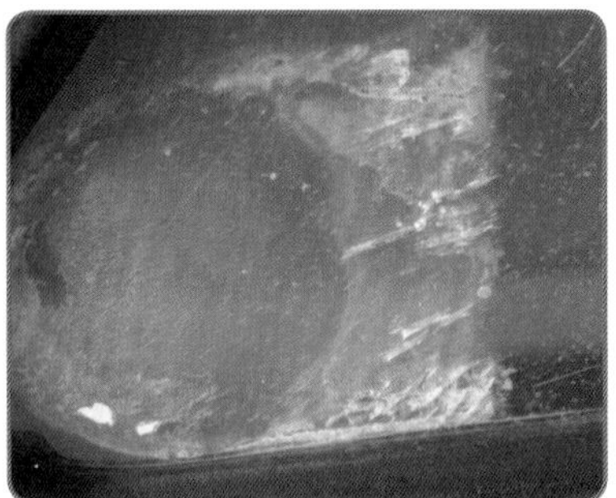

Crazing of Perspex can't be cured and replacement of the windowpane will be necessary.

Window damage repair

Cast acrylic Perspex is commonly used for boat windows, although other makes and materials are sometimes used.

Although the Creeping Crack Cure method is worth trying first, severe cracking and failure of window seals will eventually make replacement necessary. Unless it's just superficial scratching, damage to the actual windows will also render replacement necessary.

If light scratches to the Perspex are the problem, you could try to remove the scratches before you resort to replacing the window. Liquid car polish that contains no abrasives can be applied using a soft cloth, a little at a time. After the polish has dried, remove it with another clean soft cloth. Repeating this process several times may be sufficient to remove the scratches. However, if they're deep it's unlikely to prove effective.

Toughened glass has a very hard surface and any scratches will be very difficult or impossible to remove without causing abrasion marks around the scratch.

Crazing of Perspex occurs over time by the action of ultraviolet sunlight. It can go deep into the Perspex and can't be cured. Replacement is the only solution.

Window replacement

Window replacement can be a fairly straightforward job but if it seems difficult – perhaps because a window is glazed or its aluminium frames very firmly stuck to the Perspex or glass – you may need to find a local boat window specialist to help. If you can't, a company known as Eagle Boat Windows provides a mail order services to cope with the complications. Windows in their frames can be sent to them for professional repair or they can supply the necessary materials, replacement parts and advice for you to carry out your own repairs. There is

Part of a boat show display by Eagle Windows showing how a company such as this can help with window repairs and supply parts for DIY work on windows.

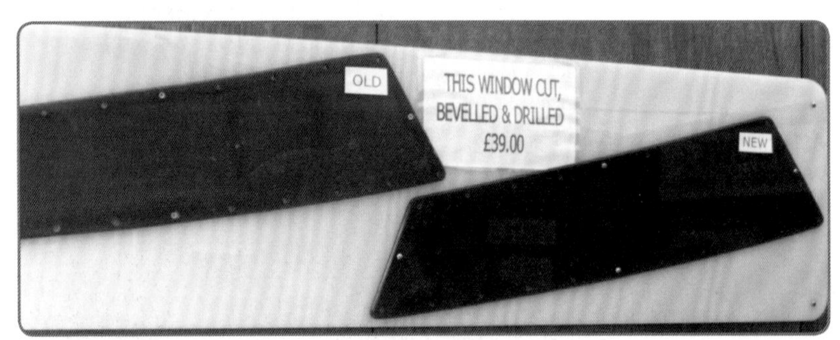

much helpful information on their website at http://www.eagleboatwindows.co.uk.

Before removing window frames, label the inside and top of each frame with its location in order to make it easier to replace them correctly. These labels can be written on pieces of masking tape attached to the frame.

On some boats, the windows and frames help to strengthen the cabin sides, so don't walk on the roof of the cabin when any part of a window has been removed. It may also be best to remove and replace only one window at a time so as to avoid the risk of distortion.

Make sure you can work reasonably comfortably and safely outside and inside the boat without cutting yourself on sharp edges. Have someone available to help on the other side of the window, to undo fastenings and help remove the windowpane or frame. Both of you need to wear suitable leather gloves to protect your hands against sharp edges and broken fragments.

The series of photos below and on the following pages show the repair of a window in which Perspex needs to be replaced. The same principles can be applied to many types of windows with aluminium frames.

The cracked windowpane needing replacement.

Drill out the flange of each rivet and push it through.

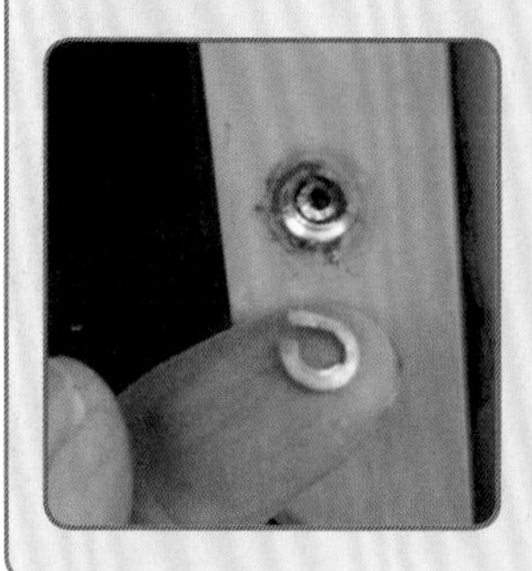

Removing a windowpane and frame

Windows made of Perspex or similar plastic are often bolted through the cabin sides with stainless steel bolts. These can be undone, perhaps with the help of some easing oil.

Loosen and remove screws or bolts in a sequence, selecting pairs that are diagonally opposite each other. If any other items are likely to make it difficult to remove the window, carefully remove or unstick them. This may involve detaching lining on the inside walls of the cabin. Be ready to hold the windowpane if it slips down at any stage.

Screws or bolts should be loosened by selecting pairs that are opposite each other.

Rivets will have to be drilled out. Start from the outside and drill out the flange of each rivet. Next, try gently pushing the rivet out through the hole. If this doesn't work, perhaps because the rivet is corroded, carefully drill it out completely.

A thin knife may have to be inserted between the window and the fibreglass or wooden sides of the cabin to

The lining and trim inside the cabin may need to be lifted carefully to get at the screws, bolts or rivets to release them.

Use a knife to break the hold of the sealant

Gently remove the frame. In this case it came away in sections.

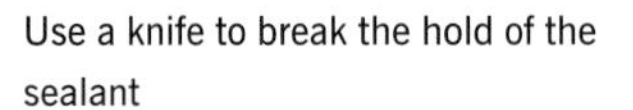

break any sealant away from the frame. Do this a little at a time all round the window. Don't try to lever the window out with the knife, though, as this could crack it or damage the side of the cabin. Aluminium frames may have become brittle with age so the frame must be taken off gently in order to avoid breaking or bending it.

If the windowpane still won't come away readily, a helper can push gently from inside the cabin while you hold it on the outside. If the Perspex or glass isn't damaged it should be possible to remove the whole sheet intact, but if it's broken you need to wear suitable gloves when removing it.

Replacing a windowpane and aluminium frame

When dealing with an aluminium frame, place it on a soft level bed of cloth to support it. Remove all traces of sealant and dirt from the frame and the area that was in contact with the window frame. If the windowpane is to be reused, all sealant should be cleaned off that too. This can be a time-consuming task, but white spirit should help. Acetone can be used on metal frames, but keep it well away from the transparent plastic windowpanes as it can turn them permanently cloudy. Take care not to scratch the outside surface of the aluminium frame and the Perspex.

Screw holes can be cleaned by drilling through them. Any sharp edges around drilled holes should be removed gently with a countersink bit.

It's important to save all the pieces of plastic from a broken windowpane. These should then be placed on a sheet of cardboard and fitted together. Draw round the shape of the window to make a template, and use this to mark out the shape and screw holes on a new sheet of Perspex. Support the Perspex carefully and securely and cut it to shape using a fine-toothed blade in either a fretsaw, a hacksaw or a jigsaw. If you're using toughened glass rather than Perspex it can usually be provided ready-cut to size by a local supplier.

With the window fully supported, mark the positions of any screw holes needed and use a sharp new drill bit to make the holes in the exact positions required. To avoid causing sudden stress to the Perspex, drill at a slow speed to start with and then increase the speed gradually.

With a helper, do a 'dry run' with the windowpane and fittings held in place. Make sure the screws or bolts fit well

It may not be possible to remove the windowpane without it breaking into pieces, so suitable leather gloves are needed.

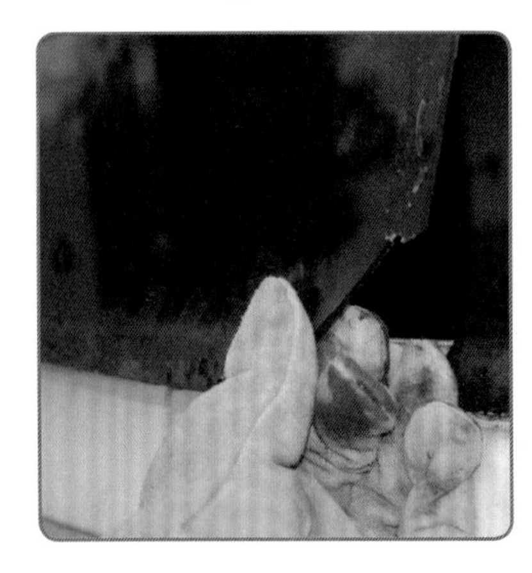

All types of window frames will have old sealant sticking to them and this will have to be thoroughly removed.

White spirit should soften old sealant making it easier to scrape off.

into the window, the frame and the cabin side, ensuring that they don't distort or exert any sideways pressure on the Perspex, which could crack it.

Silicone or a similar non-setting sealant such as butyl (as used in Arbo sealing compound) should be used when refitting the windowpane – strongly adhesive polyurethane sealants aren't suitable, as they could render the windowpane difficult to remove in the future. Run a substantial bead of sealant round the edge of the pane in line with the screw holes. Sufficient should be applied to result in an excess being squeezed out as the window is screwed or bolted into place.

Press the windowpane and frame – with more sealant on the frame where necessary – into its hole in the cabin side. Some sealant will appear in the bolt holes. Check that the screws or bolts can get through the sealant and remove any of the excess that might cause a problem when tightening the fastenings.

Don't use a powered screwdriver, which could damage Perspex by tightening screws too quickly and aggressively. Instead you should use a hand screwdriver or your fingers to lightly tighten each screw or bolt a little at a time. Alternate the tightening across the window, starting with the screws in the middle at top and bottom, and go round them all several times. This beds the window down evenly without putting too much pressure on any one part.

The final tightening should squeeze out a little of the sealant. Bear in mind that you're not intending to glue the window to the boat. The idea is to have a flexible gasket of sealant between the surfaces. Leave this to cure and then carefully cut and peel the excess off, preferably with a plastic scraper. Be sure to avoid scratching the windowpane or the frame. White spirit could be used to remove any residue that's difficult to shift.

If screwing Perspex straight onto the side of the boat without a frame, watch out for any bowing or distortion that could crack the plastic pane or the gelcoat. If the plastic has to bend to fit, it would be best to order preformed Perspex shaped to the curvature required. Thinner Perspex *might* bend enough but there's a risk of cracking. Don't use countersunk screws straight onto Perspex as the wedge shape puts stress on it and cracks will eventually develop.

Drilling screw holes in Perspex should be done slowly, gently and carefully to avoid cracking it.

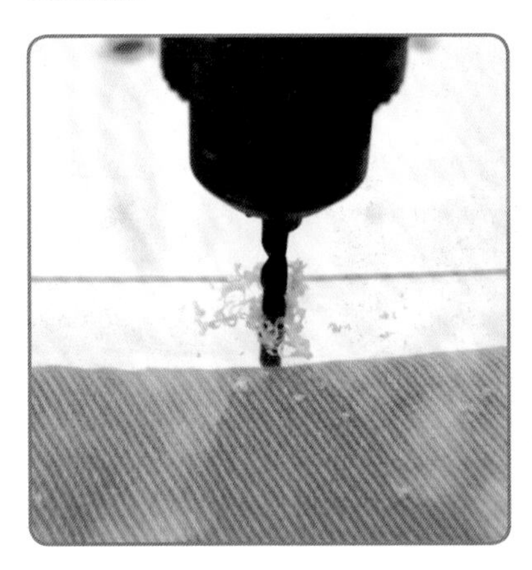

Apply a substantial bead of sealant to the frame and the surfaces to which it's to be bonded.

Screws should be tightened a little each, one at a time, to spread the pressure evenly.

Rubber Claytonrite window seals

The black rubber frames on some motor cruisers can be removed by finding the end of the central filler strip and hooking it out. Pull it out all the way round. This should loosen the windowpane so that it can be carefully pushed out without breaking it. The pane should be kept as a template for cutting the replacement, as described above.

Likewise, once you've removed the rubber seal you need to keep it in order to identify exactly the size and type that's needed to replace it. The new seal should be ordered a little longer than actually needed. New Claytonrite seals, other types of rubber seals, advice on using them and the special glazing tool required to fit them can be obtained from a number of suppliers including http://www.sealsdirect.co.uk and http://www.wilks.co.uk.

Clean the surfaces where the seal has been removed. The new rubber seal should be fitted round the aperture first to establish the exact length needed. Push it well into the bends and corners, and cut it about 25mm longer than needed, with square ends to make a butt joint. This joint should go at the top of the window.

Remove the rubber seal and run a thin bead of silicone sealant into the groove that takes the windowpane. Insert the pane into the bottom of the seal. Use the glazing tool to fit the lip of the rubber over the edge of the pane.

The filler strip that tightens the seal has to be fed through the eye of the glazing tool and worked into the channel in the rubber seal. Lubricant can be used at this stage to help the process. Cut the end of the filler strip allowing a slight overlap. Push this overlap in to make a tight joint.

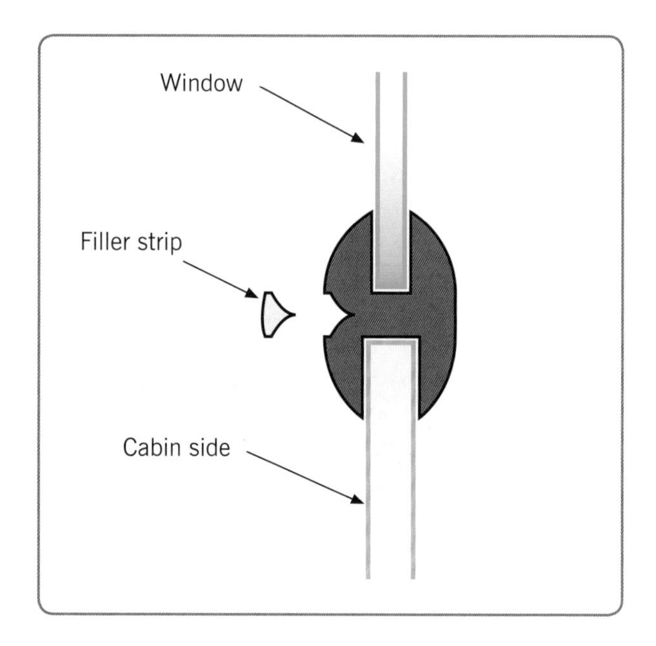

Cross-section of the Claytonrite rubber window seal. The glass or plastic pane slots into the groove on one side and the cabin side slots into the groove on the other. A filler strip is pushed in to hold them in place.

The end of the filler strip is pulled out to loosen the window.

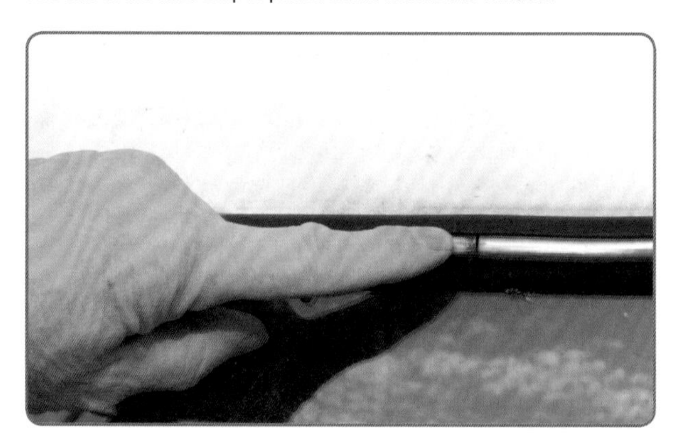

Cleaning Perspex

Windows should be kept clean but you should never wipe them when dry, as grains of dirt can cause scratches. Use warm soapy water and a soft cloth.

Damp, mould and smell reduction

A problem with boat cabins is condensation causing mould and bad smells. Wooden boats have an advantage here because the wood provides some insulation, although any condensation that does occur can cause rot in wood. GRP, on the other hand, has a colder surface, which attracts condensation unless it's insulated from temperature changes. Although some degree of cabin insulation is provided by many boat builders it may not be adequate, and any bare surfaces in the cabin and inside lockers will benefit from the following advice.

A special thick paint called 'International Anti-condensation Paint' is advertised as being able to provide some insulation in order to reduce or prevent condensation, and it's possible that several coats of this paint may solve your problems. This would certainly be a much simpler solution than cutting and sticking new headlining material to the ceiling.

However, the main method of reducing condensation is to provide adequate ventilation, particularly when our own bodies and cooking processes are generating plenty of moisture. Complications can arise with this, though, as you also need to keep rainwater, spray, nesting birds, rodents and intruders out of the cabin.

Vents are available that have been specifically designed to permit the circulation of air and the removal of water vapour without allowing rainwater and unwanted visitors to get in.

To help overcome condensation problems, consider installing one or more solar-powered ventilators. These have electric fans driven by a photovoltaic solar panel on top of the vent. The more recently developed models will work without direct sunlight, and the most expensive have rechargeable batteries so that the fan will keep operating even at night.

The main problem occurs during the long periods when a

boat is shut up and not used. Anti-condensation units that rely on moisture-absorbing granules may help, but the fact that water remains stored in their reservoir means that it can evaporate again and perhaps condense elsewhere in the cabin.

If your boat is kept in a marina, boatyard or anywhere that mains electricity is available, a dehumidifier can be used. Small ones have become available quite cheaply, and

Vents are needed to provide air circulation. In this case the louvred vent opens from the cabin into the wheelhouse.

Fitting a solar-powered ventilator

This type of solar-powered ventilator comes with a rubber ring that seals the unit against leaks. It can also be used to mark the hole to be cut in the cabin roof, both inside and outside.

A hole has to be cut in the cabin roof. This may cause some complications with headlining on the inside of the roof, so take care to locate it where there's likely to be the least difficulty and where there are no electrical wires under the headlining. Carefully take measurements inside and outside to locate the position of the vent. When you're sure you've got it right, drill a pilot hole through the roof from outside. Check inside that it's in the right position. If a circular rubber seal is provided with the vent, this can be used to draw the hole on the cabin roof.

Cut the hole through the roof and any headlining. It may be possible to do this with a circular-hole saw if you have one big enough. If not, use a combination of drilled holes and a keyhole saw. Depending on the type of headlining it may be better to use a sharp knife to cut the corresponding hole in it. Mark and drill the screw holes.

Apply a thin layer of sealant to the rubber seal and put some in each screw hole. Fit both the rubber sealing ring and the vent into the hole and screw or bolt it in place.

The vent is lowered into the hole and screwed in place. Be sure to put sealant in the screw holes to prevent any risk of rainwater leakage.

A grille can be fixed in place inside the cabin to provide a neater finish.

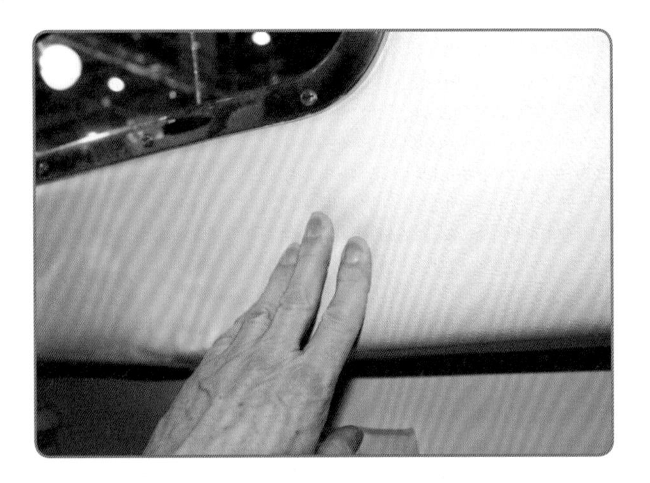

Foam-backed vinyl provides insulation and a soft surface.

Materials similar to thin carpet are used to line cabin interiors.

Sticking headlining to the awkward shapes inside a cabin takes some practice but looks good once complete.

they can be adjusted to come on only when humidity increases to a certain level. In this case cabin vents should be closed, otherwise you'll be trying to dehumidify the Earth's atmosphere!

Trying the above should remove the condensation problem. If not, increasing the insulation is the next method. Securely sticking a layer of insulating material on the curved and awkwardly shaped surfaces of a cabin's interior isn't easy, and takes careful planning. Purpose-designed and quite costly headlining materials are available, usually involving foam-backed vinyl or similar. Order more than you need, as you'll need some to practice with before you get it right.

Alternatives to commercial materials that have been used successfully on many boats, include thin carpet, carpet tiles, cork tiles and spray-on foam behind thin plywood panels.

When sticking up any type of insulation, keep the cabin doorway open and ensure there's plenty of ventilation, as harmful fumes will accumulate in the confined space. Read the instructions on adhesive products carefully. Accidental glue sniffing can lead to other accidents as you attempt to leave the boat in an intoxicated state!

Mould

An inevitable by-product of condensation is mould. Many paints, including the anti-condensation paint mentioned above, contain mould-killing chemicals, but don't expect them to last forever.

Plenty of anti-mould liquids are available and can be applied to surfaces, but take care to check whether they're safe to use in the confined space of a cabin, and ensure that you have plenty of ventilation. Strong bleach-containing preparations can give off choking fumes.

One product that's effective in removing mould inside a cabin and the

'Simply Gone' can be used to clean off mould and algae, and is advertised as being suitable to leave on GRP surfaces to prevent regrowth.

The diluted liquid is brushed or sprayed onto the mould or algae.

algae that forms on outside surfaces is 'Simply Gone', which has already been mentioned in Chapter 11. After treatment the mould turns black and is easy to remove with a wet sponge.

Smells

A locked-up cabin is very likely to accumulate musty odours – or worse. Any really bad smells needs to be investigated fully; they could be caused by leaks from a diesel engine, toilet or sink, accumulating and festering in the bilges. Decaying food and dead birds or rodents can also cause an appalling stink. Having removed and disinfected such horrors, any remaining smells are likely to be caused by the mould described in the preceding section. Improvements to ventilation and treatment of the mould should remove such odours.

However, even in the cleanest of cabins an infuriatingly persistent musty smell may still have to be dealt with. Household 'odour killers' usually just replace one smell with another that some find more acceptable. A product that actually removes smells is Adsorbex (http://www.adsorbex.co.uk), which is made from Zeolite, a granulated mineral formed by volcanic activity. An 'Adsorbex Multi Sachet' hung in a cabin can remove odours by trapping them. After a few months you place the bag outside in the sun to discharge the trapped smell, and it can then be reused. Loose Adsorbex powder can be used in the bilges, where there may be persistent smells.

Adsorbex powder and sachets help to remove odours, as does adequate ventilation.

Water and waste

Water can be carried and supplied on an open motor boat by using containers obtained from camping shops. These are often equipped with a tap, so the container can be mounted on a seat with a bowl underneath. Make sure that the container is made from 'food quality' material, otherwise it could contaminate drinking water.

Water can be provided in a small motor boat with a cuddy or cabin in the same way, though a pumped supply is more usual. Manually-operated pumps have an advantage over electric pumps in that they don't drain the battery. A variety of electric pumps are used on motor cruisers, and it's wise to have a spare pump or spare parts on the boat.

Water tanks, containers, pumps and pipes can become contaminated with bacteria and various mould growths, and should be sterilised at least annually with a suitable product such as Milton sterilising fluid or Puriclean powder. Remember to flush away the sterilising fluid thoroughly before refilling with fresh water.

Sterilising tablets or water filters can be used to improve the quality of stored water. Remember to change any filter fitted in the water supply pipes according to the instructions for your type of filter. An old exhausted filter can actually harbour bacteria, which it then adds

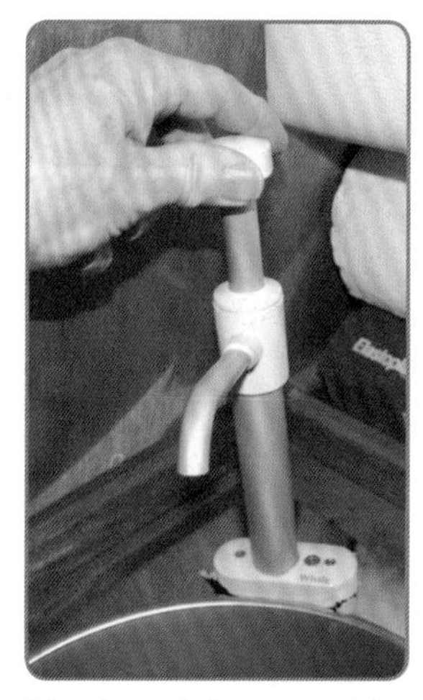

A hand-operated pump supplying water to the wash basin.

Below left: In a motor cruiser's cabin the water supply to the sink and washbasin is usually provided by an electric pump that comes on when the tap or a separate switch is operated.

Below right: An electric pump for the water supply is usually accessible in a locker under a bunk or in a cupboard.

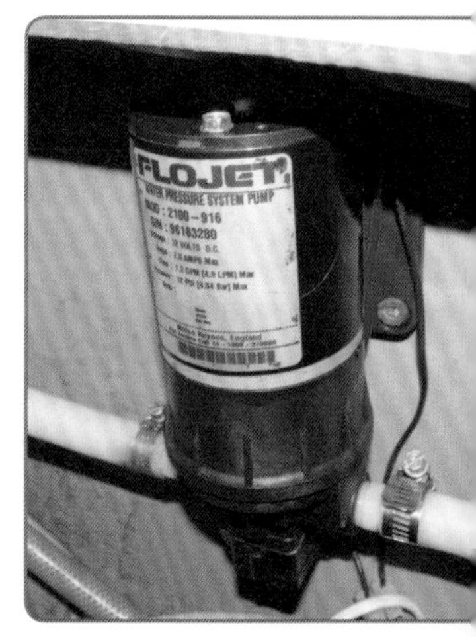

A rail-mounted barbecue device.

to the water that passes through it. If you have any doubts about the quality of the water from your tank, have a separate container of drinking water that you can trust or drink the cheaper varieties of bottled mineral water.

The simplest way to dispose of washing water is to use a bowl and empty it over the side. However, most motor cruisers have sinks and washbasins drained by a waste pipe discharging through the hull.

The main points to check regarding your water supply are that there are no leaks allowing dirty water – and smells – to accumulate in the bilges, and that the waste pipes stay firmly attached to the fitting that goes through the hull. This is a point where water can leak into the boat and is a cause of boats sinking.

Before the winter lay-up period, disinfect the drain pipe from the sink and place plugs in sink drain holes to prevent any odours. Also, in order to avoid frost damage during the winter you should drain all water tanks, pumps, pipes and any appliances that may still contain any water.

Cooking equipment

The most common fuel used for cooking aboard boats is bottled gas. However, there are alternatives. When using an open motor boat and camping ashore, driftwood can be collected for a genuine, original-style barbecue on the beach. Of course, portable barbecue kits can also be used ashore.

Some barbecue devices are available for use mounted on the boat itself, such as a pushpit rail overhanging the stern, but great care needs to be taken in order to avoid burning more than just the food. Also consider where the smell and the smoke is going, since other people may not enjoy the aroma and will prefer to breathe fresh sea air.

Portable gas stoves using disposable canisters have become available very cheaply and are fine when used ashore camping-style, and in accordance with the instructions provided with the cooker. However, they aren't designed specifically for use on a boat and don't have pan clamps to hold pans in place if the boat moves. Consequently their use aboard a boat is very risky, and they certainly shouldn't be used on a moving boat. Even on an apparently calm mooring some inconsiderate boat owner may pass too fast, creating a hazardous wash that might dislodge a portable cooker or its unsecured pans of boiling water.

Disposable gas canisters should not be stored in the cabin, but should be stored in the same way as large gas cylinders: in a flame-proof container ventilated to the outside of the boat. Even when apparently empty, the canisters leak heavier-than-air gas that must be vented overboard and not allowed to get into the cabin or bilges.

You have to be sure any cooking equipment is securely fixed in place on the cooker, to allow for the unpredictable movements of the boat. This is particularly important for seagoing cruisers. Cookers installed on cruisers may have pan clamps or a framework of 'fiddles' (also called 'sea rails') round the burners to hold pans in place, or 'gimbals' to keep the cooker level. If not already installed, such fittings can usually be purchased as extras from cooker manufacturers, including Calor, and from dealers. They're fairly straightforward to clip or screw in place.

Various types of clamps are available to hold kettles and pans in place on a cooker.

Ensure that curtains and other inflammable materials are kept well away from the cooker and won't fall onto it with the movement of the boat.

Filling a large stainless steel vacuum flask with hot water before setting off is one way of avoiding having to use a cooker whilst actually cruising, by providing the hot water needed to make soup or a cup of tea.

Gas installations

Bottled LPG (liquefied petroleum gas) installations should always be installed and repaired by a Corgi-registered fitter experienced in working on boats. Doing such work yourself involves considerable and unacceptable risks of gas leakage, fire and explosion, and not involving a Corgi-registered fitter will probably invalidate your boat insurance. Fire in the confined space of a boat is particularly dangerous and frightening, so every precaution should be taken to avoid the risk of gas explosions.

Burning gas gives off harmful fumes including carbon monoxide. Sadly, every year there are cases of deaths where people have died by inhaling these fumes on boats. Adequate ventilation is therefore vital when using gas. Permanent adequate ventilation is a requirement of the BSS certification for inland waterways and this sets the standard for all boats. A carbon monoxide alarm, similar to a smoke alarm, can be purchased and installed in the cabin.

LPG bottles should be stored and secured in an upright position somewhere that any heavier-than-air gas leakages can escape rather than accumulating in the bilges. For this you'll need a storage unit sealed from the rest of the boat and with ventilation from the base of the storage space to the outside. Make sure that such vents are always clear and unobstructed. The storage unit mustn't contain any electrical equipment because of the risk of a spark igniting the gas.

Always turn off the gas supply at the cylinder when it's not in use. This normally involves either screwing closed a valve by means of a turn-wheel on the cylinder or turning off a switch on the regulator. The regulator connected to the pipework has a sealing washer that should be replaced regularly. Be sure to buy the correct type of replacement washer for this.

The drain to the outside of the boat for any leaking gas can be seen at the bottom of this purpose-made gas storage unit, which is sealed off from the rest of the boat.

The flexible hose that connects metal gas pipes to the regulator attached to the gas cylinder deteriorates with use and exposure to sunlight. Such hoses should be replaced at five-year intervals, or sooner if there are signs of deterioration (such as loss of flexibility or cracking where the hose joins metal pipes). A date on the side of the hose should show when it left the factory.

Although amateurs shouldn't carry out work on a gas system, it's obviously important to check for leaks. LPG has a smell added to it, so warning of leaks should reach your nose. A leak detection liquid can be applied to the equipment with a brush to investigate where the leak is coming from, but the problem here is that gas will be seeping down to be trapped in the bilges while you're trying

The gas supply to individual appliances may have valves that can be turned off, but you should always turn off the gas supply at the cylinder when not in use.

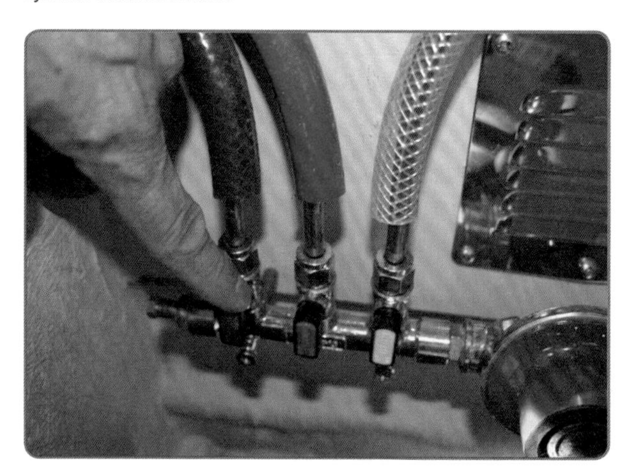

to find the leak. It's therefore best to turn off the gas as soon as you suspect a leak and get a Corgi-registered engineer to do the necessary work. A properly installed gas system will have a testing point where the engineer can use a tester to check for leaks.

At the risk of stating the very obvious, don't light a naked flame or turn on any electrical equipment that might cause a spark if a gas leak is suspected.

The use of washing-up liquid is sometimes recommended to find a leak, as the escaping gas will blow bubbles in a smear of the liquid. Unfortunately, however, washing-up liquid contains salt, which can cause corrosion of the metal components in the gas system. If proper leak-detection liquid isn't available and you decide to use washing-up liquid, it's essential to wash it off thoroughly and promptly with clean water.

A gas cooker on a boat should have a 'flame failure device' to turn the gas off if the flame goes out, thus preventing leakage of gas. When you want to light this type of cooker you have to hold in a knob for a time to disengage the device.

If the gas flame on a cooker's burner flickers yellow and soot can be seen deposited on pans, it shows the gas isn't burning fully. The cooker must be turned off and corrected by a qualified gas engineer before being used again.

Fire precautions

Suitable fire extinguishers and a fire blanket should be easily accessible in the cabin. Extinguishers must be in date and inspected regularly according to manufacturers' recommendations. A smoke alarm should also be installed.

A fire blanket and fire extinguishers should be mounted within easy reach.

Alcohol/methylated spirit cookers

An alternative to gas is the Origo cooker, which uses unpressurised denatured alcohol or methylated spirits. Origo cookers are safer than the old pressurised alcohol/paraffin stoves still found on older boats, and many people consider them to be safer than gas. They're certainly much less complicated to install safely than gas cookers. Even though they're quite expensive, you should compare their price with the cost of getting a Corgi-qualified engineer in to install or repair and refit a gas installation.

Having no gas installed and using an Origo cooker should make it much easier to get a BSS safety certificate, which is essential if you want to use your cruiser on inland waterways. Adequate ventilation is still important with this and any type of cooker in the confined space of a cabin.

Origo cookers.

Sanitary equipment

Toilets may be available in marinas, but there's no escaping the fact that if any length of time is to be spent afloat a suitable receptacle will be needed on board.

On a small motor boat with just a cuddy and a simple bucket-type toilet it's tempting to empty this overboard in the style of 'bucket and chuck it'. Stop and think, though, of the consequences of everyone doing this. The Victorians may have thought the solution to pollution was dilution but they were wrong. Pollutants, harmful bacteria, parasites and viruses can accumulate and persist to poison us – and wildlife. This was discovered on the Norfolk Broads many years ago, and the hundreds of hire boats had to be fitted with toilets that have holding tanks, to be pumped out into sewage disposal systems at boatyards.

The simplest arrangement is the chemical toilet. This can be a bucket-type container with a suitable detachable seat. You need to ensure, though, that the seat doesn't detach as the boat moves... It's also important to refit the watertight clip-on cover after use in order to prevent spillage, which inevitably reaches the bilges to haunt you for months.

A more advanced version less likely to leak is the flushing cassette toilet. This has a water tank incorporated in the top half, under the seat, and a handle is operated to flush the contents of the bowl into the holding tank in the bottom half, where a diluted chemical treats the waste and its smell. The servicing of cassette toilets mainly involves cleaning and the frequent lubrication of its moving parts, which have a tendency to stick shut if neglected.

Chemical fluids for toilets have improved in recent years

A compact portable flushing chemical toilet with its own holding tank.

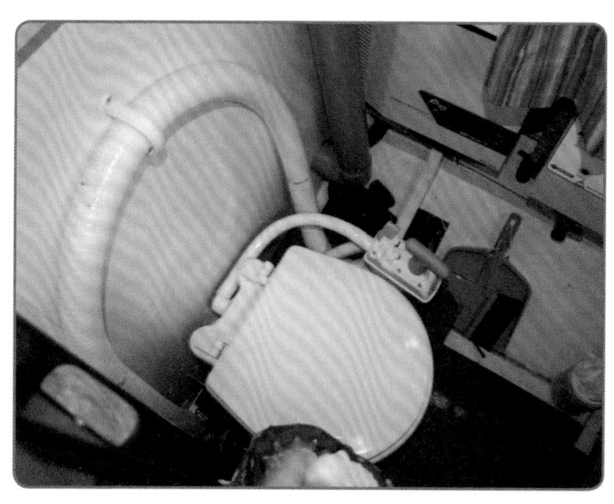

A fixed flushing toilet with a separate holding tank.

and many are much more environmentally friendly. Even so, the contents of the holding tank must still not be emptied into waterways and should be deposited in the disposal points available at some boatyards. If this is a problem, they can be emptied into a domestic sewage drain at home, a little at a time, and flushed with plenty of water from a hose, to prevent blocking the drain.

Larger motor cruisers may have fixed toilets with storage tanks that need to be pumped out at a boatyard. Similar toilets that still get away with discharging into the sea may be found on some boats but these really should only be discharged well out to sea.

Fixed sea toilets are usually found in offshore cruisers beyond the size of boats covered by this book, and their servicing is more complicated. If you do have a toilet of this type, maintenance tasks will include maintaining pipes that go through holes in the hull, and ensuring that sea water can't leak into the boat. Instructions appropriate to this type of toilet should be followed carefully and professional help should be sought when there's any risk of leakage – either of sewage or the sea water used for flushing, which could end up flushing the whole boat if not properly maintained.

Much useful information on environmentally friendly boating can be found at http://www.thegreenblue.org.uk.

Bunks and cushion care

There are likely to be problems with foam cushions on a boat – it can be difficult to keep them dry, so waterproof covers or even thick polythene bags should be used to protect them from damp clothing, dirt and the spray that always seems to find its way into a fast seagoing motor boat.

The long periods when motor cruisers aren't in use, such as during the winter lay-up, mean condensation and mould can contaminate foam cushions. To avoid this, ensure good ventilation and remove the cushions when the boat is going to be left unoccupied for any length of time. Ideally they should be kept in dry, reasonably warm storage at home.

On a well-used cruiser, cushion covers will eventually need to be replaced. Cautious owners of older cruisers may choose to replace the cushions with fire-resistant covers and what's sometimes called 'combustion modified' foam, to reduce fire risk. If the cushions have become compressed, an alternative to complete replacement is to use an extra top-up layer of foam inside the cover.

The covers can usually be removed from cushions by unzipping or by untying tapes. They can then be washed at a suitable temperature that will avoid damage or shrinkage. Stretch-covers can be ordered as replacements. Companies supplying these can sometimes provide quite cheap ready-made covers for standard-sized rectangular cushions. Unfortunately, however, on a boat the cushions are more likely to have a tapering shape, which requires covers to be made to measure – a more expensive course of action, though adequate expertise with a sewing machine can keep the cost down. That way the covers could be made from suitable material, but it may be worth considering the purchase of ready-made rectangular covers and then altering them to the necessary shape, with the excess

Cushions usually rest on the lids of storage compartments. Condensation can accumulate here so it's wise to lift and ventilate them occasionally.

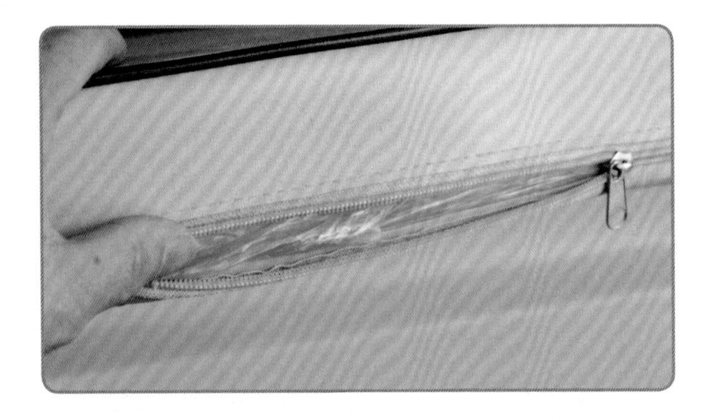

Cushion covers can usually be unzipped for cleaning.

Floor coverings

The cabin floorboards may be painted or varnished with a non-slip surface. Adding a floor covering may make the cabin more comfortable and homely, but will it provide a suitable surface to walk on when the boat is moving? If you're satisfied it will be non-slip, a clean and attractively coloured floor covering is the first thing you see as you climb down into the cabin and it certainly makes a difference.

material being hidden under the cushion. Not the most elegant solution, but one that could keep costs down. Alternatively, cushion cover companies will provide instructions that will enable you to measure your cushions and order covers to fit.

Curtains

Some crewmembers may have strong feelings about the degree of privacy available in a cabin. Being aware of this problem and finding a solution to it will help you persuade the more reluctant members to cruise with you.

The problem with curtains on windows is the fact that the boat moves and tends to open gaps between and under them. A few well-placed pegs from the washing line can help close the gaps, but more effective is a line, rail or expandable curtain wire fixed to hold the bottom of each curtain against the window.

Lights in the cabin can throw shadows on the curtains providing an entertaining shadow performance for onlookers. Thicker, lined curtains or the installation of blinds may help here.

The bottoms of curtains need to be secured back against the window.

Velcro can be used to hold curtains in place.

Blinds improve privacy.

A cockpit canopy provides shelter for the helm and extra accommodation.

Canopies and covers

On a cruiser, a cockpit canopy can extend the cabin accommodation substantially. This is usually secured in place by eyes in the cover and turnbuckles screwed to the boat, or by rubber or elastic loops on its edges that fit over hooks.

The eye fits over a turnbuckle, which is turned to secure it.

It's important to ensure that all the fittings are firm and secure. If some of them should fail during a gale, the canopy will flap and rapidly deteriorate. When some types of rubber fittings perish it can be difficult to find the correct-sized replacements. If necessary they can be replaced with elastic loops instead.

As a canopy ages the seams are likely to fail before the actual fabric does. Use a strong thread to restitch the seams as soon as there's any sign of broken stitches, on the principle that 'a stitch in time saves nine'.

Unfortunately the actual fabric of the canopy will eventually deteriorate, discolour and fail, and it can't be revived. Buying a new one is a major expense. Canopies and covers are usually made of reinforced PVC fabric or polyester and cotton, although breathable materials are available which are less likely to attract condensation. Plenty of companies provide made-to-measure covers but the material can also be purchased for DIY.

If you, or someone you know, is skilled in the use of a suitable sewing machine, it may be worth making your own canopy. The panels of the old canopy can be used as a pattern. The tough material may be a challenge for some sewing machines, so in the interests of domestic harmony take care to consult other users of the machine first. Tools are available for punching holes and fitting metal eyes to the

Elastic loops can be used to replace perished rubber fittings when necessary.

Canopy seams should be restitched as soon as any broken threads are spotted, otherwise the seam will quickly come undone.

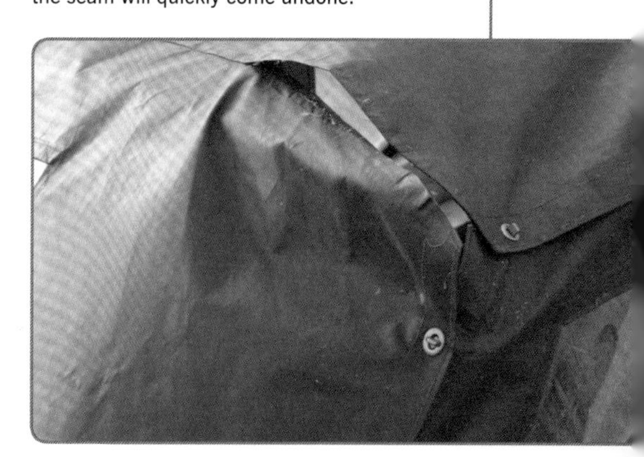

The first sign that a plastic canopy window is about to fail is likely to be a loss of transparency. It then becomes brittle and splits. Such windows can be replaced, but it's likely that at this stage of deterioration the whole canopy will need replacement.

edges of covers. Take care to get the holes and fastenings in exactly the right positions to match the fittings on the boat.

Canopy care

Cleaning the canopy regularly helps to extend its life. Use well diluted soap – such as washing-up liquid – and clean water, with a sponge. Rinse the soap off thoroughly. Don't use harsh cleaning chemicals or anything abrasive that might scratch the material. Occasional use of purpose-designed cleaning and reproofing products can be worthwhile, since these contain protection against the degradation of material caused by UV light; they can be purchased at chandlers. Alternatively the products used for cleaning and protecting car soft tops may be suitable, depending on the type of material used in the canopy. Duck muck and seagull droppings contain a chemical that may burn into the fabric, so try to remove them as soon as you can.

The press-studs and turnbuckles should be lubricated with a little Vaseline, which can also be effective in helping to waterproof canopy seams.

Sometimes, when in a hurry, canopy side panels are unzipped and thrown over the roof of the boat. However, this can crease the windows and distort and damage the zips. You should always roll up the side panels carefully in order to avoid creasing, which eventually leads to cracking of the flexible plastic windows and fabric.

Various cleaning and treatment products are available to help extend the life of canopy materials.

Laying up and winterisation

Apart from a few determined enthusiasts with suitably equipped motor boats, most boat owners in the UK lay up their boats for the winter. Many of the measures necessary to protect the stored boat have been covered above in connection with the cabin, and in earlier chapters, but the following important points should also be noted.

Insurance

Ensure your cover continues throughout the winter and that your insurance company is aware and approves of the boat's storage location and security. The darker nights of winter, along with severe winter weather, mean there are still risks that need to be covered. Insurance companies usually indicate their requirements in their policy documents and tend to expect that a boat will be laid up in a reasonably secure and safe location. They may require a motor cruiser to be ashore by a certain date and for certain months of the year. If this isn't possible or there's a delay, consult the company about it and get an extension, otherwise the insurance cover may cease to apply.

If the boat is kept away from home, the insurance company is likely to require that you or someone reliable checks it regularly, such as every month.

If taking a boat of any size home on a trailer, check that the insurance covers road transport and ensure that the trailer, which may have been neglected for months, is fully roadworthy.

Preparation for the winter

Tie the boat down to reduce the possibility of autumn gales blowing it over. The supports for boats on land will need to be strong and stable enough not only to cope with the weight of the boat but also to resist the pressure of violent gusts of wind.

Ensure the trim of the boat is angled to allow rainwater to drain off the decks and elsewhere.

Outboard motors must be removed to safe, secure storage along with any items that could be damaged by the wind or stolen. Unfortunately there have been cases of propellers being stolen for their value as scrap metal, so either remove the propeller or ensure the boat is stored in such a way that the risk is minimised.

The start of winter is also a good time to identify tasks that need to be done before the next boating season. Make a list and organise the tasks into groups that can be done at various appropriate stages during the winter. Either carry these out yourself or arrange in good time for the boatyard to do the work.

Wash and dry the boat thoroughly to remove dirt and salt, which can attract moisture. If left outside, small open boats normally used with removable outboard motors can be kept turned upside down and supported clear of the ground.

The cabin of a motor cruiser should be emptied of removable equipment such as GPS and VHF radio if possible. Drain water tanks and containers, as they could get damaged by frost. Tie labels in prominent places to remind you to replace equipment and what needs to be done to re-commission the winterised engine or outboard motor. (See Chapter 17 for more on engines).

Well-fitting covers are a useful protection when laying up a boat of any size for the winter. Ensure that they're really tight and firmly tied down – flapping covers can do considerable damage. If possible, allow some circulation of air. This helps to stop condensation in a cabin, where damp, mould and rot can affect wood and soft furnishings. Ideally bunk cushions and bedding should be taken home and kept indoors if storage space allows.

It's difficult getting the balance right between providing adequate ventilation and keeping out rain, insects and intruders. A flow of air is the best protection against condensation leading to mould and smells. Fine-meshed netting can keep out the birds, wasps, bees and flies that find boat cabins, lockers and engine compartments ideal homes for the winter.

Water left in the bilges can evaporate and cause condensation. Try to check regularly for rainwater accumulation and pump out any that appears.

The above precautions may be rather tedious, but they help to ensure a trouble-free start to the next boating season.

Winter covers help to keep a boat clean and dry but need to be carefully and firmly secured.

16 Electrical equipment

Various types of 12V batteries are available for use on boats.

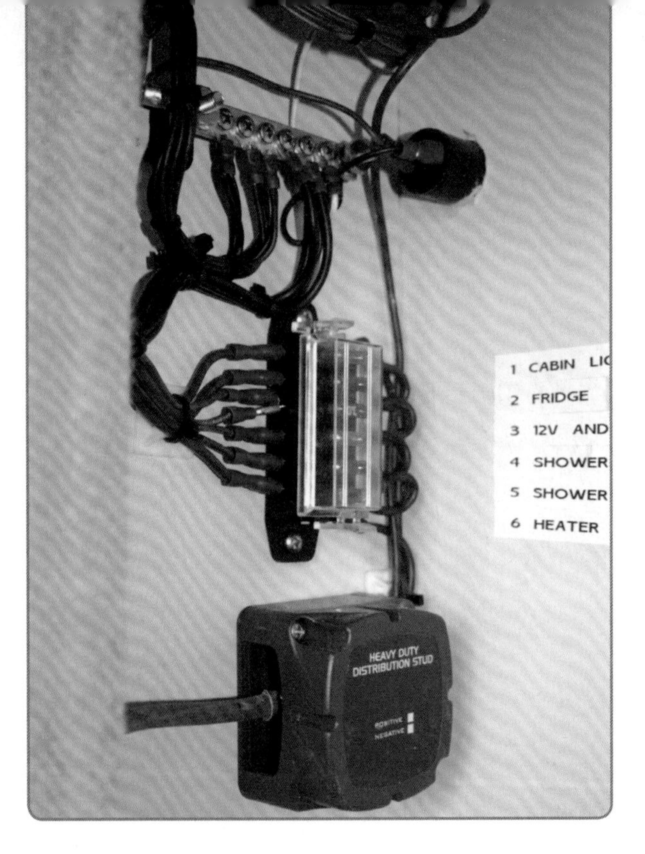

All batteries must be mounted securely in a ventilated location so that the explosive gases they emit can escape. Check the ventilation is kept clear of obstructions.

12V electricity

A 12V starter battery will be connected to the engine on motor cruisers, and to many outboard motors on other types of boat. This battery is designed to deliver a very large amount of current in a short time. It's *not* designed to be deeply discharged by supplying electricity to lights and equipment – a separate battery needs to be available for this, as it's obviously important that the starter battery is kept in good condition in order to start the engine.

The additional 12V battery for use with electrical equipment should be of the deep cycle marine leisure variety and should be securely mounted in a ventilated location. Its purpose is to supply lighting (including navigation lights) and to power equipment such as a VHF radio. Unfortunately, as the need for electricity increases so does the complexity of the wiring and equipment. Using electricity in a watery environment means that installation must be carried out to a high standard, preferably by someone qualified to do it. Good quality equipment must be used to avoid rapid deterioration, including adequate fuses and a battery isolator switch. Carrying out such installation work is beyond the scope of this book, and care needs to be taken to ensure that it's done professionally in order to satisfy both your insurance company and the BSS requirements for inland waterways. Here we are mainly concerned with maintenance tasks rather than the installation of an electrical system and its associated equipment.

Problems can arise as the amount of electrical devices expands to include depth sounding and navigation equipment, and you must take great care not to overdo things, as this can put considerable demands on the battery.

Each battery should have an isolation switch that must be turned on to start the engine and use electrical equipment. These switches vary in style and location but are usually found quite close to the battery.

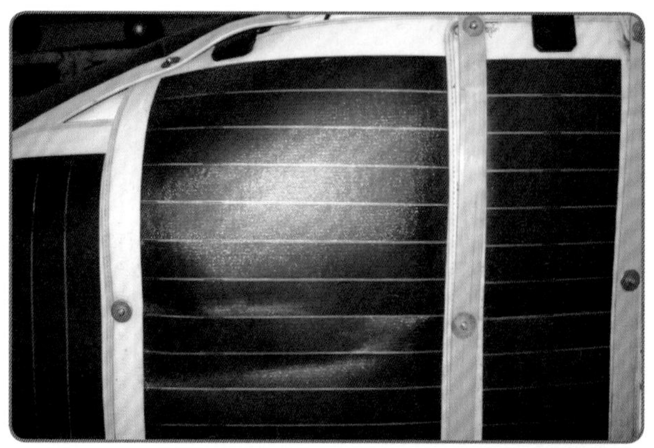

Both rigid and flexible solar panels are available to charge batteries.

Battery charging

Many outboard motors and most engine installations will charge the boat's batteries when cruising. However, running a noisy motor to charge the battery whilst stationary at a mooring is a major cause of disputes with other waterway users hoping for a peaceful time. Using a petrol generator is an alternative that might be considered, but many types of generator are as noisy as the engine, and are heavy and awkward pieces of equipment unless properly and permanently installed.

Charging using sun and wind

Photovoltaic solar panels and wind-powered chargers have been developed for use on boats. These have become much more efficient in recent years and solar panels can generate a useful amount of electricity in daylight even without direct sunlight. However, on a small motor cruiser it's unlikely there'll be enough space to mount sufficient panels to match your electricity use during a cruise. There is, though, a good chance that a substantial recharge could be achieved on summer weekdays if the boat is used only at weekends.

If you do have enough space to mount substantial solar panels or a wind generator, blocking diodes are needed in the wire leading to the battery in order to prevent the current flowing the wrong way. A regulator is also needed where substantial current will be supplied to the battery – particularly with a wind generator. This monitors the condition of the battery and controls the amount of charge reaching it. Without it the battery could be overcharged, damaged or could even explode.

Interesting advances with thin film solar panels by companies such as Nanosolar Inc in San Jose, California, promise to make electricity available from daylight at much lower cost in the near future.

Though a wind turbine can generate much more power than solar panels it can be difficult finding a suitable place to mount the equipment safely and effectively. Unfortunately some noise and vibration may also be experienced in the

The wind can provide a substantial amount of electricity to charge batteries.

If the necessary fittings have been professionally installed in a boat, mains electricity can be used to charge batteries at many marinas and at some public moorings.

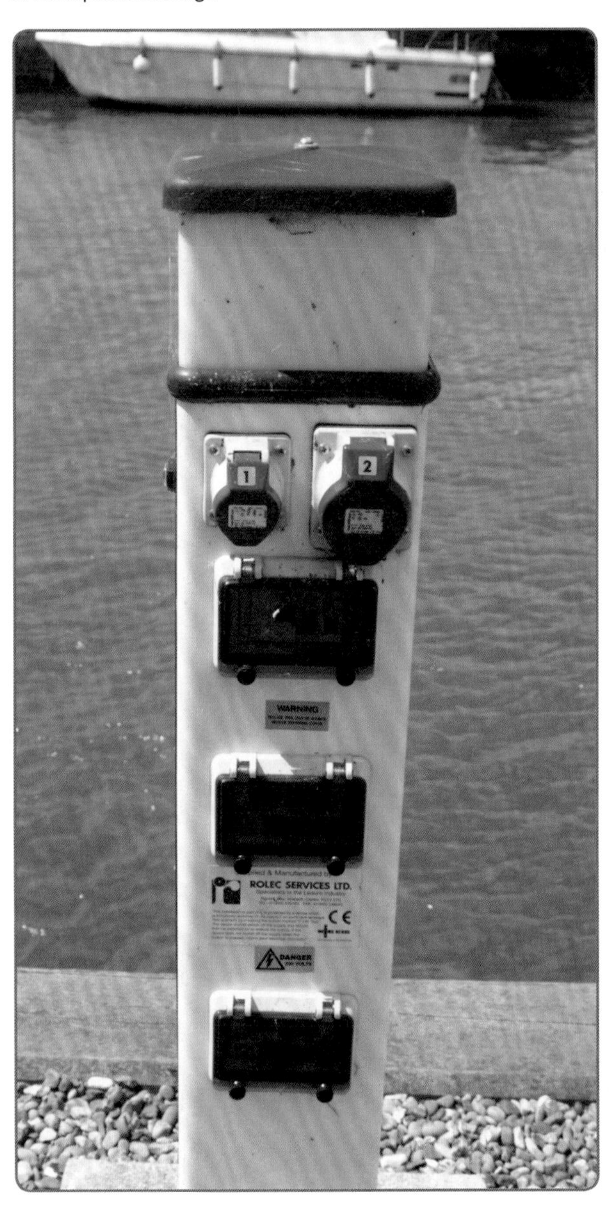

boat, but this should be much less than that felt when running the engine to charge the batteries.

Charging with mains power

Using mains shore power to recharge the battery is possible if it's available at a mooring and if all the necessary equipment and safety precautions have been installed by a suitably qualified engineer. For example, a residual current device (RCD) is an essential safety precaution in order to cut off the electricity supply when there's any risk of electrocution. So too are connectors designed for use with the power supply. Obviously, mains electricity is particularly hazardous in a wet environment and all parts of a mains system need adequate protection from rain, water splashes and bilge water as well as from the ever-present sea or river water.

If shore power isn't available, removing the battery and charging it at home between cruises may sometimes be necessary to be sure of a full charge.

Mains connected battery chargers need to be chosen to suit the type and capacity of battery. Basic chargers for car batteries are best avoided, as they can overcharge and damage the batteries used in boats. Much better are the more sophisticated automatic chargers that monitor the state of the battery and adjust the rate of charge accordingly. Gel-filled batteries also need a charger specifically designed for them.

Safety

The Boat Safety Scheme has quite lengthy regulations for electrical systems, which form part of the compulsory inspection and certification process for boats on inland waterways. The regulations are available both in printed form and online from its website at http://www.boatsafetyscheme.com.

The BSS regulations set standards, which should, as far as possible, be achieved or exceeded, by all boats used in coastal waters even though this isn't currently a legal requirement.

Battery isolator switches should be easily accessible and used to turn off the electrical supply when necessary.

Working with batteries

- Wear eye protection when working with batteries. A battery may eject drops of acid when the plugs are removed, particularly if it has been gassing during charging.
- Don't connect or disconnect any wires to the battery when it is open with plugs removed.
- Never use a naked flame near a battery.
- Have a fire extinguisher suitable for electrical fires near the battery compartment.
- Use rubber gloves when cleaning any spillage from the battery.
- Battery acid must be washed off skin and clothes immediately in order to avoid burns and damage.
- Take care to prevent salt water getting into a battery otherwise highly toxic chlorine gas can be given off.

If a spare battery is carried in the boat it should be securely fixed in a battery box.

As with all aspects of boat maintenance, check your insurance policy for requirements concerning electrical equipment installation and maintenance in order to ensure that the insurance cover is maintained.

Basic regular safety checks

Check that 12V batteries stay secured in their installed positions with adequate ventilation to the outside of the boat. The battery gives off explosive lighter-than-air hydrogen and oxygen gases, which must not be allowed to accumulate in the boat.

The battery must not be able to move and should be enclosed in a purpose-designed battery box to contain any battery acid that might leak from it.

Sealed batteries or gel batteries can be used to prevent problems of leakage. However, gel batteries are more expensive than lead acid batteries and instructions supplied with them concerning recharging with the correct type of charger must be followed.

Never leave any loose metallic objects such as spanners near a battery, where, with the inevitable movement of the boat, they may fall across the terminals and result in sparks and a fire. A short-circuit across battery terminals can melt a screwdriver in seconds.

Fuses provided in the wiring system should always be replaced with the correct rating of fuse. Always investigate and rectify the fault that has caused the fuse to blow before replacing the fuse. Ignoring the problem could result in a fire.

12V batteries are heavy and care needs to be taken to avoid injury when lifting them. Moving one from a dinghy to a boat on a mooring takes care and planning. Otherwise both you and the battery could descend into the depths.

Maintenance

Probably the most frequent cause of electrical failure, apart from a flat battery, is a loose or corroded electrical connection. A saltwater environment is inclined to increase this problem. Check, clean and tighten all connections frequently.

Keep the top of the battery clean and dry and ensure the battery terminals are clean and tight. Avoid corrosion and the appearance of the white substance that develops on battery terminals by applying Vaseline. A battery loses its charge over time whether or not it is connected. The loss rate can be one per cent per day depending on temperature

Spare fuses are kept with these electrical connections, which are normally protected behind a slide-on cover.

Apply Vaseline to battery terminals.

Top-up the battery with distilled water when necessary.

and surrounding conditions. Dirty and damp conditions accelerate the rate of loss.

Check the electrolyte level by unscrewing the plugs on top of the battery and topping up with distilled water when necessary. In most batteries this involves covering the top edges of the plates with no more than a centimetre depth of water. Any more than this and the acid solution will leak out when the battery is charged. If a flat battery is charged at a high voltage to revitalise it the resulting gassing tends to result in a reduction in electrolyte level, so it's particularly important to check this after it's been charged and the gassing has stopped.

Although a deep cycle leisure battery is designed to be deeply discharged, it will last much longer if it's seldom discharged below 50 per cent of its capacity. Occasionally using up to 80 per cent of its charge can be tolerated, but complete discharge will damage it and may mean it can't be recharged.

The use of an electrical meter is the easiest way to check the battery's charge. First, check that nothing is taking power from the battery. Turning off the battery isolator switch is the best way to do this. Then measure the voltage across the battery terminals by placing the probes directly on the battery terminals. If the voltage is between 12.6 and 12.8 or higher, it's fully charged. At 12.2V it's about 50 per cent, and at 12V, 25 per cent. At 12V or less a battery is unlikely to start an engine and at 11.7V or less it's flat. If the engine has been running the voltage will usually be high, and you should allow a little time for the battery to return to normal before taking readings.

A hydrometer can also be used unless it's a sealed or gel battery. This measures the amount of acid in the battery. The concentration becomes less as the battery discharges, so measuring it shows the battery's condition. A hydrometer can be obtained from a car accessory shop, but check it's the type to be used with a battery rather than the different type used to check the condition of antifreeze. Be aware that with a hydrometer, there's the risk of drips of acid burning holes in your clothing and skin.

Using an electrical meter to check the condition of the battery – in this case it's fully charged.

Where equipment has been installed and connected on a small motor boat it may have been connected directly to the battery, to a bus bar, to the battery isolation switch, to a circuit breaker or to a point on a switch panel that incorporates fuses. Whatever the situation, the wiring should be protected by a suitable fuse. Check the ratings of all fuses and make sure you have corresponding spares. Never be tempted to bypass the fuse with a length of wire.

Keep spare fuses in a small plastic container with a lid. Fasten this container firmly alongside the fuse panel so that you can find it easily.

If it's necessary at any time to replace a length of electrical wire always use wire which has the same diameter as the original or larger. Because of the amount of movement on a boat the wire must be able to flex without being damaged, so don't use single-strand wire. Always use multi-strand marine grade wire.

When the boat is unused in the winter, remove the batteries. Recharge them preferably every month.

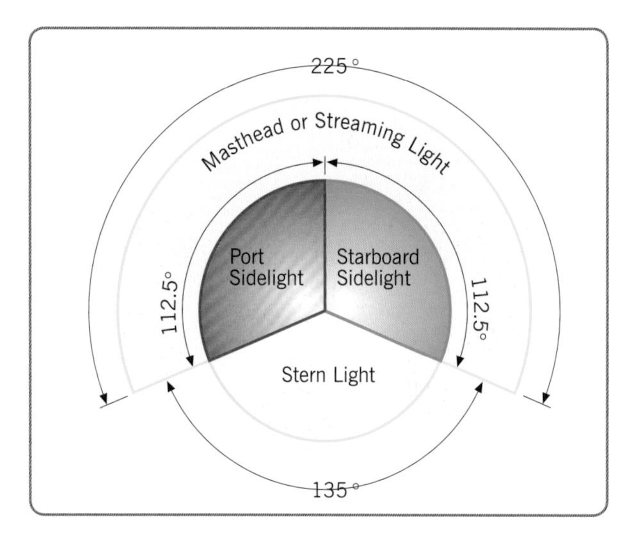

This is the 'light rose', which shows how navigation lights should be arranged to be visible around a boat.

Navigation lights

Cruising at night is only for the experienced boat owner who has learned all about it on a suitable course. You do, though, need to be prepared for an occasion where you may find yourself delayed and still cruising after dark unexpectedly. The main consideration is to avoid a collision by being seen by other vessels.

Motor cruisers should have 12V navigation lights permanently installed and those over 7m should show an all-round white light when at anchor.

Navigation lights should be arranged with red on the port (left-hand) side, green on the starboard (right-hand) side and white at the stern. A white light should be mounted at least 1m above the sidelights. This may be mounted on a small 'mast'.

On an open day boat with no 12V supply, a powerful and reliable torch and white lantern are needed, along with a set of three emergency navigation lights in red, green and white, using alkaline batteries. Spare batteries are also needed. These lights are available from chandlers.

Navigation lights can be seen mounted on these boats, including a white light on a small mast. Spotlights have also been mounted on the roof of one boat.

The lenses of navigation lights need to be checked for damage or deterioration and replaced as necessary.

A set of emergency navigation lights with internal batteries. These can be kept on any boat as an emergency back-up in case a fault develops in the 12V system.

Interior lighting

Most motor cruisers have 12V interior lights. Fluorescent lights use less electrical current than ordinary bulbs, but if you need to replace existing lights consider using light emitting diodes (LED), which take very little from the battery. LED navigation lights are also available.

On small boats with cuddies or small cabins and no 12V electrical system, LED torches and other battery-powered lights provide simple cabin illumination, provided sufficient spare batteries are carried. These can be adequate on inland waterways and very sheltered coastal creeks and estuaries.

A push-switch LED light with its own batteries.

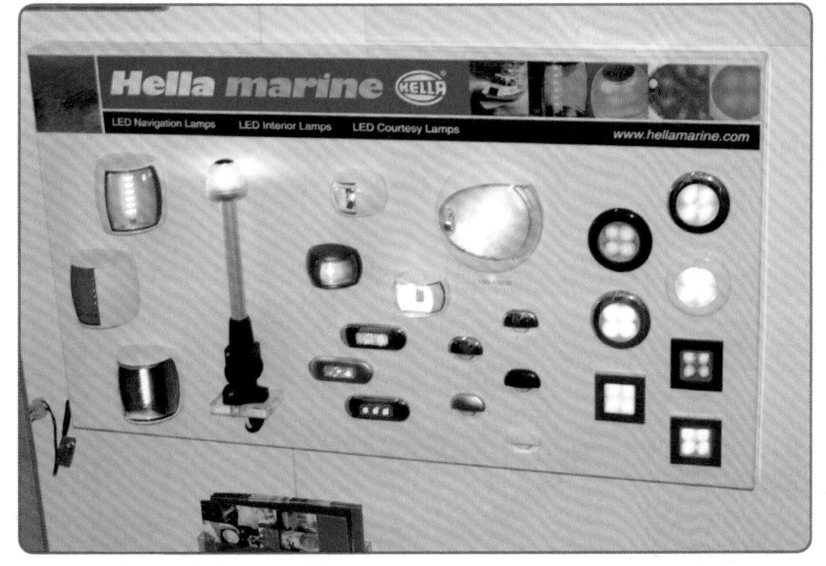

Plenty of bright 12V light-emitting diode (LED) lights are available. They have the advantage of saving battery power as they use very little electricity compared with other lights.

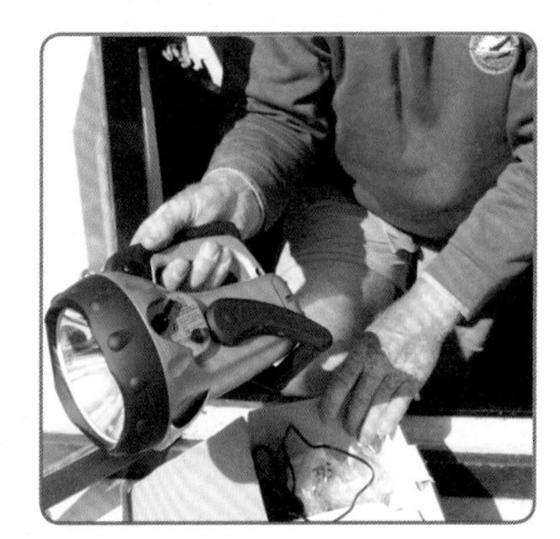

A rechargeable hand-held spotlight may also have a 12V connection.

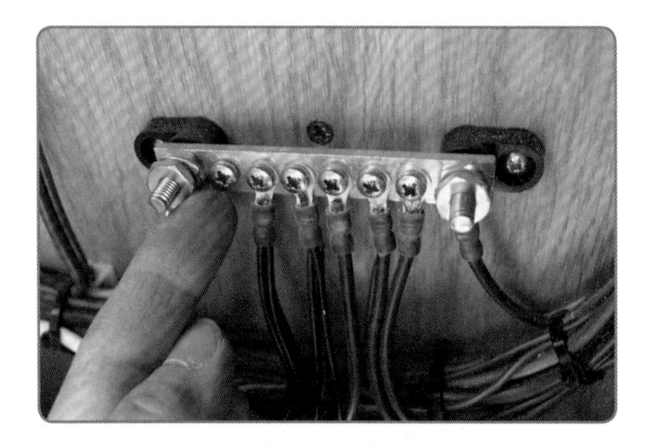

A cable for a new electrical appliance can be attached to a vacant terminal on the bus bar.

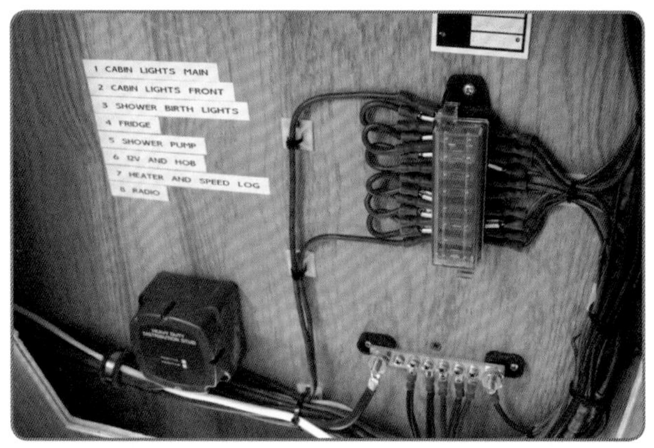

Fuses, connections and labels are neatly laid out in this Viking motor cruiser.

Neat dome-shaped, push-switch-operated LED lights powered by three 1.5V alkaline batteries are available very cheaply and can be stuck around the inside of a small cabin. These can also provide useful emergency back-up lighting on boats with 12V electricity.

Adding extra electrical equipment

The instructions that come with new or replacement 12V electrical equipment will indicate where to locate the unit, and the power supply required. In order to avoid interference from electrical currents, take care where you route the cables for the transducer of a fish-finder or for a VHF aerial cable.

Electrical items such as a VHF radio, GPS or fish-finder are normally mounted near the steering wheel. The battery is near the engine. There are many ways in which boats of various ages will have been wired and their equipment connected, and if you encounter a confusing 'birds' nest' of wires a wise course of action is to get an electrician to sort it out and identify safe connection points before you add any extra equipment, in order to avoid overloading wiring you don't understand.

In many well organised wiring systems a metal bar called a 'bus bar' is provided for connecting 12V electrical equipment. This has a number of terminals and is located behind or near the steering console, and the negative cable from the battery is connected to it. The negative wire for a new electrical unit is connected to a vacant terminal.

The heavy-duty positive cable runs from the battery to an isolating switch and then to a fuse panel, which can be found near the negative bus bar. The positive cable is connected to one side of each fuse in the fuse panel. Electrical appliance positive leads are connected to the other side of each fuse either directly or via another bus bar. When connecting a new electrical appliance check with the instructions to ensure that a correctly rated fuse is used, and change it if necessary. Label the new connection with the name of the appliance.

If wire isn't supplied with the electrical unit, use wire rated for the amperage load in a marine 12V system. Don't use household wiring, which may break or corrode in use

Electrical equipment, such as navigation and communication devices, can be connected to a 12V system, but take care to ensure that it can cope with the loads and that adequate fuses are installed.

The cables in this seagoing Guernsey motor cruiser have been well protected with plastic conduit.

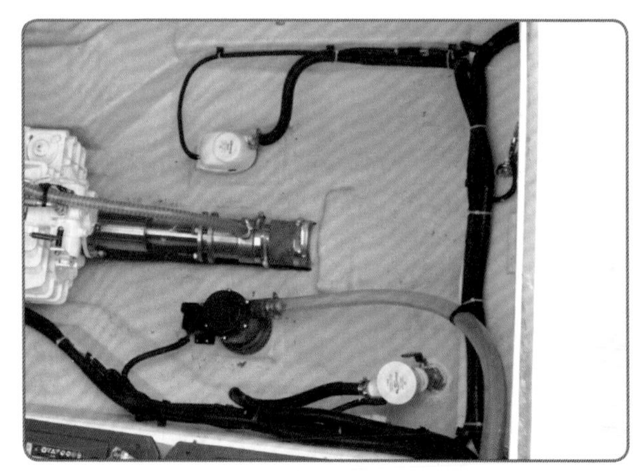

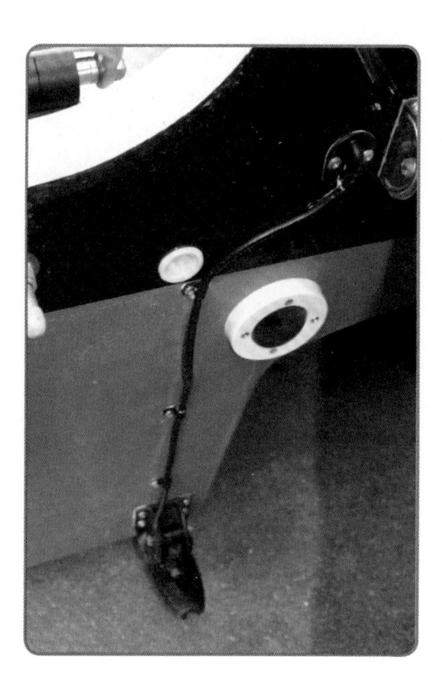

Left: A fish finder transducer mounted on the transom.

Right: A basic fish finder shows water depth information – and fish. Many more expensive sophisticated models are available, some combined with GPS and radar functions.

on a boat. Use multi-strand marine grade cable, which has a coating of tin over the copper wire to reduce the risk of corrosion. Connectors also need to be marine grade for the same reason and should be securely crimped.

When routing cables through the bilges and other compartments, they should be protected as far as possible by being threaded through plastic conduit and placed where they won't get chafed, knocked or snagged. Locations such as under the cockpit floor and under the side decks help to protect them. Secure them well above any possible accumulation of water in the bilges. Cable ties help to keep cables tidy and prevent tangles. The spiral plastic wrappings available for wiring looms also help to tidy and protect wires in those places where it's difficult to install conduit.

Label new and existing positive wires connected to the fuse panel with a waterproof marker on a plastic label, or else number each wire and list them nearby. This makes it much easier to trace faults such as a fuse that's been loosened by vibration or movement of the boat.

The fish-finder transducer

A fish-finder does find and indicate fish, but more importantly for safe navigation it shows the depth of water below the hull. Pulses are sent through the water and the time taken for the echo to return from the seabed, along with its signal strength, is measured. This provides the information for the display.

The transducer is the unit that sends the pulses. The mounting of the transducer will depend on the make and model, but it may be either in the water on the transom or else on the inside of a fibreglass hull, through which the pulses are transmitted. The installation manual will indicate exactly how it should be mounted, but the following general points should be borne in mind.

- Avoid mounting the transducer where bubbles and turbulence will pass in front of it.
- Marine grade screws and sealant designed for underwater applications should be used.
- Where a transducer is mounted inside the hull, it should be located well away from possible contact with anything that might damage it.
- It's vital that when mounted inside the hull the face of the transducer has no gaps or air bubbles between it and the hull's smooth surface.

The future

Hopefully, high capacity lightweight alternatives to lead-acid batteries will soon be developed and become available at a reasonable price. This will make dealing with electricity onboard a boat easier and help with the inevitable changeover to electric motors as the world runs out of the fuels we currently rely on.

The displays of fish finders and other equipment are mounted near the helm where they can easily be checked for depth and other information.

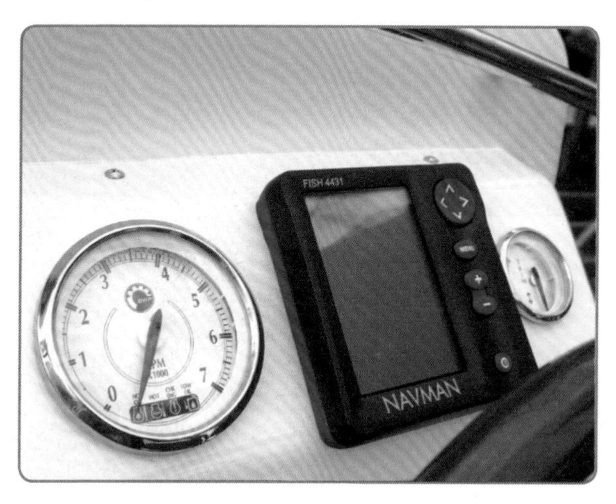

17

Engines and outboard motors

Use and simple servicing

As most motor boats don't have sails and are probably too big and heavy to be propelled by oars, reliance on the engine means it's vital that it's maintained in good condition. This chapter covers those straightforward tasks that can be carried out by the majority of boat owners in order to use and maintain their engines. Unless you have substantial mechanical knowledge and skills, more complex work is best left to the experts. In fact boat insurance companies are increasingly insisting that the servicing and maintenance of particular engines is done as per the manufacturer's instructions in order to ensure continued cover by their policy. So check the wording of your own policy to see whether it calls for the involvement of a qualified engineer – perhaps to check DIY work before the boat is used.

Petrol outboard motors

The most commonly used power unit on open motor boats and many cruisers is, of course, the petrol outboard. Even boats with inboard motors often carry an outboard motor as a wise precaution in case the engine fails and auxiliary propulsion is needed.

The general points covered below provide an introduction to using an outboard motor. They will help you to understand the basic maintenance tasks to be carried out on most engines. However, because there are so many different outboard makes and models in use, of greatly varying ages, it's impossible to cover their many variations, specific details and safety precautions here.

Consult the motor's manual

It's vitally important to consult the appropriate handbook and manual for your particular make and model. This has, in the past, been a problem if the motor is second-hand and the manual is no longer published, but the Internet has made it much easier to obtain information on particular outboards. The eBay auction website is one good source and an Internet search for particular manuals is also likely to produce results. Of course, outboard dealers and manufacturers can be helpful too. You may even find your outboard has been included in a book covering many models from one manufacturer, available from your local chandler.

The importance of accurate information is illustrated by the case of many two-stroke motors, which require a particular ratio of the correct type of oil to be mixed with the petrol. Don't just assume that the oil to petrol ratio is the same as for someone else's motor. An oil/fuel ratio of 1:50 has been used for a great many outboards, but it can vary from 1:10 for the very oldest outboards to 1:100 or twice that for automatic injection models.

In the case of the running-in period of a new two-stroke motor, the amount of oil to be added may need to be twice the amount normally used. Check the manual for the exact procedure for running-in the motor. This may also apply if parts of the motor are replaced with new ones.

Detailed manuals for the many makes and models of outboard motors are available from a variety of sources.

Two-stroke oil to be added to petrol can be purchased at chandlers.

The smallest outboards have an integral tank with the filler cap on top of the motor.

Preparing to set off

The following section is mainly concerned with the technical side of using the motor. See Chapter 8 for more on actual boat handling.

First check you have enough fuel. A two-stroke outboard motor will need the appropriate amount of the correct type of oil added – don't be tempted to use ordinary engine oil. Check the ratio of oil to petrol in the motor's manual.

Add fuel and oil to the tank well clear of the boat and away from any source of ignition. Have a fire extinguisher ready to hand. Never add fuel while the motor is running and always leave a small space for expansion at the top of the tank.

Very small outboards have an integral petrol tank mounted on top of the motor, so petrol and the appropriate oil should be added when the engine isn't hot. In order to mix them together the oil should be added stage by stage as the petrol is poured into the tank.

Remember petrol produces a heavy, highly flammable and explosive vapour, and take appropriate precautions whenever dealing with it. Avoid any sources of ignition such as a smoking cigarette. Place the tank onto the boat in a well-ventilated location to disperse any vapour away from the boat.

On four-stroke outboards the oil isn't added to the petrol and a separate lubrication system is provided. The oil level for this needs to be checked and topped up if necessary.

Always have a rope tied to the outboard and fastened somewhere inside the boat so that the motor can never drop overboard. Obviously there needs to be sufficient slack in the rope to allow the motor to turn while steering. Unscrew the clamps before lowering the motor onto the transom and clamping it there. The clamps used to fasten the motor to the transom need to be tightened firmly. They can loosen with use as vibration from the motor shakes them.

Check the condition of the manual starting rope and make sure that there's no debris round the propeller. Fishing line sometimes gets wound round the propeller hub, and if not removed this can tighten and damage the seal protecting the lower gear case.

Another line, called a 'lanyard', is provided with some motors. This is attached to a stop switch and to you, so that if you fall overboard the pull on the lanyard will stop the motor.

Lower the outboard if it's tilted up. Put levers provided for lifting and tilting the motor in the 'lock' position.

With the boat in the water, point it in the direction of

Check the engine oil level on a four-stroke outboard.

Ensure the clamps holding the outboard motor onto the bracket are kept tightly fastened, and attach a safety rope to the motor to prevent any risk of it falling overboard.

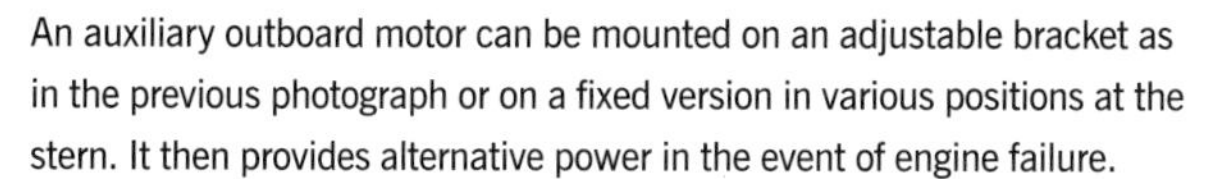

An auxiliary outboard motor can be mounted on an adjustable bracket as in the previous photograph or on a fixed version in various positions at the stern. It then provides alternative power in the event of engine failure.

Undo the fuel tank vent before starting and screw it down closed after using the outboard motor.

travel where there are no obstacles. Put the outboard in neutral to start it. If it has a separate fuel tank, connect it to the motor using the quick-connect fitting, which pushes onto the appropriate point on the motor. Fuel tanks have a vent that needs to be opened by unscrewing it sufficiently to allow air to enter. This needs to be screwed down and closed to stop leakage when the tank and outboard aren't being used and particularly when it's being transported. Forgetting to undo the vent is a major cause of embarrassment, with the motor failing to start or spluttering to a stop after running briefly. On some motors there's an additional valve to open.

Gently squeeze the primer bulb in the fuel pipe leading from the tank until it feels firm. This is a hand-operated fuel pump that pushes petrol into the carburettor. Check that there's no leakage of petrol, as this could cause a fire hazard.

Pull out the choke knob and put the throttle control and gears into their starting positions. Bear in mind that on some of the smallest outboard motors the propeller starts turning as soon as the motor is started, so in such cases you need to be particularly careful not to move the throttle control from the start position until the motor is warmed up and you're ready to move off. The boat also needs to be securely moored and tightly tied up to prevent any movement.

Check you won't hit anything or anyone when you pull the starting cord. Then get into a sitting or crouching position in order to avoid the exertion of starting the motor upsetting you or the boat. Pull it steadily until you feel resistance. This is the compression building up. Now pull with more force, smoothly and firmly. With luck the motor will start first time, but a cold motor is more likely to need a few pulls.

Having an electric start outboard motor saves you from having to pull a starter cord, but you need to remember to switch on the electricity supply before using the ignition.

When started, let the motor warm up for about three minutes, and once it's running well progressively push in the choke knob.

Check the cooling water is circulating by looking for water spraying out with the exhaust or coming out of a separate hole as a jet of water. If it's not coming out, stop the engine by using the stop control and check for blockages

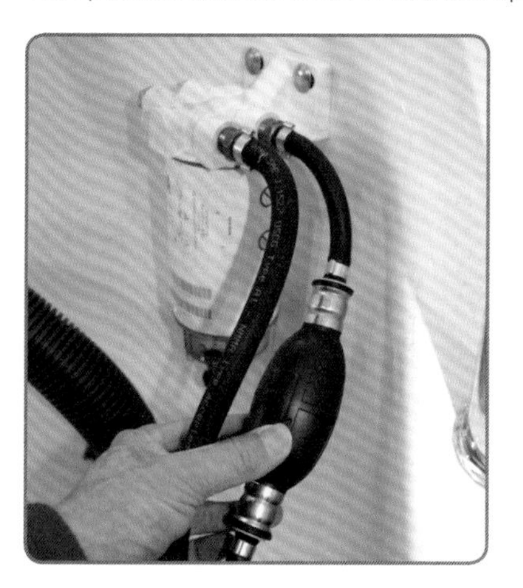

The primer bulb is squeezed to pump fuel into the carburettor before starting the outboard. On some boats the petrol goes through a filter before passing along another tube to reach the carburettor.

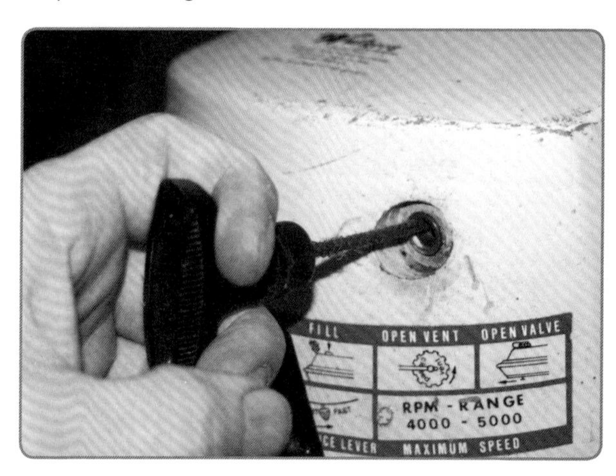

Pull the starter cord smoothly and quite forcefully when you feel the compression causing resistance.

or a damaged impeller, which pushes the water round the cooling system. *Never* run an engine without any cooling water circulating satisfactorily. It will soon seize up and sustain serious damage. For the same reason, an outboard motor should never *ever* be run whilst out of the water: the impeller would be damaged in a matter of seconds, water being necessary to lubricate and cool it. Although the motor may still run when put back in the water, it will quickly overheat and seize up if the damaged impeller isn't circulating sufficient cooling water.

Check the direction you intend to travel for obstacles including other boats and swimmers. Having cast off from the mooring, move the throttle into the 'shift' position, engage forward gear and accelerate away smoothly. On a small open boat in particular you should avoid sudden acceleration – a powerful motor can suddenly push the boat so hard that it forces the stern down and either powers the boat down under the waves or leaves crew members behind in the water.

Stopping

Slow the throttle back to the 'shift' position and put the motor into neutral as you approach the mooring or the shore. Some skill is needed to glide smoothly to a stop without power, but when you've mastered this it gives you a good sense of satisfaction. Any tidal flow, river current or wind can be used against the momentum of the boat to bring you to a halt without an embarrassing or damaging collision with the quay or slipway (as explained in more detail in Chapter 8). Push the stop button and tilt the motor up before it grounds in shallow water.

If reversing is necessary to slow down or to go backwards, check no boats or obstructions have appeared behind you and put the throttle control in the 'shift' position. Smoothly put the gear lever into reverse and go slowly, using no more than half throttle unless this is an emergency stop. Reversing suddenly and rapidly can cause a small boat to become dangerously unstable; it may be difficult to control and to steer a straight course when reversing.

A screw or cover can usually be undone to drain fuel from the carburettor before transporting the motor.

If the motor is removed from the boat, keep it upright long enough for the water to drain out of the cooling system. Never lay it down horizontally or with its lower unit higher than the powerhead, because any remaining water might run back up the exhaust and enter the cylinders. With a four-stroke motor, check your manual for the correct side to lay the motor down on in order to prevent oil leaking out or flowing to where it could cause damage.

Drain off any fuel remaining in the carburettor bowl before transporting the motor. It may be possible to undo a drain screw to do this and then catch the fuel in a rag. This avoids the rather risky situation of having petrol fumes in the vehicle used to transport the motor.

Alternatively, whenever you're about to finish using the motor the carburettor can be drained with the engine running by turning off the fuel supply. The engine will stop when the fuel has been drained from the carburettor.

If the motor has been used in sea water, it's important to flush the cooling system with fresh water, because salt is very corrosive and can also crystallise and block the water passages. It can be flushed through by running the motor in a suitably large and strong container of clean fresh water, after taking precautions to ensure that it's mounted safely and securely whilst it's running. The leg of the motor must be in water deep enough to cover the cavitation plate and up to the level that the motor is used on the boat. Some engines, however, have special attachments and equipment for flushing with a hosepipe. Follow the manual's instructions carefully.

It's also wise to run an outboard occasionally in clean water even if it's been used in freshwater locations, to remove any sand or debris in the cooling system.

Remember to close fuel tank vents and any fuel supply closures before leaving or moving the motor.

Outboard motor theft is a major problem in many areas. If the motor has to be left on the boat, tilt it up out of the water and use a suitable lockable security device to prevent it being unclamped and stolen.

Fuel Additives

'Miracle' additives are often advertised for use in improving the performance of engines and to solve all kinds of problems. However, outboard motors aren't necessarily the same as other types of motor, and although some such additives may just possibly be helpful in certain engines you shouldn't risk using them.

If really necessary, only use additives specifically designed for your make and model of outboard and follow the instructions carefully. You must, of course, add the appropriate oil to fuel for a two-stroke motor, but not for a four-stroke motor because the four-stroke outboard has a separate oil circulation system similar to a car engine.

Two-stroke and four-stroke motors

Two-stroke motors have proved popular because they're powerful, reasonably light and basic compared with four-stroke motors. Unfortunately, though, because oil is added to the petrol the exhaust produced is usually more polluting than is now generally acceptable, and there's a tendency for unburned oil to be deposited on the water.

The regulations governing exhaust emissions have not led to existing two-stroke motors being banned, although this could happen in the future on some inland waterways as it already has on some lakes in the USA and Europe. But the sale of new two-stroke motors that don't meet today's emission regulations has already become illegal in the UK, with the result that almost all new outboards are now four-stroke motors, which don't burn oil along with the petrol. They're cleaner and somewhat quieter than two-stroke motors, although many are also heavier.

However, if you're about to buy a new outboard motor for use on inland or sheltered coastal waters, you should first read about the incredibly quiet and pollution-free electric outboards later in this chapter. With an electric outboard you can forget about 90 per cent of the following maintenance tasks and the hazards associated with petrol. Big improvements have been made in the power and efficiency of electric motors, particularly for the more relaxed enjoyment of cruising inland waterways and leisurely trips out on sheltered waters.

Outboard motor maintenance

The following maintenance details apply to most of the still very common two-stroke motors often purchased with small second-hand motor boats. Additional notes are included, where necessary, for four-stroke motors.

If in doubt about the reliability of an outboard motor or your ability to carry out work on it, always consult and involve a qualified engineer. The following will help you to understand and discuss what needs to be done.

If you decide to dismantle parts of any motor according to the instructions in its handbook, take photographs with a digital camera at each stage as you proceed. You can then look at the photos to see how to put the parts back together again.

NB When the outboard motor is tilted up on the back of your boat out of the water – for example on a trailer – never get under the lower end of it, as it might drop onto you. Also, when carrying out inspections of the engine while it's running, keep loose clothing and hair well away from any moving parts in which they could become entangled.

MONTHLY CHECKS AND MAINTENANCE

Remove the engine cover and check the following:

- Check wire terminal connections are secure. Any signs of corrosion mean they should be disconnected, cleaned and tightened. Use an appropriate anti-corrosion/water dispersant spray on exposed electrical connections.

Check the wiring and spray it, and all moving parts, with water dispersant.

Check the condition of gaskets.

- If there's any corrosion developing near the cylinder head gaskets it could indicate leaky gaskets, and tightening or gasket replacement may be necessary.
- Check the fuel filters and remove any dirt and water. Take care to ensure that any washers or O rings are carefully replaced. Pump the fuel with the fuel primer bulb to check for leaks. A new filter may be needed if dirt is firmly stuck or the filter is damaged.
- With the engine running in water, operate the controls and check they're moving smoothly. Lubricate them if necessary. Never shift the gears unless the engine is running otherwise they could get jammed or damaged.
- While the engine is running, check that no water is leaking from joints between the exhaust cover, crank case and cylinder head.
- Check whether any of the bolted-on components, such as the fuel pump, coil, voltage regulator etc, have come loose, and tighten them as necessary.
- Lubricate moving parts, including the tilt mechanism and any cable controls. The steering pivot may have a grease point that needs to have a small amount of grease inserted.

Check that bolted-on components can't move and that moving parts such as the controls can move freely. Lubricate as necessary.

The fuel primer bulb on the pipe from the fuel tank should be soft and flexible. Replacements are available if there's any danger of leakage.

- Where zinc sacrificial anodes are fitted to become the subject of electrolytic corrosion instead of the outboard motor, check their condition. If more than half eroded away, they should be replaced.
- Clean the casing of the engine and check for scratches and damage. Do likewise with the fuel tank. To prevent corrosion, touch up in the appropriate type and colour any areas where paint is missing.
- On a four-stroke motor, check the level of engine oil and top up if necessary.

THREE-MONTHLY CHECKS AND MAINTENANCE

These tasks are usually appropriate at between 50 and 75 hours of use or every three months, but with low usage where the outboard motor is an auxiliary engine it may only need to be an annual event. The above monthly tasks should be included.

The following are the basic tasks suitable for DIY. They're the tasks most commonly required for the maintenance of many outboard motors. Details will vary according to the motor you have, so consult the owners' manual as much as possible. More advanced and complicated repair and maintenance work will need special tools and the skills and knowledge of an engineer trained for your particular make of motor.

Spark plugs

When removing or replacing a spark plug take care not to damage the insulator. External sparks can result from a damaged insulator and this could ignite petrol fumes, causing a fire or explosion when the engine is started.

Use a proper spark plug socket to remove the plugs. Ideally a socket with a rubber insert should be used to reduce risk of damage to the ceramic insulator.

The electrode should be between light brown and grey if the engine is operating correctly. If it's black and damp or if it's very white in colour, ask the appropriate dealer or servicing engineer for advice on how to correct this in your particular model of outboard.

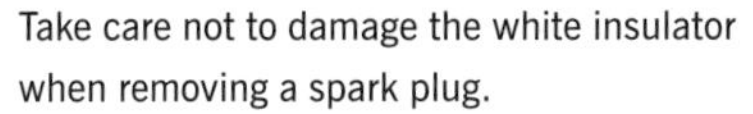
Take care not to damage the white insulator when removing a spark plug.

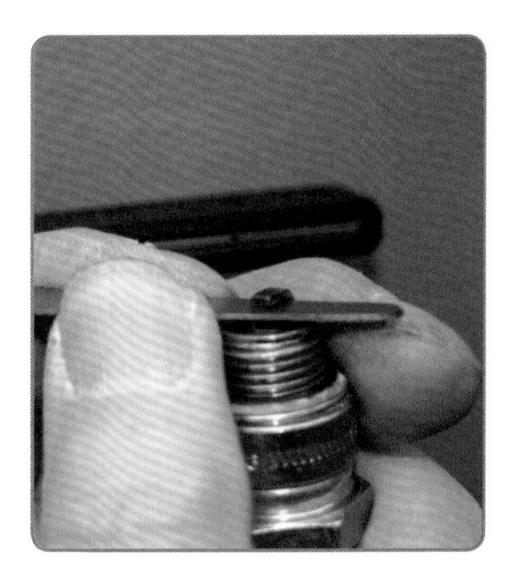

Check the spark plug gap is correct.

Replace the gasket when fitting a new spark plug. A new gasket is usually supplied with a spark plug.

Heat and deposits on the spark plug cause it to gradually break down and wear away. Carefully cleaning the plug and electrode will help, but it will eventually need replacement. In fact replacement is often recommended instead of cleaning, which might cause damage.

Using a feeler gauge, check the gap against the recommended gap size in the motor's manual.

When refitting the cleaned plug or a new plug, use a new gasket and ensure that all surfaces and threads are clean. Screw the plug in by hand for the first few turns to make sure it seats correctly and isn't cross-threaded. Ideally, use a torque wrench to tighten to the setting specified in the manual. Alternatively, a reasonable estimate of tightness is one quarter to one half of a turn past finger tight. Don't over-tighten it.

Where grease points are provided they should be filled with the appropriate type of fresh grease recommended by the motor manufacturer. Pump the grease in until all the old grease, along with any water, is forced out. Old grease should be wiped away as it emerges.

Check the condition of controls and any control cables. If worn, replace them before they break in use.

Disconnect the spark plug caps from the spark plugs and ensure the shift control is in neutral to be sure the engine can't turn the propeller. Remove the propeller and any fishing line or other debris wrapped round the shaft. If the propeller blades have any slight damage, use a file to smooth them off. Check the condition of the hub and shaft. Wipe old grease off and apply a layer of the appropriate type of waterproof grease.

Shear pin

On older and smaller outboard motors a shear pin fastens the propeller to the shaft. Check the condition of this pin, which is made of soft metal and is designed to break if the propeller hits a hard obstacle, thus avoiding damage to the drive mechanism and the propeller. When it's broken the propeller stays on the shaft but is no longer rotated by it. Spare shear pins should be amongst the spare parts and tools kept with the motor, so that replacement can be carried out whenever necessary. If the pin is corroded or damaged it should be replaced.

Other motors have a rubber bush instead of a shear pin. This slips on the shaft if the propeller hits something. It can get worn and will then need replacement if the system is to work satisfactorily.

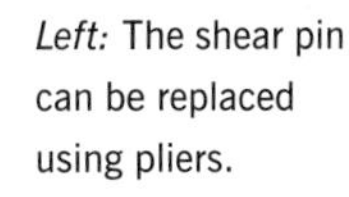
Left: The shear pin can be replaced using pliers.

Right: Since the propeller might hit an obstacle and break its shear pin, spares should always be kept ready for use.

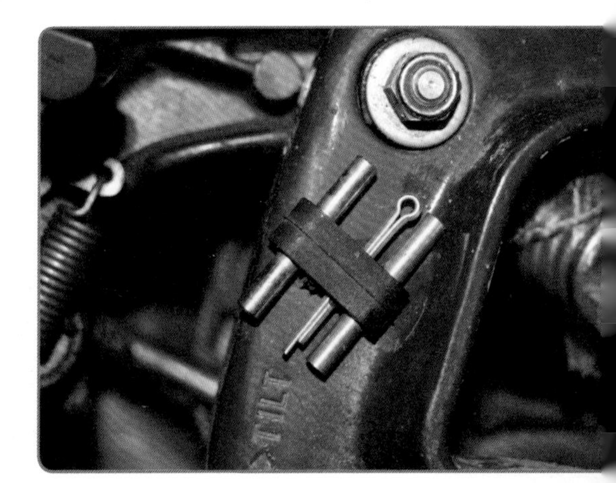

Undo the screw-in plug used for checking the gear oil level.

Gear oil

Gear case oil needs to be changed next. The gear case usually has two screw plugs in the side of the gear housing, and the oil will flow out when these are undone. Before undoing the drain plug, clean the skeg at the very bottom of the outboard motor. Then stick one end of a long piece of tape, such as masking tape, to the end of the skeg so that it hangs down into a container suitable for collecting the oil. After removing both screw plugs, the oil should flow down the edges of the tape into the container.

Examine the oil carefully. If a lot of water comes out before the oil emerges, or if the oil is milky, a bad seal has probably let water into the gear case. If you're uncertain, one way to check for water is to put the old oil into a transparent plastic or glass bottle or jar and leave it to settle for a couple of hours. You'll then see any water that will have settled to the bottom while the oil floats. If there is water, the motor will need to be further checked by an appropriate engineer, who'll replace the seal if necessary.

The oil should be a normal brown colour, possibly with a few metal filings in it. The lower drain plug may have a magnetic pickup to collect filings; if so, clean them off. The oil drain plug sealing rings should also be checked and replaced if damaged.

Be sure to use the correct type of oil according to the outboard manufacturer's instructions. Don't use oil intended for car gearboxes. The marine oil includes water-dispersant additives and in some cases may be more like the fluid used in a car's automatic transmission.

To be sure the oil goes into the gear case and fills it fully, it's most important to fill it from the bottom. If you take the apparently easier route of filling through the top hole, air is likely to get trapped in the oil. If it does, then when the oil gets hot during use the air will expand and put pressure on the seals: oil will leak out, water will get in, and the gears will be damaged.

Oil can usually be purchased in a tube like a toothpaste tube so that it can be firmly pushed up into the lower hole, but a pump may be needed to force the oil in from the bottom. This can be purchased at the same time as the oil. The oil-filling pump is inserted into the lower hole, where it should be possible to screw it onto the thread to form an oil-tight seal.

Squeeze the oil container or work the pump until oil appears at the top hole. Don't overfill, as this may result in a damaging pressure build-up when the oil heats and

Before undoing the oil drain plug stick a long piece of tape to the skeg so that it hangs down and guides the oil into a container.

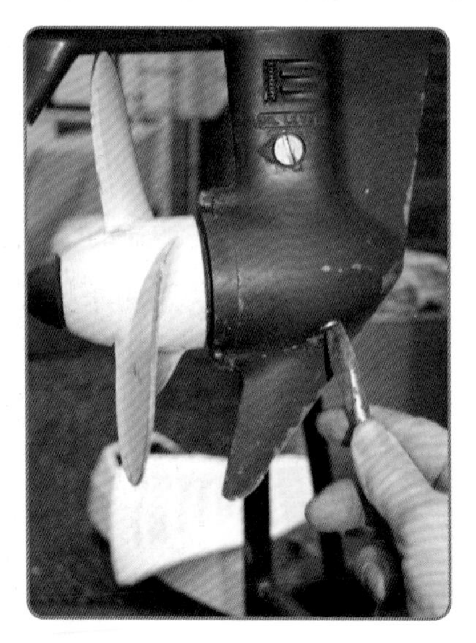

expands. Screw the plug into the top hole. Doing so helps to stop oil rushing out of the bottom hole when the pump or tube is removed.

Check the O ring or gasket is in place on the bottom plug and have it ready to screw in as you remove the pump. Screw in the bottom plug quickly and tighten it to avoid leakage. Wipe the area free of oil and look for any leaks.

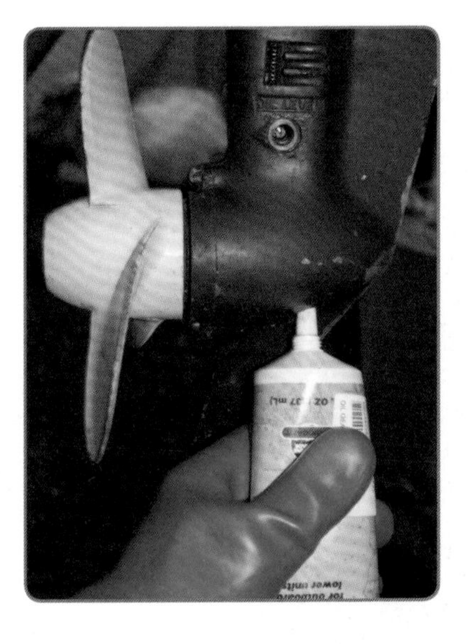

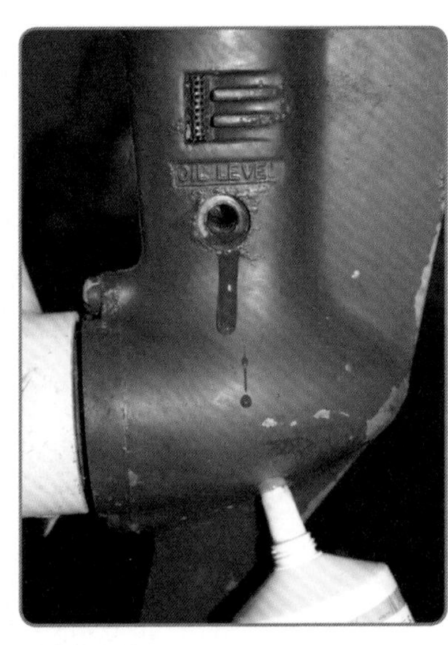

Oil should be squeezed into the lower hole, with the tube firmly pushed up the hole to prevent it running out, until it appears at the top hole.

Cooling System

Thoroughly flush the cooling system with fresh water. This is best done with the motor securely mounted to run in a large, strong and stable container of water, such as a clean dustbin. Some motors have attachment points and equipment provided for flushing by other methods, such as by attaching a hosepipe and 'flush adapter' or 'flush muffs', according to instructions in the appropriate manual. Don't try these alternative methods on a motor not designed for their use, as both you and the motor could be damaged.

The impeller, which pushes the cooling water round the system, may need to be replaced. Recommendations on the frequency of replacement vary according to make. In some cases annual replacement is recommended but others advise replacing it only when it shows signs of wear. If you give the motor a lot of use in areas where sand is drawn into the cooling system, or rely on it at times when cruising offshore, the impeller should be replaced annually to be on the safe side.

Gaining access to the impeller can be quite a complicated process depending on the make and model of the outboard. The manufacturer's manual should help but you may still prefer to involve an appropriately experienced engineer.

Checking the compression of the engine is an optional task and a job for an engineer familiar with your make and model. It can be worthwhile arranging for this to be done in order to catch any developing problems before they become a serious issue. Any variation from the normal compression figures may give early warning of wear or faults that should be rectified while the engineer has the motor in his workshop.

Even if you have the equipment to do this yourself, it can still be difficult because the actual compression figures for a particular outboard are not always easy to find, even in the appropriate manuals.

Adjustments to the ignition timing and carburettor are only needed if there are problems with smooth running of the motor. These are also tasks best left to a specialist equipped with the tools and knowledge necessary for your make and model of outboard.

Extra tasks for four-stroke outboards

As well as all the above, four-stroke outboards need some additional work, as outlined below. Four-stroke motors have an oil sump and use a pressurised lubrication system similar to that of a car.

Changing the engine oil

Warm the engine with water provided for the cooling system. This warming thins the oil so that it flows out of the sump effectively. Have a container ready to catch the old oil being drained out.

Wearing protective gloves, unscrew the drain plug, ensuring that the sealing ring comes away on the plug so

Oil for four-stroke outboard motors and their gears.

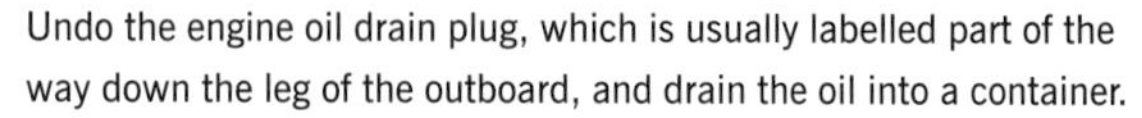

Undo the engine oil drain plug, which is usually labelled part of the way down the leg of the outboard, and drain the oil into a container.

that it's not lost in the oil as it drains out. The ring might need to be replaced if it's squashed or damaged.

As the oil drains out, check its colour. Any milky discolouration indicates that water has leaked into the oil. This usually means a cylinder head gasket is leaking internally. Unless you're experienced in this type of repair you should get the gasket replaced by someone who knows what they're doing. Don't ignore it, as severe damage to the motor can ensue.

There's a tendency for DIY motor mechanics to over-tighten oil drain plugs because the well lubricated plug screws easily into the hole. However, you'll want to be able to unscrew it again in the future so don't jam it in place.

The oil filter needs to be removed and cleaned next. If there's a problem finding and removing it, the manual for your outboard should help. On most outboards it can be put back after cleaning if it's not damaged. If in doubt, replace it with a new one. The filter sealing ring is likely to need replacement, as screwing a filter back onto an old seal could

Fill with new engine oil.

Check the belt for wear and tension.

cause an oil leak. When tightening, get it screwed on and then tighten only an additional half to three-quarters of a turn. Don't over-tighten it.

After checking the engine is in a normal operating position, fill with the appropriate type and quantity of oil recommended by the manufacturer for your model of outboard. Run the motor with cooling water for a couple of minutes and check for oil leaks. Stop the engine and check the oil level.

Check the timing belt for wear. This usually involves removing a protective cover by unscrewing it. Belts usually last several years with low to moderate use, but they should still be checked for fraying and excessive sideways movement.

Replacement of the belt may be a DIY task on some engines but this could once again be a job for the professionals if there are complications. Likewise, adjustment of valve clearances is really only for those who have experience in this type of engine maintenance.

Winterising an outboard motor

Before winter sets in, or earlier if the motor is to be stored unused for several months, a number of actions need to be taken in order to protect it from corrosion and other problems. A list is provided below, which includes many tasks covered in more detail earlier in this chapter. Many boat owners who have little-used auxiliary outboard motors do the main service at this time as well. Any developing faults that need professional attention can then be dealt with during the winter in readiness for a trouble-free boating season the following year. As well as the general list of tasks given below, owners' manuals may have some additional recommendations for particular types of motor.

- Flush the cooling system using fresh water.
- With the motor running in fresh water turn off or disconnect the fuel supply to let the carburettor run dry. In the last ten seconds spray storage oil into it.
- If a battery is used with the outboard, disconnect it, charge it and store it in a suitable dry place.
- Service the fuel filters.
- After removing the spark plugs, squirt a small amount of outboard oil into the cylinders through the holes. Turn the engine over by rotating the flywheel to distribute the oil and then replace the plugs.
- Wash and clean the outside surfaces of the motor, touch up any scratches in the paint and when the paint is dry spray the motor with water dispersant such as WD40. Any salt-encrusted crevices should be scrubbed with an old toothbrush.
- Remove and inspect the propeller. Grease the shaft before replacing it.
- Check the sacrificial anode and replace it if more than half used.
- Lubricate all moving parts and grease points.
- Check the manual starter rope and replace if necessary.
- Drain out and replace gear oil.
- On a four-stroke motor, change the engine oil.
- Check the fuel supply pipes and replace if showing signs of deterioration.
- Petrol can deteriorate over time, particularly when mixed with oil. Enquire about local facilities for the safe disposal of old fuel – a local car-servicing garage may help with this. The tank should be drained very carefully, avoiding any sources of ignition.

Storage

Having completed the above, mount the motor upright in a lockable garage or reasonably frost-proof shed. Clamp it on a support where it can't fall over, preferably arranged so that it doesn't rest on its skeg. Cover the motor with a cloth to keep out dust.

Mice have been known to take up residence under the cover of an outboard motor and then feast on its insulation and sound-proofing. If this is likely to be a problem take suitable precautions, such as the use of a trap or two.

A Minn Kota electric trolling motor may provide sufficient auxiliary power to reach a mooring in sheltered waters.

Electric outboard motors

If you use an electric outboard you can forget most of the maintenance tasks covered above. Other advantages are very easy starting, very quiet operation, no exhaust fumes, no risky petrol fumes, and the motor itself being lighter, easier to carry and quicker to prepare for use. An electric outboard can also be surprisingly effective as an auxiliary motor on a small cruiser on inland waterways and sheltered estuary waters, providing an alternative to the main petrol outboard or inboard engine that's far less likely to scare away wildlife and fish.

In recent years big advances have been made in the efficiency and power of electric outboards. Increased popularity, and regulations banning petrol motors on some waterways, have made them more widely available and more competitively priced. Originally, most electric outboards were actually 'trolling' motors for use when fishing, particularly in the huge number of lakes in North America, 'trolling' involving motoring quietly along whilst

An electric outboard motor and 12V deep cycle battery can provide several hours of very quiet cruising on sheltered waterways and is very simple to operate and maintain.

towing fishing lures. Their quiet operation also suits them to auxiliary use in inland and sheltered coastal locations where peace and tranquillity are valued.

An amusing aspect is the appearance of achieving the impossible. An electric outboard can be so inconspicuous that onlookers aren't aware of the motor. The expressions of amazement at the silent progress of the boat are most entertaining!

A disadvantage is the need for one or more 12V deep cycle leisure batteries. Lead-acid batteries are heavy but the combined weight of the electric outboard and the battery needs to be compared with the total weight of a petrol outboard plus fuel, spare parts and tool kit. It's a pity we still rely so much on lead-acid batteries, and the development of high capacity lightweight alternatives, available at a reasonable price, is not only long overdue but essential, as the world demand for petroleum exceeds supply; but progress is being made with lighter alternatives, as in the case of Torqeedo electric outboards.

Comparisons between electric and petrol outboards are difficult because most electric outboards have the motor mounted next to the propeller, providing direct drive without the loss of power involved with the gears and transmission in most petrol outboards. The electric outboard's thrust is usually measured in pounds of thrust rather than horsepower.

Minn Kota is particularly well-known for its trolling motors in the USA, and a wide range is imported for sale in the UK (see the importer's website at http://www.johnsonoutdoors.co.uk/minn-kota.htm). Other makes have also become more widely available. Although trolling motors were originally intended to be used on fresh water and for just a few hours at a time, there are now more powerful versions for use in sea water, such as the Minn Kota 'Riptide' 24V and 36V series. These can be used on small open boats and even small cruisers in sheltered coastal waters. For the open sea and strong currents, however, a petrol outboard motor still has the advantage of greater power against strong winds and tides.

Recent developments towards more powerful electric outboard motors include the Torqeedo motor and the 36V

Minn Kota Riptide motor for seawater use.

British Anzani. The British Anzani E-Pilot motor does need three 12V deep cycle leisure batteries, but these give it substantially more power and duration than the 12V trolling motors. Although the batteries are heavy, the actual motor weighs only 21lb (9.4kg). See the company's website at http://www.britishanzani.com.

Torqeedo electric outboards, which have become available from Germany in recent years, may be more expensive than trolling motors but they demonstrate big advances in efficiency. The smaller Torqeedo Travel motors fold neatly into a waterproof rucksack and are supplied with advanced lithium-manganese batteries. The larger Torqeedo

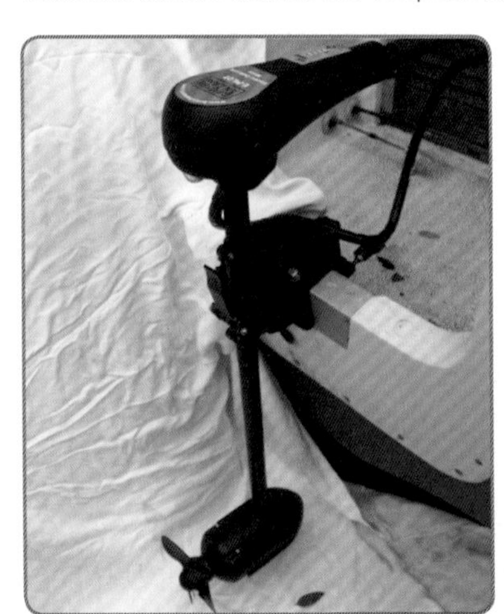

The British Anzani, in common with other electric outboards, has its underwater motor efficiently connected directly to the propeller, providing maximum power. The controls are very simple: just switch on and twist the handle to select one of three forward or two reverse speeds.

Torqeedo Travel electric outboard motors with their removable black battery packs mounted on top.

The Torqeedo Cruise 6HP outboard motor.

Cruise version is advertised as having the power of a 6hp petrol motor. Bear in mind the cost of running and servicing a 6hp petrol outboard motor when comparing purchase prices. Torqeedo outboards do produce a little more noise than trolling motors but they're still quieter than most petrol outboards. The new Torqeedo 'Cruise R Series' of motors promise even more propulsion power, including the thrust power of a 9.9hp petrol outboard. For more information see their website at http://www.torqeedo.com.

Remember, with electric outboards, there's no expenditure on petrol and oil, and virtually no expenditure on servicing and spare parts such as spark plugs. Recharging a standard 12V leisure battery is a fraction of the cost of just one litre of petrol and a suitable battery should have a life of about 200 to 300 charge/discharge cycles. It may last five years or more if well looked after.

The deep cycle leisure battery used with electric outboards should have a rating of at least 85 amp hours. Running at full speed can use the capacity in an hour or two, but easing back to half throttle makes the battery last much longer. You can, of course, use batteries connected in parallel for longer-range expeditions.

Inland waterway authorities are keen to encourage the use of environmentally friendly electric motors on boats and offer discounts on annual navigation licences to encourage their use – a significant saving, applicable, for example, to those boating on the River Thames.

Servicing electric outboards

Servicing is mainly concerned with keeping the leisure battery, or batteries, in good condition, with prompt recharging and topping-up as necessary.

The propeller should be cleaned of weeds and fishing line. Remove the propeller, following the procedure in the motor's instruction manual for removal and replacement, and cut off any fishing line that may have wound round the shaft, which could damage the seal protecting the underwater motor. Keep the leading edge of the propeller blades smooth by sanding with fine sandpaper.

Washing off dirt and salt, light lubrication of the few moving parts and checking the electrical connections are tight completes all the regular attention that's required.

Inboard engines

An introduction to the use and servicing of inboard motors is provided below. This will help you to understand the basic tasks that need to be carried out. Most of the following applies to both diesel and petrol engines.

Whole books have been written on the maintenance of such engines, and manuals are available for most makes and models (see the Appendix for details), of which there are many. If you don't have a manual, one should be available from the manufacturer or from the book section of your local chandler. If not, try a search on the Internet. Many manuals are advertised on eBay.

The appropriate manual must be consulted for more detailed information regarding your particular engine, including servicing, maintenance, repair work, winterisation and appropriate safety precautions. The Royal Yachting Association runs courses for those who are keen to do much of the work involved in maintaining their own boat engine. Two other organisations that run courses, as well as providing emergency engine repairs and rescue services, are River Canal Rescue Ltd at http://www.rivercanalrescue.co.uk, and Seastart Ltd at http://www.seastart.co.uk.

Unfortunately, in the confined space in a boat's engine compartment it can be difficult to reach parts for servicing. If in doubt about the reliability of an engine or your ability to carry out work on it, always consult and involve a qualified engineer. The following guidelines will help you discuss what needs to be done.

When going out to sea it's always best to have a reliable outboard motor, regularly serviced as described earlier, in addition to the inboard in case of engine failure.

Checks before starting the engine and setting off

Many of the safety points covered in the section on outboard motors apply equally to working on inboard engines. It's vital in the case of a petrol engine to ensure that there's no leakage of fuel and no petrol vapour that could be ignited by a spark when starting the engine. In the case of diesel fuel it's still important to check for leaks. It may be less of a fire hazard than petrol but it can still burn fiercely when it's ignited.

Take care not to get hair and clothing entangled in moving parts, and wear suitable protective gloves when handling oils and other liquids and chemicals.

All fuel-burning engines produce harmful exhaust gases, which can dangerously accumulate in a boat. Fit smoke detecting and carbon monoxide detecting alarms in cabins and ensure adequate ventilation. A 'bilge blower' fan helps to remove hazardous gases and must be operated for a time before starting the engine and during operation.

When reaching down into a cramped engine compartment there's a risk of falling head first into it. Some people have had to be rescued from this situation after their legs have been spotted waving frantically in the air. It's therefore a good idea to have a mobile phone in your pocket at such times!

This boat engine, exhibited at boat shows by Lancing Marine, is painted to show parts of the engine more clearly than may be seen in the confined space on a boat, and was used in some of the following photographs.

Tools and small items that you've taken apart have a habit of dropping down and disappearing into inaccessible corners in the bilges. It's much easier to find them if the bilges are clean, and positioning a container under the parts being unscrewed helps to catch anything that attempts to escape.

- Check the engine oil by removing the dipstick. Wipe it clean, reinsert it, remove it again and check that the level comes up to the marker. Top up as necessary.
- Check the gear oil level in the same way.
- Both oils should be a dark colour. If there's any change in the colour, and in particular if it's turned milky, this should be investigated, as water is likely to have contaminated the oil.
- Depending on the type of cooling system, it may be necessary to check the level of coolant in the freshwater reservoir while the engine is cold.

Use the dipstick to check the oil level.

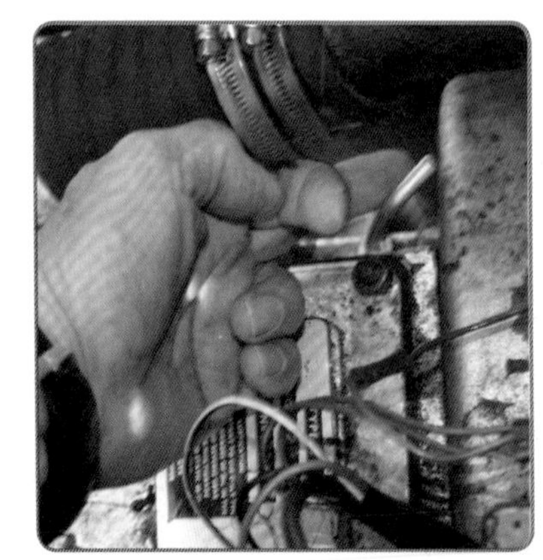

The gearbox dipstick, in this case on a Ford petrol engine.

If appropriate, while the engine is cold check the level of coolant and top it up if necessary.

The water filter cover should be unscrewed and all debris removed.

- Open the seacock, which is a tap allowing water to be pumped in to the cooling system.
- Check for leaks of oil, water or fuel in the bilges and investigate if necessary.
- Check the fuel filters and water filter. It may be necessary to clean the filters and remove dirt from filter units.
- Check all belts are tight and not worn.
- Ensure all cables, hoses and connections etc are secure.
- If fitted, operate the stern gland lubricating dispenser where the propeller shaft passes through the hull.
- Check nothing is likely to get caught up in moving parts in the engine compartment or round a drive shaft, such as a cleaning rag, rope or an empty container.
- Look outside the hull for any trailing ropes that might wrap round the propeller.
- Open the fuel shut-off fully.
- Operate any fuel primer device.
- Check for any fuel leaks using your nose and eyes. This is very important with petrol motors because of the highly inflammable vapour given off.
- Turn on the battery isolation switch.
- Check you have twice the amount of fuel likely to be needed and, in any case, that the tank is at least half full.
- On a diesel engine, operate the pre-heat for 15 seconds.

The fuel shut-off usually opens with a lever.

- On a petrol engine, pull out the choke knob. This should be progressively pushed in again as the engine warms up.
- With the engine in neutral and the boat securely moored, start the engine and allow it to warm up fully before moving off. A diesel engine benefits from being worked quite hard and should not be stopped until it has reached full working temperature.
- Check that cooling water is flowing and coming out of the hull. This is most important, since it proves that the cooling system is working.
- If all is well, check that the course ahead is clear of boats and obstacles, untie from any mooring, engage forward gear and accelerate smoothly away. More on boat handling will be found in Chapter 8.

Always switch off the fuel tap when not running the engine and when refuelling.

Regular maintenance

The checks covered above should be carried out plus the following:

Lubrication

Changing the engine oil and filter at least as often as stated in the handbook is an essential task. This will mean doing so annually even if the engine has had little use. The oil contains additives that stop corrosion but they have a limited life span.

Draining the oil should be done when the engine is warm, *ie* after it's been used. An oil drain pump is fitted to many types of engine.

An oil drain pump permanently fixed to the engine.

The place where you add the engine oil should be easy to find, although it won't necessarily be as obvious as this.

Alternatively a drain pump can be purchased which is used to extract the oil via the dipstick hole.

The gearbox oil should also be changed. Check the type required, as it may be different from the engine oil.

Old oil should be disposed of where a suitable facility is available. Refuse disposal sites run by local authorities usually have a container to receive old oil. A car servicing garage may also take the old oil for disposal.

The cooling system

Boats don't have the radiator found in a car to remove heat. Instead, there are two main types of cooling system. One is the direct raw water (sea water) system where water from outside the boat is pumped through the engine's cooling system and out through the exhaust. The other, and more common, is the indirect enclosed freshwater system, which has a tank of fresh water with anti-freeze added. Raw water is still pumped in from outside but instead of flowing through the engine, it goes through a heat exchanger to cool the enclosed freshwater system before exiting via the exhaust.

In an enclosed freshwater cooling system, the coolant should be changed every second year, including sufficient antifreeze/summer coolant, which has corrosion inhibitors.

Raw water (sea water) cooled engines should have the system flushed through with fresh water and then be drained in winter. In order to avoid the scalding steam and water that could escape when it's hot, you should only work on the cooling system when the engine is cold.

When draining cooling systems have a bowl ready to collect the water, which will contain toxic ethylene glycol that you don't want accumulating in the bilges. Remove the filler cap and unscrew the drain cocks that will probably be available to drain water from the engine. Check that these actually do remove all the water. It may be necessary to disconnect some hoses to be sure. To prevent frost damage they should be flushed and then filled with a mixture of 50 per cent antifreeze and fresh water after closing the drain cocks.

Any sacrificial anodes in the cooling system should be checked annually and replaced if more than half has gone.

The water pump impeller should be checked and replaced annually. It may be necessary to use two screwdrivers at the same time to extract the impeller, but it's also possible to purchase a special tool for this. Examine how the vanes are aligned in order to insert the new impeller the right way round. Take care not to leave any broken bits behind in the cooling system. When inserting the new impeller, clean the housing and face-plate and smear the impeller with washing up liquid to help slide it into place. Ensure the vanes are aligned the same way as the old impeller and make sure the pin engages with the slot. Use a new gasket when replacing the cover.

Check the condition of the water injection point of the exhaust system. This can corrode and leak exhaust gases and water into the bilges.

Fuel system

The 'sniff test' is useful in diagnosing fuel leaks and faults. Always use your nose as well as your eyes.

In the case of petrol engines, great care must be taken to ensure that fuel and vapour don't leak into the bilges when you're working on the fuel system, and it's wise to have risky fuel system maintenance done by an engineer. It's not

The cover should be unscrewed to access the water pump impeller.

Take care not to damage the gasket and remember to include it, or preferably a new one, when screwing the cover back on.

Removing the impeller.

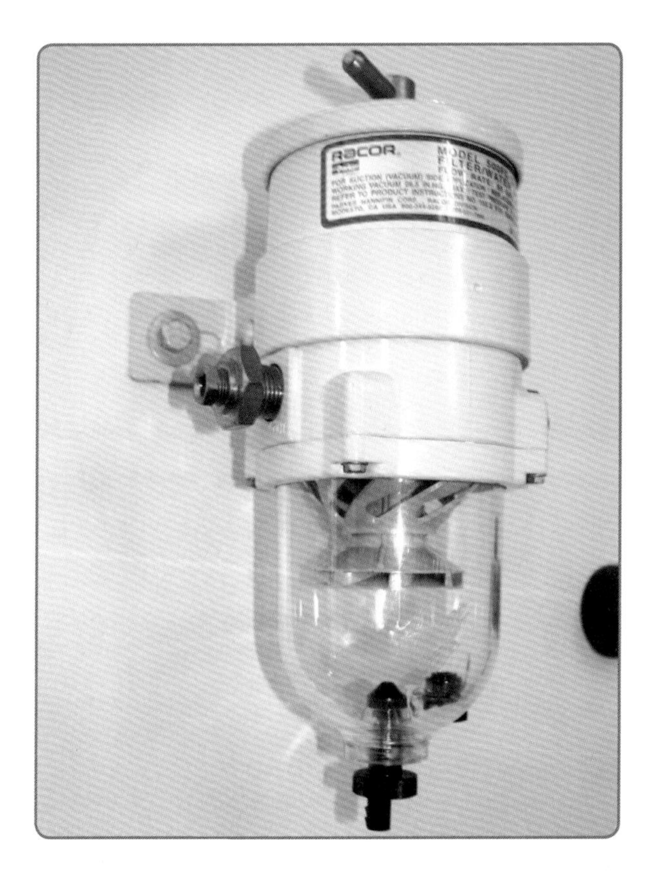

Many primary fuel filters have clear bowls so that dirt and water in the fuel can be seen and removed.

like working on a car, where the fuel and vapour can escape easily – in a boat the heavy petrol vapour can get trapped and can accumulate dangerously. It then only takes one spark to cause an explosion and fire.

Fuel filters are changed annually. There are normally two filters in the fuel system, particularly on a diesel engine: the primary filter and the engine fine filter. The primary filter should have a transparent bowl giving a view of any dirt or water. A cock or plug at the bottom of the filter bowl can be undone to drain any water or heavy sediment. Be sure to retighten it securely. If fuel is contaminated, this should be tackled urgently – by an engineer, as it could involve cleaning the inside of the fuel tank. Unfortunately the tank can be difficult to reach in many boats.

Before changing the primary filter, close fuel stopcocks. Before proceeding place a bowl or plastic bag below the filter to catch any spillage of diesel. Unscrew the filter, normally using a central bolt, and replace the filter and the sealing rings that are usually supplied with it.

The secondary filter is usually either similar to the primary filter or is a 'spin-on' type similar to a car oil filter. The latter type can be undone using a filter wrench to loosen it.

Air gets into the fuel pipes when filters are changed, so changing them is followed by 'bleeding' the fuel system to remove air and get the fuel flowing smoothly. This can be a little complicated and the exact procedure varies depending on your type of engine. It should be explained in the manual for your make and model of engine and it's worth knowing how to do it in case it becomes necessary during a cruise. One way to learn is to ask the engine dealer or engineer to do the job and show you how to it's done.

Air system

The air intake filter should be cleaned or changed annually. Paper elements can simply be replaced. Some filters have a layer of wadding that can be washed clean and replaced. Old engines may have an oil bath, in which case you need to clean the metal screen and replace the oil.

Electrical system

When working on the electrical system, first disconnect the battery.

Clean and check the tightness of all electrical connections. With a petrol motor it's particularly important to avoid sparks occurring in the engine compartment. The battery should be kept clean and dry. Grease the battery terminals with petroleum jelly – Vaseline or similar – to

Air filters vary but this type is accessible by unscrewing the bolts.

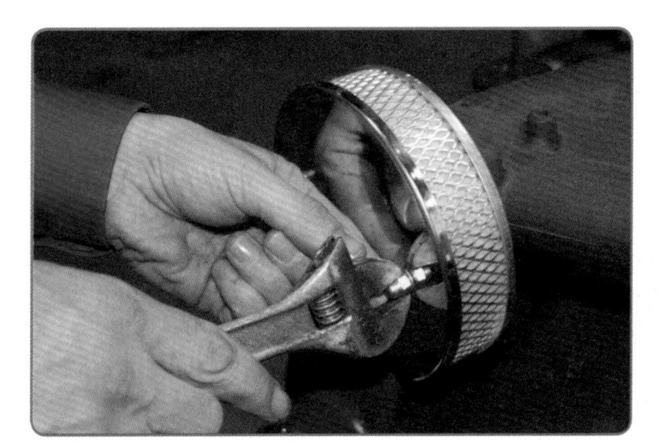

The filter is replaced between the securing mesh before bolting the cover back on.

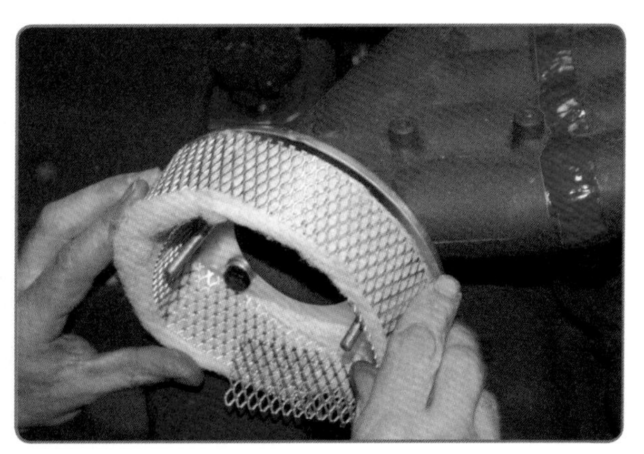

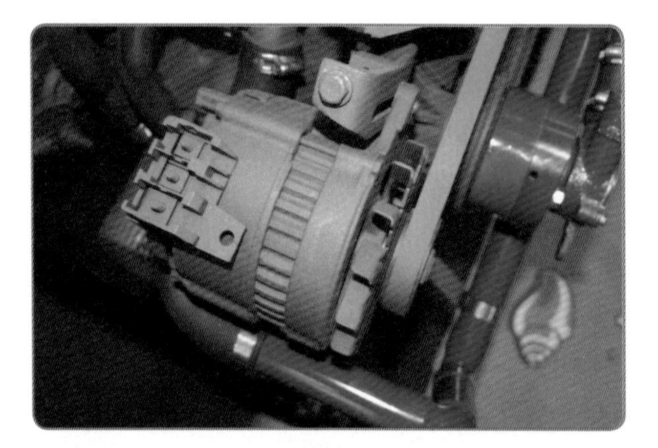

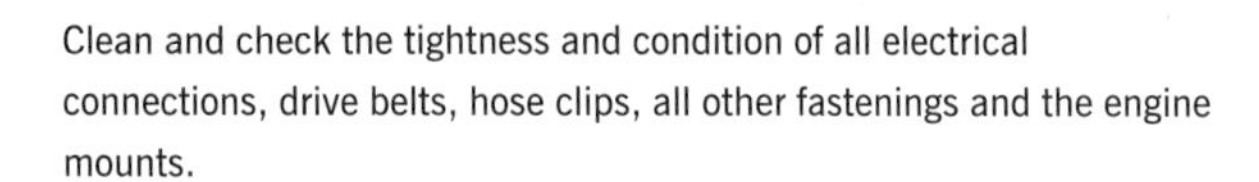

Clean and check the tightness and condition of all electrical connections, drive belts, hose clips, all other fastenings and the engine mounts.

prevent corrosion. Remember, batteries contain harmful acid, so wear suitable eye and hand protection when dealing with them.

If the boat is unused for any length of time remember to charge the battery every month or two. A small 12V solar panel connected to the battery can help to stop it losing its charge.

Check belts for wear, cracking and tightness. In most cases if the belt can be depressed 12mm with your finger it's at the correct tension.

Additional points for petrol motors

Spark plugs

See the earlier section on spark plugs in outboard motors. The same maintenance tasks also apply to inboard engines.

Distributor

To service the distributor, first remove the cap by releasing the two spring clips. Then remove the rotor arm and

Ford Water Mota petrol engines are found in some older motor cruisers. They need to be carefully maintained as they can suffer from the damp environment more than diesel engines, and it's important to prevent leaks of petrol vapour meeting sparks from the electrical system.

lubricate the inside of the cam body with a couple of drops of engine oil. Put a very thin smear of lithium grease on the cam faces and check that the points gap is correct according to the engine manual. Use the adjustment screws to reposition it if necessary. If the contact points are badly worn or pitted they should be replaced. Badly pitted points may indicate that the condenser needs to be replaced.

Fuel system

Because of the risk of petrol vapour accumulating in the boat, a suitably experienced engineer should carry out the work on the fuel system. If it's necessary to adjust the slow-running or volume control screws on the carburettor, this should be done when the engine has reached its full operating temperature. Don't be tempted to remove and clean the jets with a piece of wire. Carburettor cleaning should only be done by someone with the necessary experience and equipment, including the use of compressed air to clean the jets.

Engine drive systems

As explained in Chapter 3, there are two main ways in which the engine is connected to the propeller. Basic maintenance procedures are described here.

Shaft drive

The engine is connected to the propeller by a shaft through the hull, and steering is by a rudder. This is a comparatively simple arrangement with the engine and gears sited in a compartment that can be accessed from the cockpit or cabin. Where the shaft goes through the hull there is a 'gland' that allows the shaft to rotate but is sufficiently tight to stop water flooding into the hull.

There will always be an occasional drip of water from the gland, but as it wears over a considerable period of time its fittings will gradually allow more water in. To prevent excess leakage fastenings on the gland need to be tightened slightly. On some glands a fitting is regularly adjusted to force grease into the gland.

When tightening the gland fittings, don't overdo it. When the engine is running there should be an occasional drip still coming from it. If there isn't, or if the gland feels hot when the engine's been running, slacken the fastenings slightly.

Eventually it will become necessary to repack the gland with the material that keeps most of the water out. This must be done effectively and with the boat ashore. It's a task best left to an engineer, as the consequences of getting it wrong could include a serious leak and/or considerable damage.

This is one type of stern gland, where the shaft goes through the hull to the propeller.

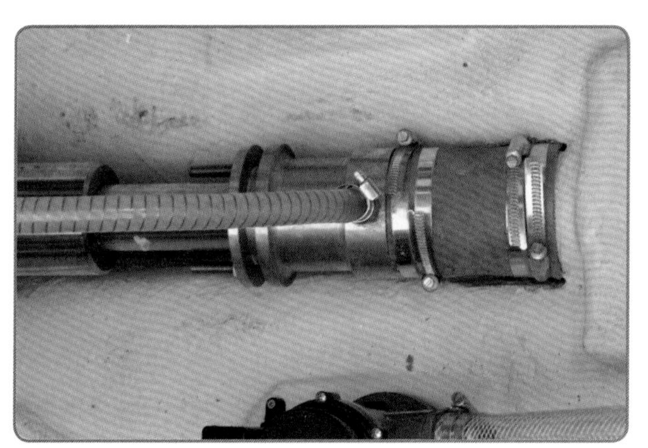

Winterising an inboard engine

Many of the above servicing tasks will be relevant for winterising most types of engine.

A major enemy of engines – particularly in a watery environment – is condensation, which causes corrosion. When you lay up your boat for winter, block the holes where moist air can enter and condense on cold metal surfaces. These include intake and exhaust ports.

Changing the oil before running the engine for the last time at the end of the boating season will help to give the moving parts a fresh coat of protective oil. Use of a lubricating water-dispersant spray will also help.

Shut the cooling water seacock and ensure water is drained out of the engine by opening any drains. Close them after draining out. Put a suitable antifreeze mixture into the cooling system to ensure that all parts are protected from frost. The exact procedure for this will depend on the type of cooling system.

Remove the battery and charge it regularly during the winter. Check the engine's manual for additional winterising tasks.

Most importantly, before using the engine again in the spring you must remember to recommission it by removing the blockages you put in the air intakes etc, replacing the impeller and battery, and restoring the cooling system and other winterised components to normal operating condition. Fixing a reminder list of these tasks somewhere prominent is a good precaution.

Outdrive

With an outdrive the engine is hard up against the stern of the boat and connected through it to a 'leg' which has gears and a propeller. This is sometimes called a 'stern drive', 'Z drive' or 'inboard/outboard'. The outdrive has some similarities with the lower parts of an outboard motor. Like an outboard it can be tilted up to access the propeller. Maintenance is more complicated than with a shaft drive, but it must be regularly serviced otherwise expensive repairs will become necessary. Servicing is done with the boat out of the water, usually during the winter lay-up period.

Continued on page 182

Reducing engine noise

Although the emphasis of this book is on simple maintenance tasks rather than improvements and the installation of extra equipment, one improvement that can make motor boating much more enjoyable involves the reduction of engine noise. In fact noise pollution from engines on inland waterways such as the Norfolk Broads has become a significant issue, and the authorities are keen to reduce the intrusive disturbance caused by motor boat engines. This can be a particular problem when an engine has to be run for hours at a mooring in order to recharge the batteries in a motor cruiser.

Although recently developed diesel engines are much quieter, a great many older engines are still in use and both their owners and the surrounding environment would benefit from substantial noise reduction. The following photographs and instructions were kindly provided by the manufacturers of Halyard Noise Insulation material.

Noise insulation installation

Step 1

Measure as precisely as possible the exact size of all the areas of the engine compartment that you intend to cover with insulation. Once you've got the exact measurements, cut the insulation material to the size you require. It would be a good idea to mark which part of the engine compartment it's been cut for, *ie* back, front, top, starboard side or port side.

The aim is to clad as much of the engine space as possible, leaving no gaps for noise to escape through and no hard surfaces for it to bounce off. Airflow must be taken into consideration when fitting the insulation. All engines require air for combustion – the bigger the engine, the more space will be needed in the engine compartment.

Step 2

The surface to which you intend to attach the insulation needs to be dry, clean and free of dust and grease. Halyard Noise Insulation material will stick to flat surfaces, but not to curved.

On GRP surfaces, attach the insulation directly to the surface using the self-adhesive backing. Note that this won't work if the GRP surface is rough or curved. Sand the surface lightly to scratch the gel coat and provide a key. Then remove all dust.

Steel surfaces that are etch-primed are ideal. Ordinary steel is also fine. This should be lightly sanded and then cleaned.

Aluminium surfaces should be sanded lightly before cleaning. The surface must be cleaned with grease-free cleaner using a lint-free wipe that doesn't leave threads, dust or paper traces on the surface.

Timber surfaces should be primed with a common wood primer. Self-adhesive materials can't be used on timber such as teak: they'll work on normal grained timber, but not on really coarse grain or cratered surfaces.

Use carbon tetrachloride, cellulose thinners, white spirit, isopropyl alcohol, Evostick Cleaner or spirit wipes. Do *not* use meths, petrol or de-greasing fluid. Be certain to follow the maker's recommendations regarding masks, eye protection and gloves.

When you clean the surface, don't wipe in circles. Instead, wipe towards one corner so that you push any dust and grease towards one point before removing it. Always clean the surface twice. The surface must be dry and free from condensation – a hair-dryer is ideal for removing condensation.

Step 3

If the surface of your engine compartment is suitable for attaching Halyard Noise Insulation using the self-adhesive backing, then this can be done now and you can skip to step 6.

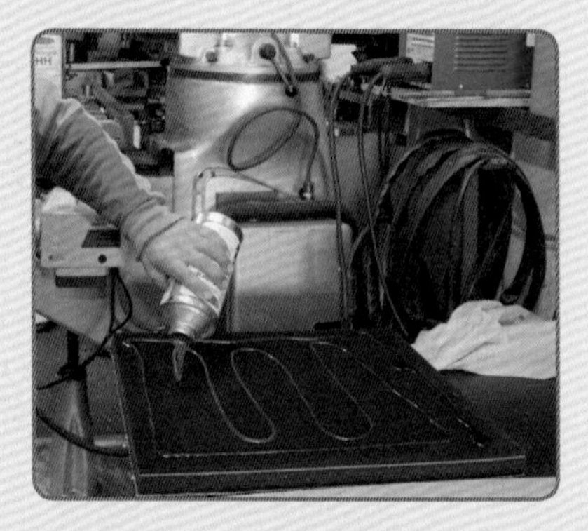

If you need to use a suitable adhesive to attach the insulation, coat the back with it, following the instructions and safety precautions set out on the adhesive container. Coat evenly in order to ensure firm attachment to the compartment surface. You should coat only one part of the compartment surface at a time, starting with the back and moving backwards out of the compartment.

The majority of adhesives will instruct you to coat both surfaces and let these become 'touch dry'. This usually means leaving the glue to dry for about 15 minutes. This is another reason why you should complete one surface of the compartment at a time.

Step 4

If you're able to remove the walls of the engine compartment then it's easier to coat them with adhesive and it can be done in a safer environment.

Step 5
Wait until the adhesive on the surface and on the Noise Insulation is 'touch dry' before fixing them together.

Step 6

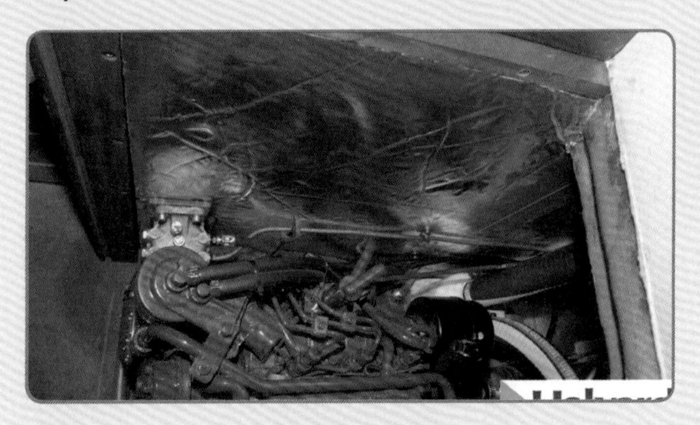

Be careful when pressing the insulation material into place. More pressure gives a better bond. Ideally the material should be 'jigged' or shored into place for 48 hours. Use vertical surfaces to support horizontal panels.

Step 7
Once the insulation is in place the bond of the adhesive will continue to strengthen over a period of 48 hours.

Step 8

Any fixings removed in order to install the Halyard Noise Insulation should now be put back in place. If there are any areas where you think the insulation could become unstuck (for example, if it's upside down beneath decking and hatches), then it should be secured in place by means of screws and washers, pins with washers, thin battens, or wire stretched across it.

Step 9
Any excess adhesive in the engine compartment should be wiped away. If it's already started to dry then leave it for 48 hours and remove it by sanding.

Additional recommendations

- As far as possible, bulkheads should totally encase the engine area. They should be free of bolted-on clutter that would force areas of bulkhead to be left without insulation.
- Insulation material should be fitted over the total surface of the engine room bulkheads, not merely between deckhead joists and in convenient clear areas.
- With engine boxes, remember that the noise will flow under the general deck area. Bulkheads should continue right down the hull, leaving limber holes for bilge water if necessary. Insulate down to, but not into, bilge water.
- With Halyard Noise Insulation all round the engine, further improvements can be achieved by adding density to the bulkheads. Halyard high-density barrier layer can be fitted between mats or carpeting and the actual deck.
- Hatches and companionways must fit neatly and should have a noise-tight cushion such as Halyard hatch tape.
- All motor boats, particularly with twin engines, will benefit enormously from 'double decking' insulation, with a 6in gap between the layers.
- Avoid leaving noise caverns either side of the engine: drop a removable bulkhead beside the engine and insulate this. Remember, fuel and water tanks collect and amplify noise.
- With twin engines try to put each engine in a separate compartment with a removable bulkhead between.

This Mercruiser outdrive is similar in some ways to an outboard motor but it's connected to an inboard engine.

Part of the necessary work can be done by an amateur, including regular topping up of oil, the draining and replacement of oil, and possibly the fitting of new anodes to prevent corrosion. However, full servicing involving dismantling the outdrive usually requires the use of special tools by an engineer familiar with the make and model. Dismantling is necessary to replace seals that prevent oil leaks and stop water entering the outdrive and mixing with the oil.

The rubber bellows where the leg joins the hull should be checked frequently for cracking or deterioration, as this could cause a leak.

Electric inboard motors

As is the case with electric outboards, most of the above maintenance work isn't needed on an electric inboard motor. Electric motors are amazingly small compared with diesel engines; even when the controls and batteries are added, they can still take up less room than the fuel tank and all the parts of a diesel engine.

Substantial advances have been made with electric motors for boats. In particular, the Lynch motor (also

A Volvo outdrive removed for servicing by an engineer who has the necessary tools and expertise.

On this outdrive, the oil dipstick is accessed by unscrewing it from the top of the unit.

The oil drain plug for this outdrive leg is at the base of the unit.

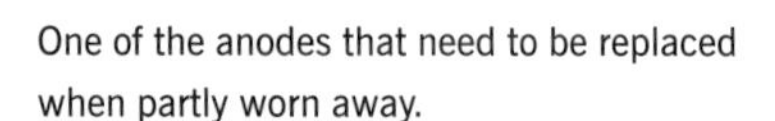

One of the anodes that need to be replaced when partly worn away.

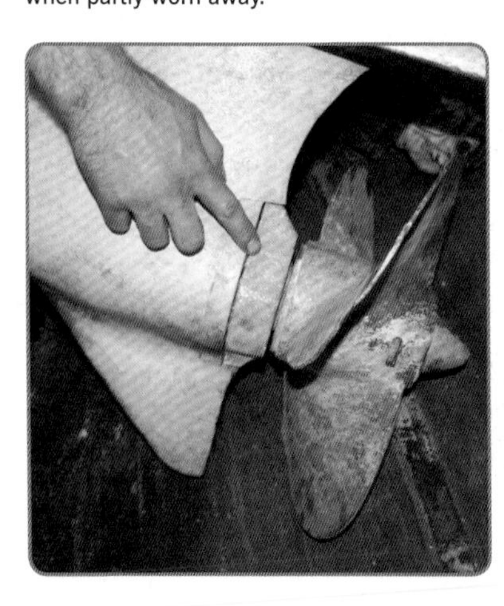

Kits of replacement oil seals are available.

Alan Curtis, engineer, is here working on the dismantled outdrives shown in previous photographs.

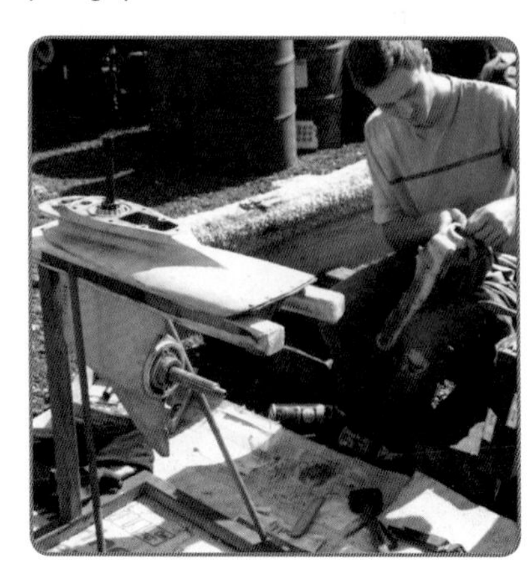

This motor cruiser, used on the Norfolk Broads, has the quiet, odour-free and simple-to-maintain electric motor shown in the next photograph.

Although the currently available lead acid batteries are quite bulky, the electric motor is nevertheless very small.

known as the Agni motor) is surprisingly powerful and very compact, as can be seen in the photographs.

Although they're still more suited to inland waterways such as the Norfolk Broads and the River Thames than the open sea, further developments are progressing rapidly. In the meantime hybrid diesel/electric motor systems are available. These have the reserve power for seagoing situations along with the advantages of silent and exhaust-free electric motoring in calm conditions.

A purpose-built vessel, the Swiss catamaran *Sun21,* recently crossed the Atlantic Ocean using only electric motors powered by solar panels. Some people may still have doubts about electric motors being able to produce high speeds, but the electrically powered speedboat *An Stradag*, piloted by Helen Loney, increased the speed record for battery-powered electric boats to 68mph on Coniston Water in November 2005.

Extensive information on all matters concerning electric motors on boats can be found on the Electric Boat Association's website at http://www.electric-boat-association.org.uk. Membership of the association gives access to many opportunities to become involved in the quiet and relaxing world of electric boating. Electric motors are set to become the first choice of power unit for many types of boat, as well as for other forms of transport.

The Lynch/Agni Motor, developed by Cedric Lynch for use in boats, is displayed along with its controls in a boat show display case. This is an indication of future trends in boat propulsion and transport motors generally.

Electricity supply companies provide 'green energy' schemes to supply electricity from wind turbines, and if the electricity used to charge your engine batteries comes from these it makes electric boating almost as environmentally friendly as hoisting sails! The use of solar panels or a wind turbine to charge the batteries is also beneficial to the marine environment and helps to conserve resources.

An Electric Boat Association rally on the Great Ouse, showing a variety of motor boats powered by electric motors. Some of the boats owned by members have a significant amount of power provided by solar panels, which work quite well even when it's cloudy.

18 Boating equipment and accessories

A large range of equipment is to be found in chandler shops and their mail order catalogues.

The huge range of equipment available for boats fills catalogues with many more pages than this book. The range and variety are fascinating but can be confusing, and some of it is desirable rather than essential. Boating magazines regularly include reviews of equipment, and articles from back issues can be ordered via their websites, listed in the Appendix.

This chapter concentrates on essential items and some strongly recommended items of equipment, where space allows. Some equipment has already been covered in earlier chapters.

Equipment in an open day boat

Storage will be limited in an open boat used for only a few hours at a time. It's therefore important to keep it clear of clutter so that you can move around unhindered. The basic essential equipment should include:

- Lifejackets or buoyancy aids (preferably with crutch straps)
- Bucket, bailer and sponge
- Paddles or oars
- Compass
- Knife
- Pliers
- Screwdriver
- Lengths of rope and cord
- First aid kit
- Anchor and rope
- Cable ties
- Nuts, bolts and screws to match those on the boat
- A selection of tools to suit the engine, nuts, bolts and adjustable fittings on the boat
- Cork or rubber bungs and epoxy putty for emergency hull repairs
- Motor fuel in suitable containers safely stored on board
- Spare parts for engine or outboard motor, including shear pins, propeller pins, oil, spark plugs and spanners
- Handbooks/manuals for operation of engine and equipment
- Copy of insurance details
- VHF radio and mobile phone
- Food and drink
- Distress flares

Equipment in a motor cruiser

In a small motor cruiser the amount of equipment will be dictated to some extent by the storage space available. The list below mostly covers items that are important from the safety point of view. Very cautious people might say they're all essential. Realistically, though, the inclusion of some items will depend on what you can afford, the size of the boat, how far from land you expect to cruise and for how long. Practical aspects concerning some of these items are covered further on in this chapter.

In addition to the items listed above, basic equipment should include:

- Lifejackets with crutch straps
- Distress flares
- First aid kit and sunscreen cream
- Safety harness and clip-on lifeline, often linked with lifejacket
- Horseshoe lifebuoy with floating line and light
- VHF radio, fixed and/or hand-held
- Mobile phone
- Hand-operated signalling horn and whistle
- Fire extinguishers
- Fire blanket
- Smoke alarm
- Carbon monoxide alarm
- Boat hook or two to pick up moorings
- Adequate waterproof and windproof clothing and non-slip shoes
- Sleeping bags and pillows in waterproof bags
- Tool kit including knife and tools to match the boat's fittings
- Motor fuel and motor spares, including shear pins, propeller pins, oil, spark plugs and spanners
- Auxiliary outboard motor for use if main engine fails
- Bilge pump as well as bailer and bucket
- Fenders
- Compasses – fixed and hand-held
- Anchors, chain and warps
- Spare ropes
- Navigation lights plus emergency battery-operated alternatives
- Torches, batteries, 12V spotlight
- Temporary hull repair materials, *eg* bungs and epoxy putty
- Binoculars
- Charts of waters to be navigated
- Tide tables
- Copy of insurance details
- Illustrated table of emergency signals
- Fish finder (echo sounder) to measure depth
- GPS (Global Positioning System) to establish position at sea for navigation purposes, possibly combined with radar as a chartplotter
- Radar reflector
- Wristwatch
- Barometer
- Padlocks, security devices and their keys

Food and drink will also be needed according to your personal preferences. The quantity will depend on the length of your cruise, but you should always take some with you even on a brief trip, in case you go aground and get stuck out on the water – or mud – for longer than expected. An emergency drinking water supply, in addition to the cruiser's own water supply, is strongly recommended.

Buoyancy aids.

Even a dog can have a buoyancy aid, complete with a handle to lift him back on board.

Lifejackets and buoyancy aids

True lifejackets and buoyancy aids are both often just referred to as 'lifejackets' for brevity, but there is a difference.

A buoyancy aid is like a padded waistcoat. Its built-in foam will help to keep someone afloat who's conscious and can swim. The padding of the buoyancy aid will also help to keep them warm. This type is ideal for people who expect to get wet enjoying activities like waterskiing. Buoyancy aids incorporating impact vests are designed to be strapped on particularly firmly for this purpose. They help to absorb the impact with the water on falling in.

Buoyancy aids also tend to be cheaper than lifejackets, and some people are happier to rely on their permanent built-in buoyancy than on the quick inflation of a lifejacket.

Modern lifejackets are usually of the inflatable type and are designed to turn an unconscious person onto their back in order to keep their face out of the water. They're often regarded as the best life preserver for people on a boat who don't normally go into the water. A tube is provided for the wearer to inflate it and there may be a gas cylinder inflator that can be activated by pulling a cord. In addition to the pull cord and inflation tube, self-inflating lifejackets have a device that activates the gas cylinder automatically if it gets wet.

The RNLI's advice is very thorough on the subject of life preservers and encourages the wearing of crutch straps between the legs to prevent the jacket or buoyancy aid rising up and over the head. It also recommends having a spray hood with a lifejacket. This helps to keep spray and waves off the face in order to make breathing easier without inhaling or swallowing water, and preserves some body heat. A whistle, reflective tape and possibly a light fixed to a lifejacket all aid location during search and rescue.

Buoyancy is measured in Newtons (N). There are four European standards for life preservers:

- A 50N buoyancy aid may be sufficient on inland waterways. It doesn't have enough buoyancy to protect those unable to help themselves and is unlikely to turn a person over from a face-down position in the water.
- A 100N buoyancy aid/lifejacket is recommended for those in sheltered and calm water. It may not have

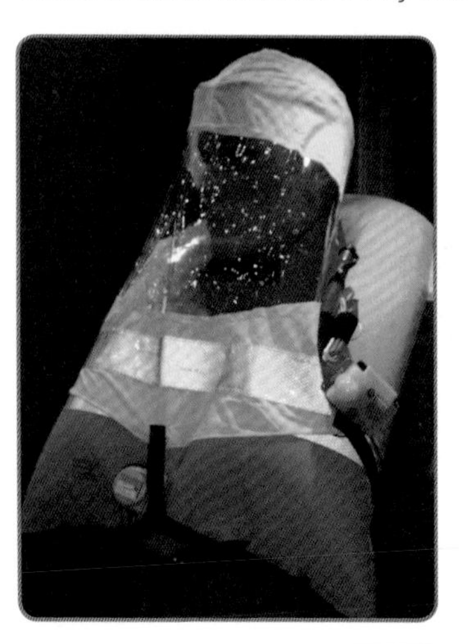

Left: An inflated lifejacket with spray hood and reflective strips that make it much easier to see someone in the water at night.

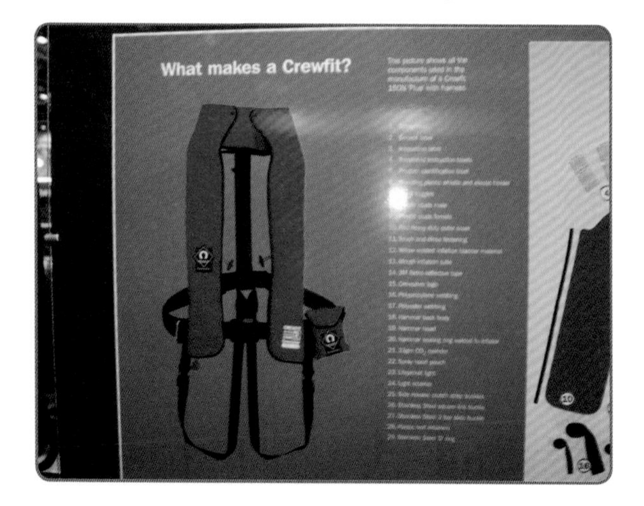

Right: An illustration of an inflatable lifejacket with crutch straps from a Crewsaver lifejacket display. This is the make of lifejacket used by most lifeboat crew members.

enough buoyancy to protect a person who's unable to help themselves and may not roll an unconscious person onto their back, particularly if they're wearing heavy clothing.

- A 150N lifejacket is recommended for general use on coastal and inshore waters, including rough weather. It should turn an unconscious person onto their back so that their face is clear of the water. Its performance may be affected if the user is wearing heavy and/or waterproof clothing.
- A 275N lifejacket is recommended for offshore cruising. It's intended primarily for extreme conditions and those wearing heavy protective clothing, which could stop lesser lifejackets turning an unconscious person onto their back.

Many lifejackets are fitted with a harness, which can be clipped via a safety line to suitably strong points on the deck of a motor cruiser. This helps keep you from losing balance on the deck of a cruiser and should prevent a 'man overboard' situation. Additionally, traditional good advice is 'One hand for yourself and one for the boat' – in other words, hold on to something with one hand whenever doing something for the boat with the other.

Selecting lifejackets for children requires special care in order to ensure a good fit. In particular, the buoyancy aid or lifejacket mustn't be able slip up over the child's head when in the water.

Even though many choose not to wear one unless sea and weather conditions are risky, putting on a lifejacket when boarding a boat should, ideally, be as automatic as fastening a car seat belt.

Lifejacket maintenance

A buoyancy aid can be checked visually for wear, chafing, splits and loose stitching. It can be tested by wearing it and going for a swim. This also helps to show how effective and how good a fit it is – a particularly important consideration as children grow up and possibly pass theirs on to a younger sibling.

Manually-inflated lifejackets can be tested by inflating them to the correct pressure, using the manual inflation tube, and leaving them for 24 hours. There should be no loss of pressure. To release the air completely, press the valve in the inflating tube and press the jacket down on a flat surface.

Older lifejackets, such as those obtained when buying a second-hand boat, must be checked and serviced. The RNLI Lifejacket Rogues Gallery displays some life-threatening lifejackets and equipment that should have been discarded and replaced long ago.

Inflatable lifejackets should be checked for abrasion, splits and wear every month and professionally serviced at least every two years. Don't forget to check the straps and fastenings.

The automatically-inflating type of lifejacket has a small CO^2 cylinder, which must be replaced after it has inflated the lifejacket and at regular intervals according to the manufacturer's recommendations and instruction manual. All too often this cylinder is neglected and corroded. Check regularly that the cylinder is screwed in hand-tight.

Trained RNLI volunteers demonstrate at boat shows how to inspect lifejackets, including the inflatable types. The accompanying photographs are from a display and demonstration at the Southampton Boat Show. Procedures vary according to make and type so it's most important to follow the instructions provided with the appropriate kit of parts sold by the manufacturer. If you have the slightest doubt about replacing a lifejacket's cylinder yourself, arrange for the manufacturer or dealer to do it for you.

Lifejacket manufacturers and dealers have websites with servicing information. Examples include http://www.lifejackets.co.uk and an online video for the Crewsaver

The RNLI's Lifejacket Rogues Gallery showing useless and dangerous equipment.

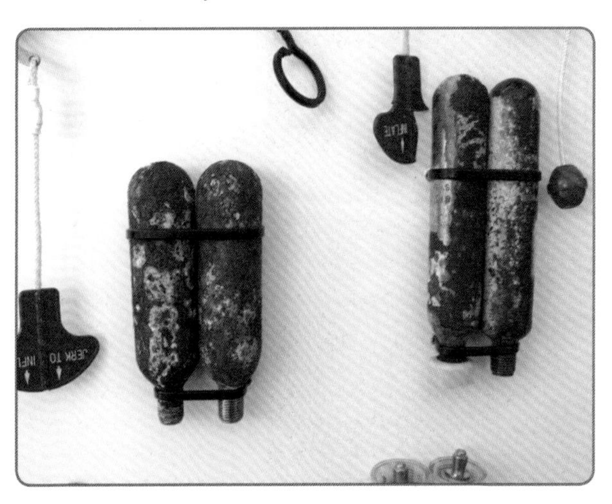

Corroded gas inflation cylinders found attached to lifejackets that would not automatically inflate when most needed.

Kits for replacing inflation cylinders on lifejackets are available from manufacturers and dealers. The instructions must be followed carefully, or else someone qualified to do so should replace the cylinder.

Above and below: Obviously a lifejacket can't be test-inflated using its cylinder as this would discharge it, but the jacket should still be test-inflated regularly using the manual inflation tube. Leave it for 24 hours to check that it remains fully inflated and that there are no leaks.

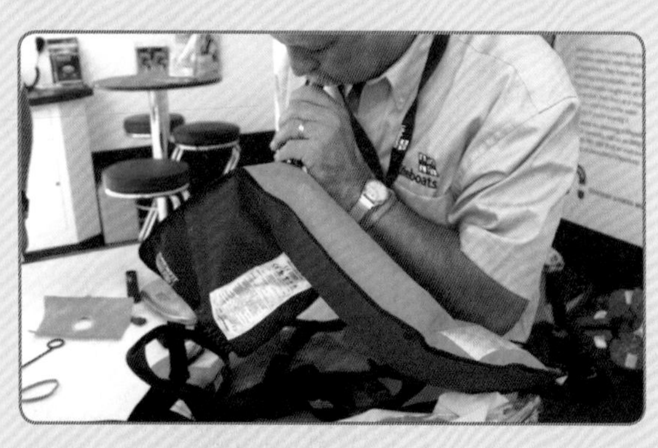

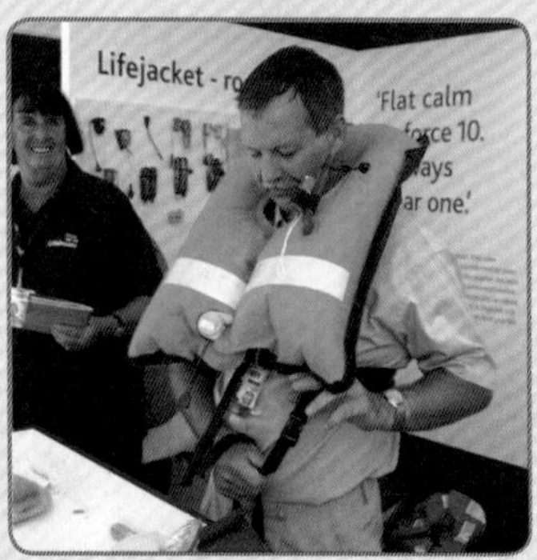

An inflated lifejacket in position, with crutch straps in place to prevent it rising up and over the wearer's head.

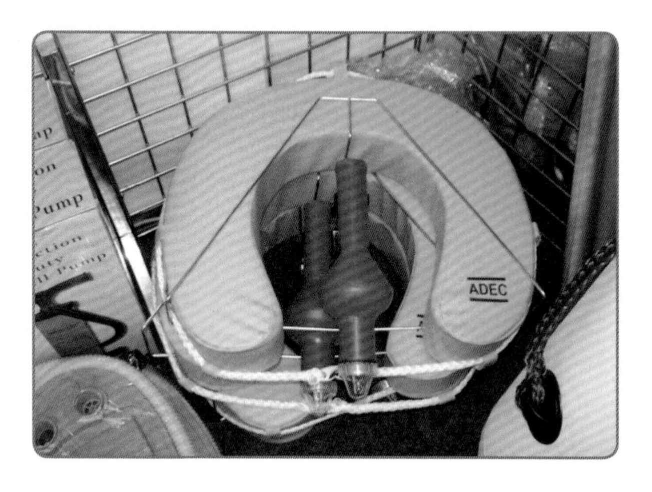

Horseshoe lifebuoys with floating lines and lights. A metal frame is included to mount the lifebuoy in an easily accessible position on a boat.

make of lifejackets at http://www.crewsaver.co.uk. Click on 'Inflatable Lifejacket Manual'.

Ensure the crew never use lifejackets as cushions, always dry them after use, and always store them in dry conditions.

Horseshoe lifebuoy with floating line and light

A lifebuoy mounted on the rail of a motor cruiser should be easily accessible to throw to someone in the water so that they can be pulled towards the boat. Ensure the end of the attached floating line is tied securely to the boat. 'Man overboard' rescue procedures are taught and practised on boating courses.

Distress flares and signals

The following may seem rather alarming but you shouldn't let it put you off boating. Most distress flares never need to be used, but they should nevertheless be part of a boat's safety equipment.

If you get into difficulties you need to be able to attract attention and call for help. One recognised method is, if possible, to stand and slowly raise and lower both outstretched arms. However, audible signals are more effective. If you're near the shore or other boats shout for help or give the SOS signal using a whistle or hand-operated signalling horn: three short blasts, three long blasts, and three short blasts.

Distress flares should be used in an emergency situation, to attract attention and pinpoint your position. A white flare isn't a distress signal but is used to warn other boats of your presence and to avoid a collision. Other types of flares include packs of mini flares compact enough to be carried in a pocket, and red parachute rocket flares.

When first boarding a boat, instructions concerning emergency equipment and procedures, including instructions provided with each flare, should be read by all members of the crew, and followed carefully in the event of an emergency.

Each flare will have an expiry date, and it needs to be replaced at this date otherwise it may not work when you most need it to. In fact an out-of-date flare may misfire and cause damage and injury. For this reason as well as the obvious risk of giving a false alarm, old flares should never be used as part of a firework display.

Out-of-date flares must be disposed of properly according to the regulations current at the time. When buying replacements, ask the seller for the current procedure regarding disposal. He may even be able to dispose of your old ones for you. The local coastguard or fire station should also be able to provide advice on disposal facilities.

More detail on choice and use of flares can be found on the RNLI website and the Pains Wessex website at http://www.pwss.com.

Mobile phone and VHF radio

The RNLI strongly advises the use of a VHF radio rather than a mobile phone. The radio needs to be licensed before it is used. The fact that it's also necessary to gain a qualification and licence to use a VHF radio is good because it helps to ensure that radios are used properly. However, there's a tendency for this to put some boat owners off owning one. RYA-approved training establishments and many boating and sailing clubs arrange the short courses and tests necessary for this qualification.

Harbour masters and coastguards listen for calls on VHF radio and can be contacted for advice and information about navigation, hazards, weather, moorings and marina berths, etc.

In an emergency a mobile phone is useful as a back-up device, to call 999 and ask for the coastguard if there's a problem with the radio. But this isn't as effective or reliable as sending a Mayday call on a VHF radio. With VHF transmissions, rescuers can pinpoint the location of a vessel and other boats can hear the

Hand-operated signalling horn.

Hand-held red flare. Used to show location of a vessel in distress.

Orange smoke flares, hand-held and floating. The dense orange smoke signals position, *eg* to an aircraft.

Flares show the lifeboat and helicopter where you can be found and rescued.

A VHF radio can be installed in the cabin where 12V electricity is available on a motor cruiser.

Portable VHF radios with rechargeable batteries are an alternative.

distress signals and come to its aid. A fixed VHF radio will have more range than a mobile phone and has the substantial power of a 12V battery behind it. A mobile phone by contrast has limited range, poor signal strength and much less battery power.

Where 12V power isn't available, a hand-held VHF radio, using internal batteries, can be used. A wide range of these is available, including radios that are waterproof and can even float if accidentally dropped. A hand-held VHF radio also provides a back-up to a fixed radio and can be used in a tender away from a motor cruiser.

The RNLI often provides demonstrations on the use of emergency equipment and procedures, and the RYA and many boating clubs provide courses that are essential to gain the qualification to use a VHF radio.

Navigation lights

Navigation lights are covered in Chapter 16.

Bilge pumps

In a cruiser with a 12V electricity supply an electric bilge pump can be installed. This can have an automatic float switch that turns the pump on when water accumulates in the bilges, which is particularly useful when a boat is left afloat. It removes rainwater that may get into the bilges and helps reduce the risk of sinking if a leak occurs.

The 'belt and braces' approach is appropriate here. Even with an electric pump it's wise to still have a manually-operated pump and one or two buckets for bailing, just in case the battery is flat or gets swamped with water.

Fenders

Few boats are built with sufficient fendering or rubbing strips to cope with mooring alongside quays and other boats. Horrible grinding noises as GRP rubs against concrete or steel can be avoided with sufficient carefully placed fenders. Most plastic fenders are inflatable and

A 12V electric bilge pump kit with automatic float switch.

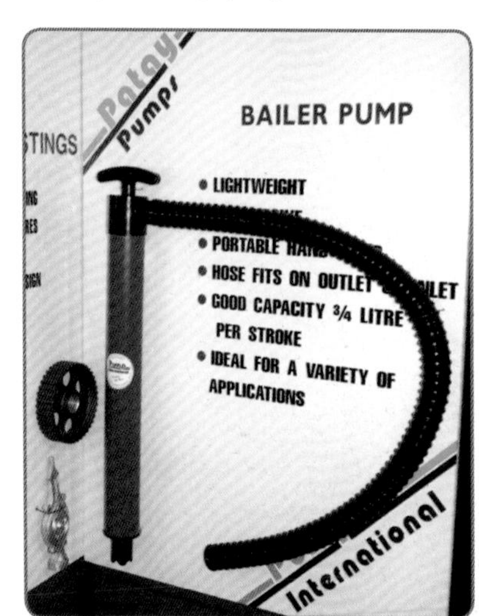

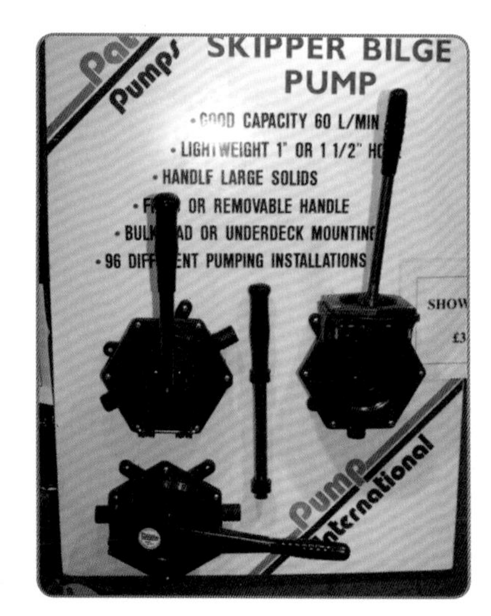

Hand-operated bilge pumps.

A selection of inflatable plastic fenders.

Fenders come in a variety of shapes and sizes to suit different boats and situations.

should be reasonably firm but not rock hard. If you can press your finger about half an inch (15mm) into the middle of a fender it should be about right for absorbing shocks without itself harming the boat.

Fenders that are dirty with mud and grit can scrape the gelcoat, so it's best to keep them clean. Some boat owners use fabric covers on fenders to further reduce any risk of chafing.

Echo sounder or fish finder

The electrical device originally called an echo sounder is now more usually referred to as a fish finder. This change indicates the increased sensitivity of such devices not only to the seabed but also to fish, which makes them particularly appealing to boat owners who want to do any fishing. For actual motor boating, a clear indication of depth and the shape of the seabed helps to avoid running aground. More on fish finders can be found in Chapter 16.

GPS

Global positioning or satellite navigation ('satnav') devices have become widespread and their mass production has reduced their price. If you have the necessary electricity supply they certainly aid navigation. In fact a portable hand-held GPS with alkaline batteries is worth considering if 12V power isn't available on a day boat. These devices also give an accurate indication of speed over the seabed or riverbed, which is important for navigation calculations and to avoid exceeding speed limits.

The very sophisticated chartplotter/radar/fish finder systems displayed at boat shows are quite expensive and more appropriate for offshore cruising and ocean-going vessels, although high tech enthusiasts may have fun with them – and why not, if this improves their boating experience?

A fish finder gives a clear indication of depth below the boat.

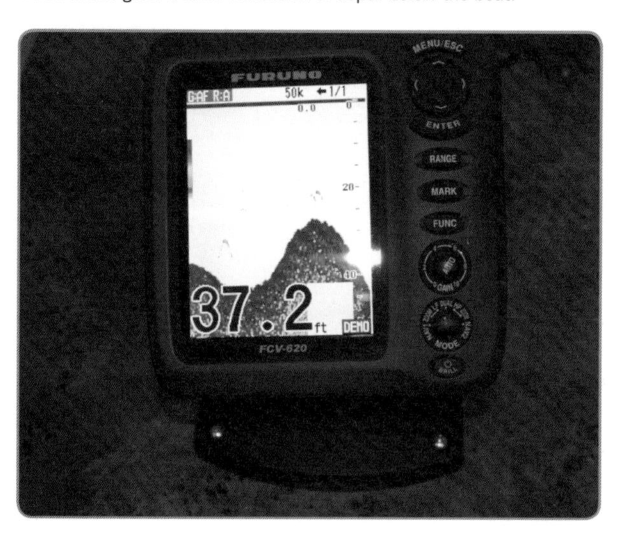

Below: Navigation is much easier with GPS equipment.

Right: A hand-held GPS with rechargeable batteries is useful on an open boat with no 12V electricity supply or as a back-up alternative.

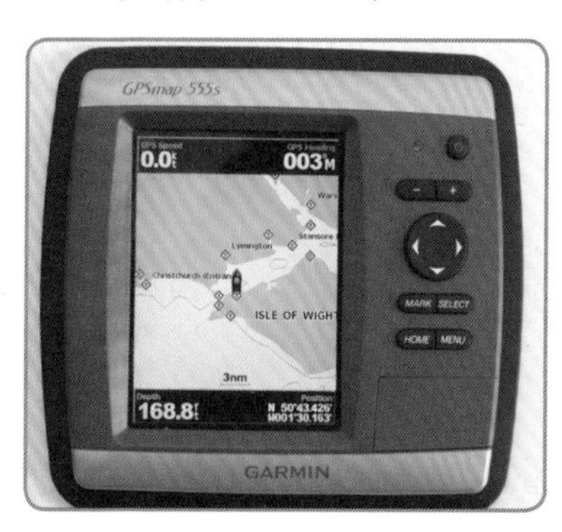

Clothing and footwear

On warm summer days with a light breeze, plenty of people wear ordinary casual clothing to enjoy boating on inland or very sheltered estuary waters. However, non-slip footwear is essential, along with clothing that will maintain sufficient body heat, bearing in mind that it's almost always considerably colder out on the water than inland. Be prepared for sudden changes in the weather. A waterproof outer layer should always be taken on the boat ready for a sudden unexpected downpour.

In cool conditions wetsuits are necessary for waterskiing and similar sports. These work by trapping a layer of water under the neoprene material of the suit, next to your skin. Body heat then warms the water, providing protection from the cold. The suit, or impact jacket, also provides some protection against the impact of hitting the water at speed. Wetsuits are available in various thicknesses and the thickest – mainly for winter use – are called 'steamers'. A wetsuit must fit well in order to work properly.

The more expensive drysuit is fully waterproof, with water-tight seals around openings for neck, wrists and feet. Thermal layers need to be worn under this suit to keep you warm.

Wet boots made of neoprene work in the same way as a wetsuit. Gloves can also be made of neoprene. As well as providing warmth, gloves reinforced with leather protect the hands from chafing and can provide extra grip.

The highly specialised and fashionable clothing available for boating is expensive. However, the latest breathable waterproof garments make life more comfortable and may be considered worthwhile by a boating enthusiast who gets afloat at every opportunity whatever the weather.

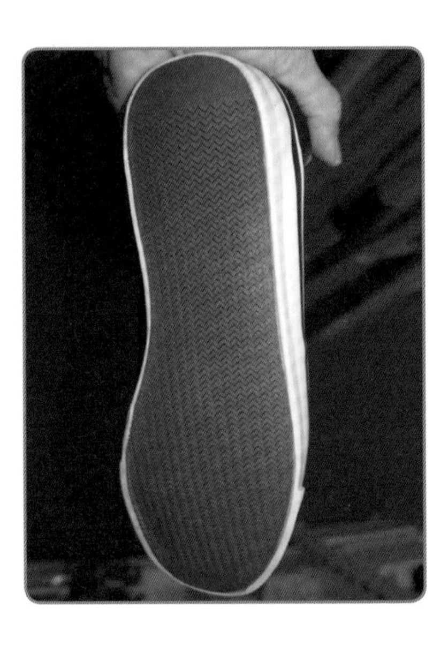

The most important feature of boating footwear is secure non-slip soles and heels.

Wetsuit care

The following tips will help prolong the life of a wetsuit and similar neoprene garments for many years:

- Never clean the wetsuit in a washing machine, and don't dry-clean it. Rinse it by hand in clean fresh water to remove salt and dirt. Stains can be removed with a mild shampoo or special wetsuit cleaner.
- Dry it away from direct heat, suspended on a large thick hanger that will spread the load and not cause distortion.
- Zips that get stiff or clogged can be cleaned gently with an old soft toothbrush and lubricated by rubbing them with a candle or beeswax.

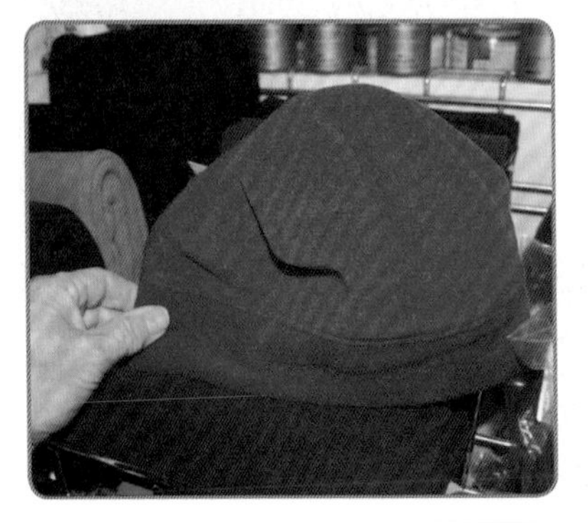

Windproof and waterproof clothing is available for boating activities. A hood or hat is strongly advised, as much body heat is lost via the head. You may also need a hat for sun protection.

A wetsuit is needed for those who want to enjoy high-speed activities outside the boat.

- Avoid contact with petrol, aerosols, oil and solvents.
- Take care not to damage the material with a broken or sharp fingernail.
- Check for tears in the neoprene. Small repairs can be done with neoprene glue. It may be possible to repair larger tears with neoprene material glued and stitched with strong polyester thread.
- Store the suit unfolded in dry, well-ventilated conditions.
- A wetsuit not often used may lose its elasticity and seem to have shrunk. Elasticity can be restored by soaking the suit in lukewarm water and then drying it thoroughly away from direct heat.

Locks and security devices

Unfortunately, outboard motors and other equipment are sometimes stolen from boats left on moorings and in less secure storage facilities. This varies considerably according to the location. In some areas boat owners leave outboard motors, trailers and equipment without any security devices at all and seem to have no problems, but elsewhere anything not securely fastened soon gets stolen.

It's better to be safe than sorry. If the outboard motor can't be removed and locked away, use a purpose-made security device, locked as in the accompanying photographs. Try to put loose equipment where it's under lock and key or else take it home. Clearly, it's as important to lock the cabin of a motor cruiser as it is to lock the doors of a car. A range of outboard motor locks is available from OML Ltd, and there's plenty of useful information on their website at http://www.outboardmotorlocks.co.uk.

Check what your insurance company requires regarding locks and the precautions that should be taken against theft. A trailer needs to be locked with a hitch lock or wheel clamp when left, whether or not the boat is on it.

Like Neighbourhood Watch schemes on land, there are Boatwatch schemes in harbours and at waterway mooring locations. Enquire from the local police station, harbour master or marina office what applies locally and get your boat and outboard motor, etc, registered with whatever scheme is available.

A battery-operated burglar alarm in a cabin may help, but only if there's someone available and willing to respond.

1

This simple cylinder lock is slid onto the outboard motor clamps and locked into place.

3

2

4

Left: Check the dial that's fitted on many extinguishers to show its condition.

Right: An automatic fire extinguisher can be mounted in the engine compartment. This operates when a fire causes the temperature of the extinguisher to rise above a certain level.

Fire extinguishers

As explained in Chapter 15, suitable fire extinguishers and a fire blanket should be mounted where they're easily accessible. Check regularly that the dial on the fire extinguisher shows it's still in suitable condition and replace it when it reaches its expiry date, which will be printed on the body of the extinguisher.

Fishing tackle

Whilst clearly not essential, a rod and line can add an extra level of enjoyment to motor boating. To keen sea anglers the main reason for owning a boat is to go out and find fish. However, many other boat owners may also want to have a minimum of tackle ready for those occasions when fish make themselves obvious. The fish finders referred to earlier will help with this, but in coastal areas you should also watch out for gatherings of sea birds, which are attracted to shoals of small fish on the surface – as are the larger fish that feed on them, such as mackerel. Having a spinning rod and some artificial lures ready will provide you with the opportunity to enjoy catching some of them. Having caught a few mackerel, a strip of the skin and flesh can be used as bait for other species.

The fishing aspect of boating will particularly appeal to younger members of the family. Although there are some awfully inadequate 'fishing kits' sold by seaside souvenir shops, proper fishing-tackle shops sell more suitable equipment including much-improved types of telescopic fishing rods that can easily be stowed away on any boat. The tackle shop staff will provide advice on the basic level of tackle needed for occasional fishing, and you may get drawn into the fascinating world of angling. Plenty of books and magazines are available to help to develop your skills and increase your success. Some are listed in the Appendix.

Although a licence is currently not required for sea angling for pleasure, check with the local authority, tackle shop or harbour master if there are any byelaws or regulations restricting local fishing, particularly in an estuary.

Regarding angling on inland waterways, the situation is rather more complicated. You must have a national rod licence, which can be bought at any post office. Additionally, in most cases you also need permission, a permit or club membership in order to fish each length of waterway. The boat registration and licensing authorities listed in the Appendix help with information on this. Additionally it's important to read some of the information in the many publications available in print and on the Internet regarding angling techniques and how to handle and return the fish you catch.

Three informative websites, which include numerous links to other relevant websites, are http://www.worldseafishing.com, http://www.anglersnet.co.uk and http://www.dofreefishing.com.

An automatic fire extinguisher can help to prevent fire damage such as this.

Breakdown services

Although it's not 'equipment' as such, many boat owners find it reassuring to have membership of a boating equivalent of the AA or RAC roadside assistance and rescue services. In this case the help usually arrives by boat. Assistance from both of the following organisations is available 24 hours a day, every day of the year.

River Canal Rescue Ltd has a range of membership options which provide assistance on inland waterways, available via an emergency telephone number. An engineer can be called out to deal with engine problems and to arrange for the boat to be towed back to suitable moorings if necessary. Its website is at http://www.rivercanalrescue.co.uk.

Seastart Ltd provides a similar service for its members in the most popular coastal boating areas. It's important to read the full details of exactly what they provide and where, which can be found on their website at http://www.seastart.co.uk.

Both of these organisations also provide other services, including courses on engine maintenance and other aspects of boating.

In areas not covered by these organisations – or if you prefer not to join – you should have the phone numbers of nearby boatyards with you, in case you need help or advice. In a dangerous situation or serious emergency you can, of course, contact the emergency services, including the Coastguard and RNLI.

Sources of equipment

Chandlers are the obvious source of supply for most items. Their online mail order operations have made their products more accessible and, as a result of greater competition, often cheaper. Many motor cruisers are used as caravans, 'mobile homes' or 'country cottages' afloat on inland waterways and in marinas. Although this may offend a few narrow-minded boating purists, there's absolutely nothing wrong with using a boat in this way if it gives you pleasure and provides relaxation in a very different and attractive environment, with the possibility of a little cruising if you feel so inclined.

In this case, the contents of caravan accessory shops will be of considerable interest, and some of the domestic equipment available can be used in the cabin of a comfortable cruiser. Bear in mind, though, that equipping and maintaining the boat itself should still be carried out using products designed to cope with a marine environment.

Details of how to make the cabin a home from home, and the vast array of domestic equipment available, isn't covered here, however, as we're concerned with actual *boating* equipment and maintenance.

Boat shows and boat jumbles

Boat shows provide not only the opportunity to see equipment and compare prices and specifications but also to learn from the experts how to use all the items displayed. Special reduced price offers are usually available for some equipment.

A cheaper alternative is the boat jumble, described in Chapter 4. The mixture of second-hand and reduced price new equipment found at such events is fascinating, and the atmosphere is invariably friendly. Having said that, caution needs to be exercised if you're considering the purchase of items affecting safety. You need to bear in mind all the points raised in this book about the strength and reliability of equipment you'll rely on when the wind and waves increase unexpectedly. Bear in mind too that some people believe equipment stolen from other boats sometimes finds its way into boat jumbles, though the regular presence of police at such events has reduced this risk.

Websites

Websites such as eBay and those that advertise boats for sale, as described in Chapter 4, also have sections containing a large range of used and reduced price chandlery. Although a huge amount of equipment is purchased in this way, it's important to be sure it's safe and fit for its purpose.

New and second-hand equipment is available quite cheaply at boat jumbles, but you should check the quality and reliability carefully.

19 Motor Boat Manual
The future

Motor cruiser displayed for sale.

Selling and trading up to a bigger boat

Plenty of boat owners start with a small motor boat and then, after several years of enjoyable boating, decide to move up to a more substantial boat for cruising coastal waters and staying aboard overnight. It may be possible to achieve this by buying a bargain 'project' boat requiring improvement and then selling it at a small profit after carrying out the necessary work and using it for a season or two. In this way it's possible to finance, at least partly, the move upmarket to a bigger boat.

An inspiring example

Dave Flint and Alison Shearing progressed from an 18ft Norman river cruiser to a larger Norman 25 and then to a much larger RLM 31 Bahama motor cruiser in need of renovation.

In each case they improved these bargain project boats to a high standard, which enabled them to trade up and eventually achieve their ambition of going to sea in a cruiser they were confident would be both seaworthy and comfortable. They were able to enjoy the process of improving these boats and then greatly enjoy cruising with each of them for a time before selling on and using the proceeds to buy another, larger boat. Along the way their skills and knowledge improved enough for them to take on the more ambitious task of rebuilding the Bahama cruiser, and

Dave Flint and Alison Shearing started by renovating small Norman cruisers.

The RLM 31 Bahama motor cruiser being worked on ashore.

they're now the proud owners of a very smart and well-equipped cruiser worth more than the total cost of purchase and renovation.

Much more information and many photographs of the work on their boats can be seen on their website at http://www.leomagill.co.uk.

Examples of many other such projects can be found on the Norman Boats Appreciation Society's website at http://www.normanboats.co.uk, and on the other boat owners' association websites listed on page 37 in Chapter 4. These websites provide much useful advice that supplements the earlier chapters and will help you to apply the principles covered to particular types of motor boat.

Selling a boat

Preparation for selling a motor boat involves carrying out many of the tasks described in this book in order to present it in a way that will be most appealing to a buyer willing to pay a fair price. Bear in mind in particular the advice on buying a second-hand boat outlined in Chapter 4. A buyer may well arrive with a copy of this book under their arm and check those very points!

It may seem obvious but it's surprising how many boats for sale haven't been cleared of personal possessions, rubbish and dirt. A good clean and polish makes a big difference. It shows that the boat's likely to have been well cared for. Pay particular attention to cookers, sinks, washbasins and toilets. Tidy up and coil ropes neatly. Replace or clean any mooring lines that are frayed or green with algae. Remember, buyers will want to see the engine so do your best to make it look clean and efficient. Remove any bilge water and clean inside lockers.

The hull of a cruiser may well look mottled and shabby at the end of the boating season but a coat of antifouling primer makes a big difference to that important first impression.

The first thing anyone sees on stepping down into a cabin is the floor, so make sure it's clean. A new floor covering makes a difference. The next thing to hit a potential buyer is the smell, so provide enough ventilation and deal with anything causing an off-putting odour. Use of a dehumidifier can help remove any dampness and condensation, which can be a problem when a boat's cabin is closed up for periods of time. A motor boat may well be perfectly sound but the above points can be a serious obstacle to a sale – particularly if a critical family member accompanies the buyer.

On inland waterways, it's an advantage if the BSS certificate has a few years left to run. A buyer could be put

Dave and Alison's cruiser ready for them to enjoy the fruits of their labours.

off if they immediately have to arrange a safety inspection and may well make this a condition of buying your boat anyway.

Be ready for the question 'Why are you selling this boat?' Bear in mind that potential buyers may ask the owners of nearby boats about the history of your boat and how you've used it, so take care to provide accurate answers to searching questions.

Prepare an inventory of exactly what's included with the boat: this can be attached to the printed details and to the receipt in order to avoid any misunderstandings. One or two extras, such as a spare anchor or auxiliary outboard motor, could be kept in reserve and thrown in later during negotiations in order to close the deal.

When deciding on the price, bear in mind that you'll probably get offers below what you're asking. The buyer is very likely to want a survey, engine test and sea trial, so you should try to avoid agreeing any price reduction before these take place since a surveyor is sure to find some aspects that the buyer could use to knock the price down. You need to decide whether you'll arrange and pay for any remedial work to be carried out or whether you'll reduce the price to cover the cost of the buyer doing the work.

Cruising the RLM Bahama 31 into the heart of the fascinating old city of Lincoln.

Paperwork

Have the necessary paperwork ready to answer questions – and prove your answers – about ownership, receipts, VAT, costs of mooring and insurance, professional repairs and servicing and any surveys that you or a previous owner had

An ambition realised: venturing out to sea off the coast of Norfolk.

done, along with details of work that may have been carried out to satisfy the surveyor. You're likely to be asked to provide details of previous owners in order to establish the boat's history, legality and freedom from any financial liabilities concerning unpaid loans secured on the boat.

A future buyer will want to see the necessary European Recreational Craft Directive documentation for a qualifying boat built since June 1998. Anyone selling a boat without the necessary paperwork to prove this compliance risks prosecution. The latest rules and procedures for compliance should be available at http://www.berr.gov.uk. Put 'European Recreational Craft Directive' into the search box.

Advertising

It may seem to make sense to put a 'For Sale' sign on your boat. However, if the boat is moored in an easily accessible public place with no supervision, this may not be wise. For some strange reason a 'For Sale' sign can attract the attention of vandals whose warped minds seem to assume that the boat has been abandoned. Others may feel that the sign's an invitation to walk all over your boat and to open the canopy and peer inside.

An advertisement including the phrase 'Well equipped; ready to use', helps to inspire confidence. Put adverts in as many websites, magazines and notice boards as possible at the same time. This helps to drum up plenty of enquiries that should include at least some seriously interested potential purchasers. You can then honestly refer to the high level of interest and to all the other enquiries you've had when negotiating the price. Many websites, such as http://www.boatsandoutboards.co.uk and http://boatshop24.co.uk, take adverts for assorted types of boat free of charge or for only a small fee. Indeed, the Internet has brought a big improvement to the process of buying and selling boats, although you do have to be careful to avoid 'scams' where someone posing as a buyer is really trying to steal the boat, extort money or extract banking details from you. The boat-selling websites give warnings and details of the current scams in operation so that sellers can avoid them.

The auction website eBay may be worth considering. Plenty of boats are advertised there. However, many people prefer to try straightforward advertising at a set price before taking the auction route.

One or two photographs can usually be included. Give as much information as possible in the space allowed and then make it clear that extra pictures and full details can be provided before buyers view the boat. The extra photographs can be put on your own website or emailed to enquirers. They could even be printed and posted by snail mail.

This approach is an effective way to avoid wasting the time of both seller and buyer. If a potential buyer is given detailed information and plenty of pictures showing different views of the boat – including the inside – they'll only travel to view it if they're very seriously interested. In fact, some have been known to say, even before viewing, that they'll definitely buy the boat if it's exactly as in the photographs and description. They may want to reserve it on the basis of 'first refusal' subject to a satisfactory survey.

It greatly helps the sale if a mooring can be arranged and advertised as being available with the boat – either the existing one or a nearby alternative mooring – subject to the approval of the marina, boatyard, club, navigation authority or other owner of the mooring.

Most potential buyers will want to see the boat at the weekend, so you obviously need to bear this in mind and not plan to use it away from the mooring at weekends.

Brokerage

If the boat's moored a considerable distance from home, so that it's difficult to arrange accompanied viewing, it may be

Plenty of opportunities exist to trade up and cruise further afield.

best to put the sale in the hands of a broker. Check the agreement carefully to establish exactly what the charges are and what they include. Ask what advertising they'll carry out. Discussing with a broker the possibility of selling your boat will gain you useful insight into the state of the market. The broker will also provide advice on how to prepare your particular boat for sale. Comments from people viewing the boat should be reported back to you, which will provide ideas for improvements that will enable you to sell it more quickly.

Some brokers act as an agent for a boat remotely and don't provide accompanied viewing. However, a much better arrangement, if possible, is to have it on display on the broker's premises where people frequently go to view advertised boats.

Remember to inform your insurance company that your boat is being put up for sale, where it's being displayed, and who's responsible for showing and demonstrating the boat to potential purchasers. Don't assume that brokers provide insurance cover for the boats they're selling: your own insurance cover needs to continue until you're sure the sale has been fully completed.

The prospective purchaser is usually expected to pay for the cost of launching/craning in for a sea trial, recovering onto hardstanding, surveying, engine testing and the eventual transport to the boat's final destination.

You may find that a broker is prepared to take your boat in part exchange for another, larger, motor cruiser. Part-exchange is also a possibility if a dealer is keen to sell you a new boat. Take care, though, to investigate exactly what your boat is really worth by looking at the prices of similar boats for sale before you negotiate a part-exchange deal. As with selling and buying motor vehicles, you may well do better by selling your boat yourself.

Future ambitions

Those with a small motor cruiser often become more ambitious and adventurous, having gained substantial experience of boating in a variety of weather and tidal conditions, and may want to exchange their boat for a larger cruiser, able to cope with longer voyages.

This is an exciting and rewarding challenge. However, owning a larger cruiser, and embarking on offshore voyages further afield, requires much greater knowledge and skills than are covered in this book. It's essential to gain the extra skills and knowledge by crewing with experienced and qualified skippers. This can be an enjoyable process in itself but should be combined with Royal Yachting Association approved courses, in order to gain the skills necessary for navigating offshore. You'll also learn about the appropriate rules, regulations, and paperwork. For example, many countries require a Certificate of Competence to be produced on arrival. This can be obtained by completing an appropriate RYA course.

Many boating clubs organise courses and cruises in company, which provide help for those who've never ventured out to sea with their boats. *Motor Boats Monthly* magazine has a cruising club for cruising abroad in company. Details are provided on the website at http://www.mbmclub.com/mbm/cruising_club. *Anglia Afloat* magazine also occasionally organises a cruise in company along the coast of East Anglia, and some Internet boating forums arrange cruises in company. An example is the Norfolk Broads discussion forum website at http://www.the-norfolk-broads.co.uk.

Motor boats of all sizes provide you with a choice of ways to escape into a different environment for relaxation, enjoyment, pleasure and – if you so desire – high-speed thrills, exploration and adventure. The choice is yours.

Appendix

This is a list of contact details for the motor boat information, products and services mentioned in the *Motor Boat Manual.* Sadly, space doesn't permit the listing of every one of the many organisations and companies involved with boating.

The majority of people have access to a computer at home or at work and Internet access is now available to all, with assistance, through public libraries and other facilities. Putting the name of a product or service into an Internet search engine will produce plenty of contact details. Additionally, the first group of organisations listed below maintain their own detailed lists of boating organisations and commercial companies.

Sources of information and contact details

Royal Yachting Association
An extensive range of information and contact details is available, including boating clubs, boat owners' associations and training courses.
RYA House
Ensign Way
Hamble
Southampton
Hampshire SO31 4YA
United Kingdom
Tel 023 8060 4100
http://www.rya.org.uk

Boats and Outboards
A very comprehensive boat advertising website. On the website, select 'Services' for companies according to category, and 'Directory of Marine Traders' for an alphabetical list.
Friday-Ad Ltd trading as Boats And Outboards
London Road
Sayers Common
West Sussex BN6 9HS
Tel 01646 680720
http://www.boatsandoutboards.co.uk

Yachting and Boating World
IPC Country & Leisure Media Ltd publish several boating magazines including Motor Boats Monthly, Motor Boat and Yachting, Practical Boat Owner *and* Classic Boat. *Magazine subscription offers, marine directories, boats for sale, articles and forums are included on their website.*
IPC Country & Leisure Media Ltd
The Blue Fin Building
110 Southwark Street
London
SE1 OSU
Tel 020 3148 5000
http://www.ybw.com

British Marine Industries Federation
This is the trade association for the UK marine leisure industry.
Marine House
Thorpe Lea Road
Egham
Surrey TW20 8BF
Tel 01784 473377
http://www.britishmarine.co.uk

The Motorboat Museum
Wat Tyler Country Park
Pitsea Hall Lane
Basildon
Essex SS16 4UH
Tel 01268 550077
http://www.motorboatmuseum.org.uk

Sources of inland navigation licences and inland boating information in print and on websites

These organisations also provide information and publications on waters where fishing is available, as many boat owners enjoy fishing with rod and line.

British Waterways
British Waterways covers most canals and some rivers including the Severn, Trent and Yorkshire Ouse.
64 Clarendon Road
Watford
Herts WD17 1DA
Tel 0845 671 5530
http://www.britishwaterways.co.uk
and
http://www.waterscape.com

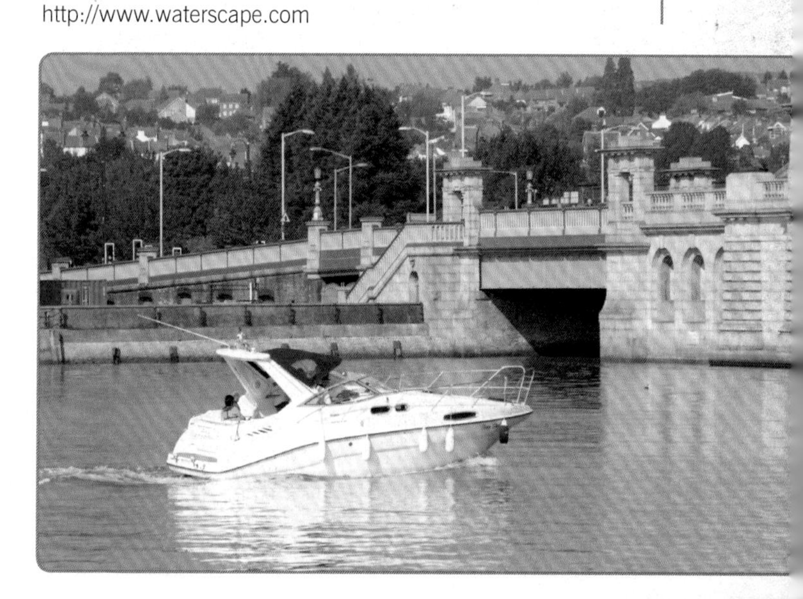

The Environment Agency
The Environment Agency licenses boats on the River Thames, the River Medway and many East Anglian rivers with the exception of the Norfolk and Suffolk Broads, which are licensed by the Broads Authority. The Environment Agency also administers the National Rod Licence, which must be obtained before fishing inland waters (it can be purchased from Post Offices or online from the Agency's website). Flood warnings are put on their website and arrangements can be made for you to receive warnings of imminent flooding for most UK rivers and waterways. The Agency operates from regional offices which are listed on its website, or you can contact the national office for information on which office to contact for boat registration and licensing.
National Office PO Box 544
Customer Contact Centre
Rotherham
S60 1BY
Tel 01709 389 201
http://www.environment-agency.gov.uk

The Broads Authority
The Broads Authority covers the Norfolk and Suffolk Broads and associated rivers.
18 Colegate
Norwich
Norfolk
NR3 1BQ
Tel 01603 610734
http://www.broads-authority.gov.uk

The Inland Waterways Association
The IWA is a very helpful source of information and publications concerning canals and rivers, including the safe use of these and their facilities. This information is freely available on their website, but everyone interested in inland waterways is encouraged to become a member. Excellent voluntary work has been and is still being done by many members to reopen waterways and make them navigable. Many events are organised by the IWA. The Association's Waterways Magazine *and newsletter are available online.*
Island House, Moor Road
Chesham HP5 1WA
Tel 01494 783453
http://www.waterways.org.uk

A few waterways are independent of the main licensing organisations listed above and require a separate licence to be purchased. Their contact details, along with information on each main waterway, can be found on the Inland Waterways Association website at http://www.waterways.org.uk/Waterways/PrincipalNavigations and http://www.waterways.org.uk/Partners/NavigationAuthorities.

A very large number of helpful links to other websites are also provided at http://www.waterways.org.uk/Partners, including boating clubs and many inland boating organisations.

Sources of safety information and other boating information

Royal National Lifeboat Institution
West Quay Road
Poole
BH15 1HZ
Tel 0845 122 6999
http://www.rnli.org.uk

European Recreational Craft Directive
Paperwork that has to accompany boats built since June 1998 should provide the necessary information on this directive, which sets statutory standards of boat construction. If you want all the latest information on the regulations, put 'Recreational Craft Directive' into the search box on the website.
Ministerial Correspondence Unit
Department for Business, Enterprise & Regulatory Reform
1 Victoria Street
London
SW1H 0ET
Tel 020 7215 5000
http://www.berr.gov.uk

HM Coastguard and Maritime and Coastguard Agency
Spring Place
105 Commercial Road
Southampton
Hampshire
SO15 1EG
http://www.mcga.gov.uk

Boat Safety Scheme – For inland waterways.
64 Clarendon Road
Watford
Hertfordshire
WD17 1DA
Tel 01923 201278
http://www.boatsafetyscheme.com

The Inland Waterways Association and the inland navigation licensing organisations listed above also provide safety information.

Magazines

Magazines are an excellent source of up-to-date information, news and articles. Most are available through newsagents, but it's well worth visiting their websites for discounted subscriptions, boating news, archived articles, reviews and reports on boats and equipment, discussion forums and advertisements for new and second-hand boats. Many of the boat owners' associations and clubs listed on the Royal Yachting Association's website (see above) also publish very informative and entertaining magazines and newsletters. Fishing magazines are included below, as this is a sport often associated with motor boating.

All at Sea
http://www.allatsea.co.uk

Anglers Mail
http://www.anglersmail.co.uk

Anglia Afloat
For East Anglia.
http://www.angliaafloat.co.uk

Angling Times
http://www.gofishing.co.uk/anglingtimes

Boat and Yacht Buyer
http://www.boatandyachtbuyer.co.uk

Boat Fishing Monthly
http://www.boatfishing-monthly.co.uk

Boat Mart
http://www.mby.com

Boat News
Available in print and free to download at http://www.boat-news.co.uk

Boat Trader
http://boatshop24.co.uk

Boats and Yachts for sale
http://boatshop24.co.uk

Canal Boat
http://www.canalboat.co.uk

Canals and Rivers
http://www.canalsandrivers.co.uk

Classic Boat
http://www.classicboat.co.uk

Coarse Fishing
http://www.gofishing.co.uk

Electric Boat News
(and Association membership)
http://www.electric-boat-association.org.uk

Hotribs
Online Rigid Inflatable Boats magazine
http://www.hotribs.com

Motor Boat and Yachting
http://www.mby.com

Motor Boats Monthly
http://www.motorboatsmonthly.co.uk

Practical Boat Owner
http://www.pbo.co.uk

RIB International
Rigid Inflatable Boat magazine
http://www.ribmagazine.com

RYA Magazine
http://www.rya.org.uk

Sea Angler
http://www.gofishing.co.uk

Sports Boat and RIB Magazine
http://www.sportsboat.co.uk/

The Sea
http://www.theseamagazine.com

Total Sea Angler
An online free magazine website
http://www.totalseaangler.com

Total Sea Fishing
http://www.totalseamagazine.com

Trout and Salmon
http://www.gofishing.co.uk

Trout Fisherman
http://www.gofishing.co.uk

Wakeboard
http://www.wakeboardmag.co.uk

Watercraft Boatbuilding Magazine
http://www.watercraft.co.uk

Waterski and Wakeboard
http://www.britishwaterski.org.uk

Waterways Magazine
The Inland Waterways Association magazine, free to download at http://www.waterways.org.uk/Library/WaterwaysMagazine

Waterways World
http://www.waterwaysworld.com

What Boat?
http://www.whatboat.com

World of Powerboats
http://www.worldofpowerboats.com

World Sea Fishing
An online free magazine website
http://www.worldseafishing.com/

Yachting Life Magazine
Mainly on sailing but includes some aspects of motor boating and is mainly for the North of England, Northern Ireland and Scotland
http://www.yachtinglife.co.uk

Companies mentioned in this book

Andy Seedhouse Boat Sales
2 Quayside
Woodbridge
Suffolk IP12 1BH
Tel 01394 387833
Email sales@andyseedhouse.co.uk

Blakes Paints/Hempel
'Blakes' is the brand name for Hempel in the UK.
Swanwick Marina
Swanwick Shore Road
Southampton
Hampshire SO31 7EF
Tel 01489 864440
http://www.blakespaints.com

Boatline
Calf Cottage, Sydney Street
Ingham
Norwich
Norfolk NR12 9TQ
Tel 01692 581177
http://www.boatlineuk.com

Bruce Roberts Yacht Design Offices
Plans and kits for self-build.
Tel +34 952 86 47 66 or + 34 616 685 200
Email boatdesigns@gmail.com
http://www.bruceroberts.com

C Claims Adjusters
PO Box 8
Romford
Essex RM4 1AL
Tel 0208 500 0147
http://www.cclaims.co.uk

Calor Gas Ltd
Calor Gas Ltd
Athena House, Athena Drive
Tachbrook Park
Warwick CV34 6RL
Tel 0800 626 626
http://www.calor.co.uk

Eagle Boat Windows
Unit 2, The Sidings Business Park
Engine Shed Lane
Skipton
North Yorkshire BD23 1TB
Tel 01756 792097
http://www.eagleboatwindows.co.uk

Electric Boat Association
150 Wayside Green
Woodcote, Nr Reading
Berkshire
RG8 0QJ
Tel 01491 681449
http://www.electric-boat-association.org.uk/

Essex Boatyards Ltd
Motor boat sales, maintenance and repairs.
Essex Marina
Wallasea Island
Essex SS4 2HF
Tel 01489 576888
http://www.essexboatyards.com

Halyard (Marine & Industrial) Ltd
Whaddon Business Park
Southampton Road
Whaddon
Salisbury SP5 3HF
Tel 01722 710922
http://www.halyard.eu.com

Henkel Loctite Adhesives Ltd
Including Plastic Padding marine products.
Technologies House
Wood Lane End
Hemel Hempstead
Hertfordshire
HP2 4RQ
Tel 01442 278100
http://www.loctite.co.uk

International Paint
Akzo Nobel Decorative Coatings Ltd
Crown House
Hollins Road
Darwen
Lancashire BB3 0BG
Tel 08447 7094444
http://www.international-paints.co.uk

Lancing Marine
Lancing Marine
51 Victoria Road
Portslade
Sussex
BN41 1XY
Tel 01273 410025
http://www.lancingmarine.com

Marinestore Chandlers and Mail Order
Marinestore Chandlery
Shipways Yard
North St
Maldon
Essex
CM9 5HQ
Tel 0845 241 2313
http://marinestore.co.uk

Pains Wessex Ltd
Distress flares.
Chemring Marine Ltd
Chemring House
1500 Parkway
Whiteley
Fareham
Hampshire
PO15 7AF
Tel 01489 884130
http://www.painswessex.com

Riverside Marine and leisure Ltd
Motor boat sales including Viking and Seamaster motor cruiser sales and boat maintenance and repairs.
Riverside Marine and Leisure Limited
Pike and Eel Marina
Overcote Lane
Needingworth
St Ives
Cambridgeshire PE27 4TW
Tel 01480 468666
http://www.boatsaleuk.com

Tony Preston Professional Yacht Services
12 Solent Road
Drayton
Portsmouth
Hampshire PO6 1HH
Tel 023 9237 1579
http://www.tppys.com/

Whisper Boats
Kits for self-build boats
1 Home Farm Cottages
High Street
Babraham
Cambridgeshire
CB2 4AG
Tel 01223 832 928
http://www.whisperboats.co.uk

Further reading

These are the books referred to in the text along with some other suggested reading, which will help to expand on the topics covered. Books on skills involved with boat handling and navigation are best read in conjunction with courses and crewing with experienced skippers.

Ball, Ian. *Sea Fishing Properly Explained* (Right Way, 2008).

Barrell, Emrhys. *The Nicholson Boating Handbook and Waterways Guide* (Nicholson, 2007).

Bartlett, Tim. *RYA Navigation Handbook* (Royal Yachting Association, 2003).

Bartlett, Tim. *RYA VHF Handbook* (Royal Yachting Association, 2006).

Bate, Brian. *The Trailer Manual* (Haynes Publishing, 2006).

Billingham, Nick. *Narrow Boats – Care and Maintenance* (Helmsman's Books, 1995).

Burnett, Andy. *Inland Boat Owners' Book* (Waterways World, 2000).

Calder, Nigel. *Marine Diesel Engines: Be Your Own Diesel Mechanic – Maintenance, Troubleshooting and Repair* (Adlard Coles Nautical, 2006).

Campbell, Geoffrey. *The Good Launch Guide* (CSL Publishing, 2005).

Clymer. *Outboard Motor Manual* series (Clymer Publications).

Cumberlidge, Jane. *Inland Waterways of Great Britain* (Imray, Laurie, Norie & Wilson, 2009).

Cunliffe, Tom. *RYA Manual of Seamanship* (Royal Yachting Association, 2005).

du Plessis, Hugo. *Fibreglass Boats* (Adlard Coles Nautical, 2006).

Featherstone, Neville, and Lambie, Peter. *Reed's Practical Boat Owner Small Craft Almanac* (Thomas Reed Publications annual publication).

Garrod, A.E. *Practical Boat Owner's Electrics Afloat: A Complete Step by Step Guide for Boat Owners* (Adlard Coles Nautical, 2001).

Goring, Loris. *The Care and Repair of Marine Petrol Engines* (Adlard Coles Nautical, 1990).

Gougeon Brothers. *Wooden Boat Restoration and Repair* (West System and Gougeon Brothers, 1990).

Imray. *Nautical Charts Series and Pilot books* (Imray, Laurie, Norie & Wilson, regularly updated).

Jinks, Simon. *RYA Motor Cruising Handbook* (Royal Yachting Association, 2009).

Judkins, Steve. *The Complete Knot Pack: A New Approach to Mastering Knots and Splices* (John Wiley & Sons, 2003).

Mellor, John. *Cruising: A Skipper's Guide* (John Wiley & Sons, 2000).

Naujok, Michael. *Boat Interior Construction* (A. & C. Black Publishers Ltd, 2002).

Poiraud, Alain, Ginsberg-Klemmt, Achim, and Ginsberg-Klemmt, Erika. *The Complete Anchoring Handbook* (International Marine, 2007).

Ransome, Arthur. *Swallows and Amazons* (Red Fox, new edition 2001).

RNLI. *Sea Safety – The Complete Guide* (Royal National Lifeboat Institution, 2007).

Russ, Mel (editor). *The Sea Angler's Step-by-Step Guide to Bait and Rigs* (EMAP Pursuit Publishing Ltd, 1999).

RYA. *International Regulations for Preventing Collisions at Sea* (Royal Yachting Association, 2009).

RYA. *Boat Safety Handbook* (Royal Yachting Association, 2007).

Seddon, Don. *Diesel Troubleshooter* (John Wiley & Sons, 2001).

Sherman, Edwin. *Outboard Engines* (International Marine Publishing Co, 2009).

Tibbs, Chris. *RYA Weather Handbook* (Royal Yachting Association, 2005).

Watts, Dennis. *Sailing Boat Manual* (Haynes Publishing, 2008).

White, Peter. *Outboard Troubleshooter* (John Wiley & Sons, 1996).

Wilson, John. *John Wilson's Fishing Encyclopedia* (Boxtree Ltd, 2000).

Glossary of terms

If you're new to boating don't let all these terms put you off – our long seafaring traditions have resulted in a large and sometimes strange vocabulary. The words are listed here not because you have to learn them all but in order to help you when you come across them. Some other relevant terms and abbreviations are also included.

Aft At or towards the back of a boat.
Amidships In the centre of a boat.
Anchor well Storage facility for an anchor.
Antifouling Paint which contains chemicals to prevent underwater growths on the hull.
Astern Travelling backwards or referring to what is behind.
Auxiliary A second engine kept in reserve to be used if the main engine fails.

Bail To remove water from a boat.
Bathing platform A platform fixed to the stern of a boat from which bathers can easily enter and exit the water.
Beam The widest part of a boat.
Beaufort Wind Scale Used in measuring wind strength.
Bilge The lowest part of the inside of the hull.
Bilge blower A fan mounted in the engine compartment that expels dangerous fumes and gases (such as carbon monoxide and explosive petrol vapour) from the boat.
Blistering Water can penetrate the gelcoat surface of a fibreglass boat, causing blisters through osmosis.
Block Pulley used on a boat.
Boat pox American term used when a fibreglass hull has a 'rash' of many blisters in the gelcoat.
Boot top A line painted along the waterline of the hull.
Bow The front end of a boat.
Bowline Knot for making a loop at the end of a rope.
Broach A term used when a boat is broadside to the waves or wind and possibly in danger of capsizing.
BSS Boat Safety Scheme. The inspection of cruisers on inland waterways is legally required, the examiner issuing a four-year certificate if satisfied.
Bulkhead Vertical partition across the width of a boat.
Buoy A floating object used as a marker and for mooring.
Burgee Triangular flag displaying a club's identity.

Catamaran A boat with two hulls.
Cavitation plate A horizontal plate situated above the propeller on an outboard motor or outdrive leg. Its purpose is to keep sufficient water over the propeller, particularly when the boat is on the plane.
Chine A sharp angle in the shape of the cross-section of a hull, usually where the side meets the bottom.
Cleat Fitting on a boat for securing a rope.
Coaming A vertical structure or low 'wall' round the cockpit or hatch of a boat, designed to keep water out.
Cockpit The area of a boat from which the crew control it.
Cowl A removable cover over the engine of an outboard motor.
Cruiser A boat suitable for making journeys by water and for staying aboard overnight, usually having accommodation in the form of a cabin.
Cuddy A small shelter on a boat not big enough to be called a cabin.

Davits Small curved cranes with pulleys used to raise and lower a dinghy at the stern of a motor boat.
Day boat A boat used for one-day excursions with sufficient space to accommodate a number of people comfortably.
Dinghy Small rowing or sailing boat.
Displacement The weight of water a boat displaces when it is afloat.
Dodgers Rectangular sheets of fabric either side of a cruiser's cockpit, intended to provide some shelter from the wind and spray.
Draught The depth of a boat below the waterline.

Ebb tide The tide going out towards the sea.
Echo sounder An electrical device that uses sound echoes to find the depth of water.
Engine well The cavity in the hull in which the engine is installed.
Ensign The maritime flag of a country.

Fairlead A fitting that guides a rope.
Fender Pad or pads fixed round or hung from a boat to protect it from damage against harbour walls, other boats, etc.
Fiddles A framework of steel rails round the burners on a cooker to hold pans in place when the boat moves.
Fish finder An electrical device that uses sound echoes to find the depth of water; similar to an echo sounder but has the increased sensitivity necessary to show fish on its screen.
Flood tide Tide rising as it comes in from the sea.
Flukes The blades of an anchor.
Fly bridge A high-up steering position on top of the cabin of a motor boat.
Foredeck The part of the deck at the front of a boat.
Freeboard The vertical distance from the water's surface to the gunwale.

Galley The kitchen area of a boat.
Gelcoat The top surface layer of a laminated fibreglass hull or other moulding.
GPS Global positioning system, used in establishing position at sea for navigation purposes.
GRP Glass-reinforced plastic. The term 'fibreglass boat' is often used to refer to a GRP boat.
Gudgeon Fitting on the rudder that hinges on the pintle.
Gunwale (pronounced 'gunnal') The top edge all round the sides of a boat at deck level.

Head Name for the toilet and its compartment on a boat.
Helm The tiller or wheel that's gripped in order to steer a boat. Sometimes used to refer to the person who does this.
HIN Hull identification number.

Keel A weighted extension of steel or some other heavy material below a boat, designed to stop it moving sideways and enable efficient forward progress. Also used to describe the structural centreline of a boat.
Kill cord A cord attached to the engine stop device at one end and to the helmsman at the other so that the engine will be stopped by a pull on the cord if the helmsman falls overboard.
Knot Unit of speed – one nautical mile (2,000yd) per hour.

Lanyard A thin rope used for holding things in place.
Launch To place a boat in the water; also a term for a small motor boat.
Lee The side of a boat away from the wind. 'In the lee' means sheltered from the wind.
Leeway The sideways movement of a boat caused by the wind.
Lee shore Shore onto which the wind is blowing from the sea.
Limber holes Holes drilled in the bulkheads and interior frame of a boat to allow water to drain through to a place from which it can be pumped out.
Log A book for recording a boat's movements, speed and distance travelled, or a device for measuring the speed and distance.
Lunch hook A small anchor for use in calm conditions for a temporary stop.

Mayday A distress call; the main term used when calling for help because there is an extreme emergency.
Mooring Permanent anchorage or place to tie up a boat.
Moused Term used to describe a shackle that's been bound with wire to stop it coming unscrewed.

Neap tides Tides with the smallest range of rise and fall.

Offshore wind A wind that blows away from the land.
Onshore wind A wind that blows towards the land.
Outdrive See 'stern drive'.

Painter Rope secured to the bow of a dinghy to tie it up for mooring or for towing behind a cruiser.
Pilot house A compartment providing shelter for the helmsman, also called a wheelhouse.
Pintle A pin-shaped part of the rudder hinge that the gudgeon fits onto.
Planing Skimming over the surface of the water when a boat's speed is high enough to lift it sufficiently.
Port side The left-hand side of a boat when looking forwards.
Pram dinghy Mainly used to describe a dinghy that has a blunt bow instead of a pointed one.
Pulpit Metal guard-rail fitted at the bow.

Quarter The rear end of the side of a boat.

Range of tide The difference between high and low water.
RIB Rigid inflatable boat.
RNLI Royal National Lifeboat Institution.
Rode The rope and chain attached to an anchor. Sometimes called a warp.
Roller A cylindrical revolving fitting over which rope or chain can run smoothly, as in the case of a stem head roller, which is used with an anchor chain or rope.
Rond anchor A type of anchor used to moor to the bank on inland waterways.
Rowlocks Fittings used as receptacles and guides for oars.
Rubbing strake Strip of wood or other material along the side of a boat intended to absorb impact and friction with mooring posts, harbour walls, etc.
Rudder Device for steering, mounted at the stern and controlled with a tiller or steering wheel.
RYA Royal Yachting Association.

Sacrificial anodes Lumps of metal, usually zinc, attached to the hull near metal fittings, beside propeller shafts and to the underwater casing of outboard motors. Zinc gets attacked by electrolysis before the other more 'noble' metals, protecting them from corrosion.
Samson post Strong attachment point for ropes for mooring and anchoring.
Scope The length of the rope used with an anchor.
Screw Another name sometimes used for a propeller.
Seacock Tap that controls the flow of water for cooling an engine or flushing a toilet on a boat.
Sea rails Term sometimes used instead of 'fiddles' for the steel rails round the burners on a cooker to hold pans in place.
Shackle Metal fitting used to join chain or parts of rigging.
Shaft A rod that connects the engine to the propeller.
Sheave A pulley over which a rope runs.
Shoal An area with shallow water.
Side deck The part of the deck on the side of a boat between the cabin and the gunwales.
Skeg A fixed fin on the hull designed to keep a boat moving in a straight line and, on some boats, to protect and support the rudder or propeller shaft.
Slack water The period when the tide hardly moves between high water and low water.
Sponsons The inflatable tubes of an inflatable boat or RIB.
Spring tide The tides with the greatest range, including the highest tides of the regular four-week tidal cycle.
Springs Mooring ropes used diagonally in addition to the main bow and stern lines, to stop a boat swinging and moving excessively when tied up.
Stanchion A post supporting a lifeline at the edge of the deck on a cruiser to prevent crew falling overboard.
Starboard side The right-hand side of a boat when looking forwards.
Stem The forward edge of the bow of a boat.
Stem head The fitting at the bow over which mooring and anchoring ropes pass.
Stern The back of a boat.

Stern drive A drive leg with gears and propeller mounted on the stern of a boat and connected to the engine. Also called an outdrive or Z drive.
Stern gland A device fitted round the propeller shaft to prevent water from flooding in but which at the same time allows the shaft to rotate.
Stern tube A tube through which the propeller shaft passes from the engine to the propeller, acting as a bearing for the shaft.

Tackle A combination of pulleys and ropes designed to make it easier to pull or lift.
Tender A small boat used to get out to a boat on a mooring.
Thwart A seat arranged across a boat.
Tiller A spar fixed to the rudder for steering.
Topsides The external area of the hull above the waterline.
Transit A navigation term used to describe the observation of two or more objects in line.
Transom Flat, near vertical stern of a boat.
Trim The level balance of a boat from front to back and side to side.
Trimaran A boat with three hulls.
Trim tabs A pair of flaps attached to the transom. They are adjusted to get the boat level and to encourage a boat onto the plane as it gathers speed.
Trip line A length of line attached to the crown of an anchor with a float at the other end of the line. This can be used to free the anchor if it gets stuck.

Warp A rope used when mooring a boat.
Wash Wake turbulence in the form of surging waves left behind a boat as a result of its movement through the water.
Whipping A binding of twine on the end of a rope to stop it fraying.
Winch A device used to wind in ropes.
Windlass A type of winch normally used to raise an anchor.
Windward Towards where the wind is coming from.

Yaw Unintentional swinging of a boat off course from side to side, often caused by waves.

Z drive See 'stern drive'.

Acknowledgements

Much help, guidance and advice has been gratefully received from the following:

The many friendly and helpful people involved with boat shows, boating activities, boating product supply, boat building and maintenance, marinas and boating clubs.

The late Maurice Perry, my uncle – a lifelong boating enthusiast from whom I gained much of my knowledge of boating matters.

My wife, Rita, who has shared my enthusiasm for boating, and read the proofs.

My son, David, for his great help with the work on our boats and with information technology.

Louise McIntyre of Haynes Publishing, for her helpful advice and guidance in writing this book.

Advice, technical assistance and help with access to locations for photography
Nick Barke of Essex Boatyards Ltd
Martin Ingram and Lesley Johnston of Blakes Paints/Hempel
Rob McKelvey of Eagle Boat Windows
International Paints
Max Campbell of Whisper Boats
Henkel Loctite Adhesives Ltd
Marinestore Chandlery and Mail Order
David Taylor and Alan Curtis, Riverside Marine and Leisure Ltd
Peter Clark of C Claims Adjusters (Romford)
Andy Seedhouse Boat Sales
The Electric Boat Association
The Motorboat Museum, Basildon
Boatline Quayside Club

People building and improving their own boats
Dave Flint and Alison Shearing
Ian and Christine Davies
David Pertwee
Tim Pettigrew
Max Campbell

Photography
All photographs are by the author with the exception of those (and some of the information in their captions) kindly supplied by:
Nick Barke of Essex Boatyards Ltd: photographs of GRP deck repairs, page 102 and damaged boat page 101.
Tim Pettigrew: photographs of boat repairs, pages 106.
Max Campbell of Whisper Boats and Simon Tomlinson: photographs of the building of boats, pages 12 and 89.
Pains Wessex Ltd: photographs of flares in use, page 189.
Bruce Roberts-Goodson of Bruce Roberts Yacht Design: boat building photographs, pages 87 and 88.
Tony Preston of Tony Preston Professional Yacht Services and Lesley Johnston of Blakes Paints/Hempel: repair and painting photographs, pages 96, 97, 98 and 100.
Peter Clark of C Claims Adjusters (Romford): photographs of fire damaged boat, page 194.
Halyard (Marine & Industrial) Ltd: photographs of noise insulation installation, pages 180 and 181.
Dave Flint and Alison Shearing: boat renovation photographs pages 197, 198, 199 and Lincoln photo page 12.

Project Management: Louise McIntyre
Page design: James Robertson
Copy editor: Ian Heath
Index: Peter Nicholson

Index